ADVANCE PRAISE

"Stefano Pelle's book brings to my mind with some nostalgic sentiments many memories of my expatriate life which made me read it as a flashback. It is certainly worth keeping in mind many of the chapters for someone who is undertaking an overseas professional life as it can be considered as a breviary and a guide helping in getting the right attitude for being accepted in the new environment. In today's world, professionals need a lot of flexibility and willingness to go where job opportunities are. Emerging markets in general and BRICs in particular offer, as Pelle suggests, opening for open minds.

If China was the 'Mecca' ten years ago, I would, and again Pelle seems aligned to this statement, recommend not to overlook opportunities in Africa. Have a safe journey with this book at hand."

—**Carlo Donati**
Former CEO, Nestlé Waters

"*When Not in Rome, Don't Do as the Romans Do* is an outstanding contribution to cross-cultural management literature. Stefano Pelle in this 'tale' provides a vivid description and many 'backstage' insights, based on his own experience, on main managerial, cultural, and life issues that managers should acquire when dealing with international expansion in Emerging Markets. I truly recommend this book to all business students, academics, and managers interested in learning valuable cross-cultural managerial clues."

—**Michele Quintano**, PhD
*Professor of Marketing at
UniParthenope (Naples), LUISS (Rome) and
ESADE Business School (Madrid)*

"Going through this engaging book, I was reminded of the Sanskrit term 'anubhoot satya,' which loosely implies the truth that is felt, first hand. What Stefano has wonderfully captured are his experiences both personal and professional, in lands and cultures spanning from India to Middle East, Russia, and Africa. This cross-cultural vantage point is unique as it's genuine, vibrant, and insightful. Be it the keen understanding of the business realities of the emerging markets or the sensitive understanding of their social framework. 'I realized that I was wrongly linking poverty with sadness ... people can have just the money to survive and still be content and joyful.' I particularly enjoyed his take on the India experience be it the wedding adventure replete with a pachyderm or the understanding of the Indian concept of 'chalta hay' attitude and 'jugaad' or naming of his pet as Lucky Singh. This is one enriching read."

—**Prasoon Joshi**
*Executive Chairman and CEO,
McCann Worldgroup India and
President, South Asia*

"Peppered with personal anecdotes and insights he gained during his stint in India as an expatriate, Stefano's book makes for an entertaining read. I was able to draw parallels with my own experiences when running a start up and was able to empathize with some of the challenges Stefano describes."

—**Manu Anand**
Chairman and CEO, India Region, PepsiCo

When Not in Rome, Don't Do as the Romans Do

When Not in Rome, Don't Do as the Romans Do

A CandyD Italian in Emerging Markets

Stefano Pelle

www.sagepublications.com
Los Angeles • London • New Delhi • Singapore • Washington DC

Copyright © Stefano Pelle, 2013

All rights reserved. No part of this book may be reproduced or utilized in any form or by any means, electronic or mechanical, including photocopying, recording or by any information storage or retrieval system, without permission in writing from the publisher.

First published in 2013 by

SAGE Response
B1/I-1 Mohan Cooperative Industrial Area
Mathura Road, New Delhi 110 044, India

SAGE Publications Inc
2455 Teller Road
Thousand Oaks, California 91320, USA

SAGE Publications Ltd
1 Oliver's Yard, 55 City Road
London EC1Y 1SP, United Kingdom

SAGE Publications Asia-Pacific Pte Ltd
33 Pekin Street
#02-01 Far East Square
Singapore 048763

Published by Vivek Mehra for SAGE Publications India Pvt Ltd, typeset in 11/13pt Adobe Garamond Pro by Diligent Typesetter, Delhi, and printed at Saurabh Printers Pvt Ltd.

Library of Congress Cataloging-in-Publication Data Available

ISBN: 978-81-321-1087-3 (PB)

The SAGE Team: Sachin Sharma, Dhurjjati Sarma, Anju Saxena and Dally Verghese

*To my mother, the person to whom I owe the most in my life,
and
to my sons, Aadam and Samar, my greatest lifetime achievements*

Thank you for choosing a SAGE product! If you have any comment, observation or feedback, I would like to personally hear from you. Please write to me at contactceo@sagepub.in

—Vivek Mehra, Managing Director and CEO,
SAGE Publications India Pvt Ltd, New Delhi

Bulk Sales

SAGE India offers special discounts for purchase of books in bulk. We also make available special imprints and excerpts from our books on demand.

For orders and enquiries, write to us at

Marketing Department
SAGE Publications India Pvt Ltd
B1/I-1, Mohan Cooperative Industrial Area
Mathura Road, Post Bag 7
New Delhi 110044, India
E-mail us at marketing@sagepub.in

Get to know more about SAGE, be invited to SAGE events, get on our mailing list. Write today to marketing@sagepub.in

This book is also available as an e-book.

CONTENTS

Prologue   ix

1. My Pre-expatriate Life   1
   - Where I Come From   1
   - My Career Path in Italy   4

2. Italy and India: So Different and So Similar   10
   - Money, People, and Politics   10
   - Emerging India; Emergency in Italy   13
   - A Bridge between Italy and India   17

3. Welcome to India   22
   - Landing in New Delhi   22
   - Of Roads and Spirituality   24
   - Of Friends and Celebrations   30
   - Cars and Arts   37
   - The House in Rajokri and the House of Hope   41

4. Working in India   50
   - Indian Talent   50
   - The *Chalta Hay* Attitude   58
   - The Inspector *Raj*   62

5. The Perfetti Van Melle India Success   69
   - How It All Began   69
   - The First Crisis and the Re-launch Years   74
   - North Meets South and Rural India   78
   - Fiscal Incentives and Masala Munching   83

6. Conquering South Asia ... 89
   - Exporting in the Subcontinent ... 89
   - The Bangla Opportunity ... 91
   - Tigers and Monks ... 94
   - Attacking Pakistan ... 99

7. An Indo-Italian Wedding ... 103
   - Marriage in India ... 103
   - A Single's Life in Delhi ... 106
   - My Big Fat Indo-Italian Wedding ... 112

8. The Russian Roulette ... 120
   - The New Faces of Russia ... 120
   - PVM's Industrial Adventure ... 124
   - Competing in Eurasia ... 127

9. Settling Down in the Middle East ... 131
   - UAE at a Glance ... 131
   - Living and Working in Dubai ... 137
   - Arab Spring and the Middle East ... 144

10. Real Estate and Emerging Markets ... 153
    - An Expatriate's Perspective ... 153
    - Investing in India ... 156
    - Middle and Far East Opportunities ... 161

11. Starting Up in the Dark Continent ... 167
    - Africa Shining ... 167
    - Making Inroads in Africa ... 172
    - Fifty Countries, Thousand Cultures ... 176

12. The BRICs over the Past Decade ... 182
    - Projections and Actuality ... 182
    - The BRICs Get Their Act Together ... 186
    - BRICS and the Green Revolution ... 189

Epilogue ... 196
Acknowledgments ... 200
About the Author ... 202

PROLOGUE

Buongiorno!
Namaste!
Though the meaning of these two words is not exactly the same, such are the traditional ways of greeting somebody in Italian and in Hindi, respectively. If you are reading this book and you happen to be one of the over 1.2 billion people living in India, you are certainly familiar with the second of the two words. As part of the Indian sense of hospitality, the word is often accompanied with a gesture of respect performed with joint hands and a movement of the head. Beware that the head moves vertically and not horizontally: that would be the nodding gesture instead, the meaning of which keeps on confusing Europeans dealing with Indians, since in Europe such head shaking means "NO" and not "YES." If you are Indian, you know this perfectly, hence my apology to you. In case you also happen to follow Indian politics, you are certainly familiar with another Italian in your country, a very famous, though not universally popular, personality of the vibrant and entertaining Indian political life. The one who writes has little to do with that personality, apart from sharing the Italian origins. Such origins are still a matter of pride for me. Despite the not-so-rosy economy of the "Bel Paese" (literally the Nice Country, as Italy is often called), our country still remains one of the largest world economies, with an immense artistic heritage and wonderful places where many would dream to retire. However, the same origins are rather an embarrassing, though undeniable, reality for the better known Italian, whose legitimacy to be in her current role despite such origins has been often the cause of criticism and attack from rival parties. In fact there are other common grounds between me and that person: one is the fact of having (or rather having had in one of the cases) an Indian spouse; another is the fact of having spent a considerable part of our lives in India: few decades for the person and almost one for me. I do not live permanently in India anymore, but I still have a home there, the construction saga of which will be described in

some of the pages to follow. It is just in such a home that this book has seen its birth. According to the Indian perspective that everything happens for a reason (i.e., the law of karma), even an irritating event such as a mosquito bite can be seen as the cause and effect of important events. And this was the case with this book. In a still December night in Goa, I was peacefully spending my Christmas holiday when one felon "macchar"[1] not only managed its way through the several mosquito nets and repellants that allow my mosquito paranoia to subside, but also had the gut to bite my right leg through the bed spread and the night dress. Woken up by this and kept awake by the high decibel trumpet blowing of a "pao"[2] seller, I could not help but think about different issues going through my head. Some concerning the dozens of activities planned for the following day to complete my house there; some linked to the endless emails that one keeps on receiving despite the holidays; others more generally about recent facts. Among these, some correspondences and a telephone call with the publisher of my previous book, who had, to some extent, hinted about me writing a new book in the near future. While I had at that moment denied that such a possibility could even be considered due to my extremely busy schedule, the thought had kept on buzzing in my mind. Probably a part of this had already at a subconscious level started reconsidering a new script. We all know that there is always enough time in a day, provided that we assign the right priorities. Therefore it did not take long before the decision of giving up some of the activities of the busy schedule was taken in favor of finding again the almost forgotten pleasure of remembering, telling, and sharing. Since it was four in the morning and I was roaming around in an unfinished holiday house, I did not have many writing tools with me. Therefore the first words of this book were written on whatever piece of paper was available at that moment (viz., an airline fast track card). And that is how the journey started.

A few words to introduce the reader to the content of this book. He will have by now realized that the book, which is a sort of autobiography, is candid (or CandyD, hence in the title I also become such) not only due to my willingness of being frank and my simple language, but also due to a much sweeter link he is about to discover. Compared to the business orientation of my previous book,[3] this one has a more general tone and targeted audience.

---

[1] Mosquito in the Hindi language.
[2] Typical Goan bread.
[3] Stefano Pelle, *Understanding Emerging Markets: Building Business BRIC by Brick* (New Delhi: SAGE Response, 2007).

The Emerging Markets are a common link between the two books; this last focuses in fact on such countries and markets, since my life and works during the last one and a half decades in many of the same have certainly been more challenging and exciting than the years spent in Italy. Also thanks to a suggestion highlighted by a friend journalist, who had read my previous work and had wished to see more of my day-to-day experience in it, I have tried to alternate business topics, concerning the several markets where I have been working, to the narration of everyday life facts and anecdotes lived in first person or gathered during the last 14 years as an expatriate. This should allow the reader (both a professional interested in business and a leisure one) to find useful material while browsing through the following pages. Even the chapters dealing with business matters are not written for business people only, since I tried telling stories that could be understood by any person with average culture and common sense. So is the case of the chapter dealing with the history of Perfetti Van Melle in India (PVMI), the local India subsidiary of the Perfetti Van Melle Group, a European conglomerate more known for its brands (e.g., Mentos, Alpenliebe, Chupa Chups) than for its corporate name. Other chapters are more narrative and easy to read, with topics ranging from typical problems of the daily life in emerging markets to local habits in different countries and social and political matters of the same. A common thread throughout the book is the issue of cross-cultural understanding while living or operating in emerging countries. I have gone through innumerable situations when a one-sided biased perspective would have led to failure in business deals or problems in personal life; more so being an Italian married to an Indian wife, currently settled in the Middle East and with responsibility over a geographical area extending from Bangladesh to Senegal.

Due to such strong links with India that has become part of my life and that I consider my country of adoption, Italy being my country of birth, I decided to include in this book an essay containing a brief comparison between these two countries. They are separated by several thousand miles of geographical distance but united by a number of historical and sociopolitical similarities, many more than a lay person may expect. The essay in the second chapter is the link between the introductory first chapter, where I briefly share my origins and the initial part of my career in Italy, and the third one where I start narrating about my new life as an expatriate in India. Hence, the second chapter is a stand alone one. Those who think to know very well both the countries may even skip it without prejudice to the flow of the book. The subsequent three chapters narrate in chronological order my experiences of almost nine years of living and working in the Indian subcontinent. I moved from Rome, where I hail from, to New Delhi in 1998, a few years after the opening of the Indian economy. It was still a time of transition from an introverted self-sufficiency seeking social democracy to a more liberal and entrepreneurial nation, where capitalism and the West were looked at with a mixture of suspicion and admiration. My move was to some extent traumatic: leaving a well-settled and organized life in an Italian city where I had worked and lived since birth and landing in a completely new world through the huge, messy, and polluted New Delhi did prove quite challenging at the beginning. But all new experiences must be faced with an open mind, and I thought I had the right attitude for a life change at that point in time. Working in a completely different environment and culture (or better in many cultures, given the amazing diversity of India) was the true challenge of the adventure. However my work was the reason for me to jump into this and I thought that if I succeeded in that, all the rest would have fallen in place. My previous job had been in the Italian Railways based in my own town Rome: from this, managing a sugar confectionery company (here we come to the CandyD link) in a different continent was a major leap. But I was determined not to let my employers down since they had believed and bet on my success in such a position. Hence I decided that for the subsequent few years, my work would have been the focal point of my life and all the rest would have stayed in the background. I could afford doing that also because at that time I was single and the rest of my family in Italy was well settled and not in need of my support. Head down into my new job, I spent the first few weeks listening and learning, while talking as less as possible. My company had been in India since 1994 and, after initial teething issues, had a reasonably good success. However 1998 had been a difficult year, with sales de-growing and several operating problems. My predecessor took some time to hand over the company to me and I cannot say that it was the easiest job takeover of my career. However, little by little things started heading towards the right direction, the growth path was revived, and a virtuous circle started, with innovation generating good results and financial resources that allowed new investments in all round innovation. The same company happens to be today the undisputed market leader in sugar confectionery in India, with the closest competitor having less than half its market share. Given the success recorded, India became the base to expand into other South Asian countries, where in the span of a few years we set up factories, gained significant positions, and became among the strongest market players.

All this is told in the first part of the book, where a brief chapter is also devoted to one of the most characteristic events of Indian life: wedding celebrations. The second part, from Chapter 8 onward, covers my professional and personal experiences in some of the other countries where I have worked and lived from 2006 onward. Starting from Russia, where I was given the opportunity to revive one of the most troubled companies we have had in the PVM Group, hence having the chance to travel often and getting to know better another of the BRIC countries. That was a very interesting period for Russia, since the once superpower that had seen its international might collapse after the fall of the Berlin wall, was on its way to regaining part of its power thanks to the abundance of its natural resources and the thirst of its surrounding countries for the same. The local middle class was expanding and its hunger for Western brands was growing. Walking in the streets of Moscow one would see plenty of branded products and luxury retailers staffed with consumers, while a few meters away there were beggars sleeping under bridges and families still sharing the same kitchen and bathroom as in the old USSR times. Next follows a chapter on the Middle East and in particular the UAE, where I moved in 2007, at the peak of the Dubai craze. At that moment the whole world seemed to have realized that there was a happening place in the Middle East where business was easy and profitable, cars and fuel were dirt cheap, and people could wear half sleeve clothes and swim in the sea almost throughout the year. Hence the number of residency applications growing by the thousands every week and the consequent sky-rocketing prices of real estate. The Middle East was also the ideal base to start looking at new markets where our Group had hardly any presence. My move there would give me the opportunity to travel to new African markets, discover new cultures, new businesses, and face new challenges, the gist of which is narrated in Chapter 11. The last chapter of this book goes back more specifically to the topic of my previous one, the BRIC countries, and tries to understand if the picture painted by Goldman Sachs in 2003 has evolved in line with the forecast made in their original paper focused on these countries.[4] The most recent developments for this cluster—which from an original acronym invented by an economist is becoming a proper geopolitical alliance—among which the BRIC leaders' meetings and their conclusions, are also briefly dealt with in this section. Interestingly the issue of climate change seems to have eventually become a priority even for such countries. The agreement reached in Durban in December 2011,[5] though only drafted in a general document with some in principal statements to be further articulated later, represents a good step forward towards the solution of an impasse lasted for years between developed and emerging nations.

---

[4] "Dreaming With the BRICS: The Path to 2050," *Global Economics Paper* No. 99 (October 2003).

[5] After several days of negotiation, a last minute agreement was found on the conclusive day of the meeting on climate change on December 11.

1

MY PRE-EXPATRIATE LIFE

Where I Come From

"You are the youngest of five brothers? Hats off to your mother: One must be a General to handle such a family!" She is an outstanding person indeed. Energetic, pushy, assertive, and present: these are the first four adjectives coming to my mind when I think about her; but also loving, friendly, giving, and ready to help whenever needed. My parents were originally from the south of Italy but they had moved to Rome when both my grandparents had been elected members of Parliament. "It was a different way of doing politics," my grandmother used to say. "Politicians were gentlemen and they cared about their constituencies. Today they are selfish and greedy." These words were spoken in the late 1970s, but they are even more relevant today after more than 40 years. My father was a lawyer but he practiced the law profession only during the initial years of his career. He later turned into an entrepreneur in the construction and healthcare industries. He had had one sister and two extremely intelligent brothers, one of whom had graduated in law at the age of 19, when in Italy one would normally have started university at that age. My father was also very intelligent, but was not a genius like his brothers. Every person who had interacted with him remembers him as a true gentleman. My mother had studied as a doctor, but the birth of her first son and, after 13 months, of her second one put a full stop to her studies. Despite very good university records she was unable to complete her graduation since, whenever she was about to re-start her studies after the delivery of a child, one more would knock on the door. With a total of five sons she really had her plate full. Later in her life, when all the children had grown up, she started a trading activity in jewels and fashion. I guess I have taken after my mother in my curiosity, perseverance, the love for people, and my multi-tasking capability. Values like uncompromised honesty and integrity, planning and precision, as well as a balanced approach to risk-taking are instead part of my father's heritage. My parents used to say that they had persisted till the fifth son (which was me) with the hope of having a girl. But this was to remain a hope only. There must be a dominant male chromosome in my family: we five brothers had eight children altogether, all of them boys.

My childhood was happy and well balanced. In spite of our family being well off, our parents never allowed us to think that we could live a comfortable life by enjoying the family assets. We had to earn our rewards through hard work. We never missed anything but, rather than with gadgets or branded apparels, we were brought up with our elder brothers' clothes and a very busy schedule of sports, music, and other learning activities. My brothers had been top performers throughout their educational path. The first two had finished the equivalent of an MBBS six months in advance against the course schedule and with the highest marks. The third one had studied law and the fourth economics. My mother used to repeatedly say to me: "You must be the best of all your brothers, since you have the advantage of learning from their experience and mistakes." It was a tough task to be the best of a smart bunch and I did take her remarks seriously. The Italian education system foresees thirteen years of schooling, out of which five are of primary grade,[1] three of intermediate and five of secondary. When starting secondary school one can select a major. The choice for me could have been between Sciences and Humanities, but since all my four brothers had studied Humanities in the same private Catholic institute there was indeed no choice for me but to follow the family tradition. Throughout my schooling I was a top performer—also thanks to the good reputation left by my brothers in that institute. I finished my high school with 60 out of 60 marks. An episode of my school career had become quite famous in my institute. My professor of ancient Greek, a Catholic priest crazy about pop music, was once overwhelmed by my reciting by heart an entire page of the Gospel in ancient Greek.[2] He gave me the highest marks, but, thinking that it was not enough to acknowledge my effort, he also presented me with a banknote of 10,000 lira (about six dollars at that time).

---

[1] This excludes Kindergarten, which is not compulsory.
[2] It was an edition of the Gospel according to Mark, το εὐαγγέλιον κατὰ Μᾶρκον the second book of the New Testament.

Chapter 1: My Pre-expatriate Life | 3

Though I had very good marks and eventually excellent final results, I did not really study that hard during my secondary education. I used to love motorbikes even at that time and had bought a scooter with my own savings. I used to keep it hidden from my parents who were—rightly so—terrified by the thought that a teenager could ride a motorbike in Rome. Homework hours were often replaced by riding trips with friends and I remember those happy years with a mix of nostalgic and joyful feelings. Unfortunately it was a motorbike accident that would mark one of the saddest episodes of my teenage years, in which one of my closest school friends passed away after sliding over some tram rails on a wet spring evening. At the age of 17, boys are in a period of their life when they think that they can do anything, they are invincible and nothing can stop them. Such an episode marked the lives of a small group of inseparable friends who had to face, for the first time, the cruel reality of the fact that life can end at any moment. Since then the concept of impermanence has stayed in my mind, often guiding my decisions. I did study very hard during the university years. At that time we had only two exam sessions during the academic year—in autumn and summer. I remember studying 14 hours a day for my seventh summer paper during the second decade of July while my friends used to go sun bathing to the beaches near Rome; by July end everyone had a nice tan while I was as pale as an aspirin. But the efforts yielded good results eventually. I was the first one in my batch to complete my Master's degree in Economics with 110/110 *cum laude*, beating by five months the next student after me. While trying hard not to waste my time in the compulsory military service in Italy I enrolled myself in a second degree in Political Sciences, which I completed a few years later. Working hard while studying during the weekend was much tougher than studying only and my final marks were limited to 107/110 this time. Even today at nights I sometimes have unpleasant dreams of the endless weekends spent locked in my room studying hard while my colleagues were enjoying the well deserved break from work. My first impact with work was an internship during university in one of the major audit multinationals. I worked there as an assistant auditor for two months, being posted in the offices of oil and pharmaceutical companies. That short period proved long enough for me to realize that auditing was not where I wanted to build my career. Having completed the Master's and cleared the military service issue, I received several job offers in banks and other industries but I had decided to be rather selective and start my career in a company that would give me sound foundations for future growth. Johnson and Johnson (J&J) Italy was to be that company. I still remember the lengthy selection process I had had to go through. It had started with a written screening test for hundreds of applicants in the huge ballroom of a hotel; continued with a few group discussions with the candidates short-listed from the first selection and finished with individual interviews with several J&J management team members. Out of the approximately 2,000 initial applicants I was one of the two hired as permanent employees; two more were given an internship opportunity that might have led to being hired after six months.

My Career Path in Italy

I joined as Assistant Product Manager in the Marketing Department of J&J Italy. On my first day there I was called to the office of the Marketing Director, a South African who had the reputation of being very tough. After a brief introduction about the organizational structure of the company, and more specifically the Marketing Department, he shared with me that I was to work in a very interesting part of the business, a franchise called SANPRO.[3] I had no idea of what that could be and was rather shocked when he took a pack from his display window, picked a small plastic pouch, opened it, and showed me a product the existence of which at that time I was hardly aware: a panty shield. He touched the external surface of it explaining about its smoothness and dry feeling; removed the back release paper to show me how it was sticking to the back of the pad thanks to a special glue; tore the pad to show me the pulp inside it and its absorbing power. "You are lucky since you will work on sanitary protection: there is a lot to do and to learn from such products." Certainly quite a bit to learn for me! Despite the initial surprise, it took me only a few days to start understanding the actual meaning of his words. The working environment was young, stimulating, and very professional. We would spend long hours in office, starting from 8 a.m. and finishing usually around 8 p.m., at times working during weekends. The company was located in the countryside about 40 kilometers from Rome, on the direction opposite my house. In order to reach the workplace before 8 a.m.—since after five minutes' tolerance half an hour of pay would be deducted from the salary— I used to leave home around 6:45 a.m. and come back after 9 p.m. During the autumn and winter seasons I would not see the sun light in my house during the week. Nobody forced us to leave the office that late, but work was exciting and we were made to feel important and told we were managers despite being the latest joiners, and that compensated for the long and hard work

---

[3] Short form for "Sanitary Protection."

and the relatively low initial salary. I was obsessed with my work and would think about it the whole day, each day of the week. So taken was I by my products that I used to casually discuss about them with women I happened to meet socially and they were stunned—perhaps a bit embarrassed too—by my detailed knowledge of their feelings about such rather intimate accessories. That was the beginning of my career and I still cherish those years for the vast learning and the close friendship bonds I developed with colleagues. Even today I am in touch with a few of them and when I travel to Rome we organize former J&J employees' dinners, where we talk of the common past and the most recent experiences.

I spent the first two and a half years of my career there and later moved on to an opportunity offered by a mineral water company belonging to the Danone Group, at that time called the BSN Group. What attracted me to this new position was the opportunity of operating in several markets. The Group had a portfolio of businesses called "Branches," among which was the mineral water branch. Evian was their international brand of still water, at that time already very well-known and distributed in many countries all over the world. They had other brands, among which was another French sparkling water called Badoit, that was believed to have too much of salts, sodium in particular, to become a universally accepted international water. Hence they bought Ferrarelle, a very well-known Italian mineral water with a large share of the Italian market, and decided that this water was to become their international sparkling water. I was given the responsibility of that project which involved the coordination of several countries in Europe, America, and Asia and the development of an international marketing mix. The job gave me the opportunity of using the knowledge of the marketing tools I had developed with J&J in the Italian market across foreign countries: it represented an enriching experience and a widening of my perspective. Working with a French group was an interesting cultural experience. I had the chance to improve my knowledge of the French language and way of working. While the company was based in the vicinity of Rome, I traveled very often to Paris since I had to work very closely with the Evian marketing department based there.

I also used to visit other countries where we had planned to launch the brand. The very different working culture, more formal compared to the American one I had experienced in J&J, and a foreign language I did not fully master made my first weeks rather challenging. However, after a few months, I had drastically improved my French and had adapted to the new working environment; hence I was able to comfortably manage the project and was very excited to learn about the markets of many different countries. We created a very premium marketing mix, including a new bottle still used today, which was designed by me with the help of a graphic studio in London. We tested the water in France and in the USA, launched it in Switzerland and Belgium and started exporting it to select countries in Asia. The strategy studied foresaw to initially introduce the brand in the HORECA[4] channels with the objective of creating a premium image, and subsequently start selling in supermarkets also. The exposure I had through working across several markets was perhaps one of the triggers of my choice to work abroad, which, sometime later, would take me to India. After three years of learning and traveling I was offered, through a head hunter, the opportunity to create and manage an entire marketing department and to shift from the FMCG to the services industry, namely civil aviation. I decided to accept the offer from Iberia, the Spanish national carrier, to head the marketing department of their Italian subsidiary. Creating almost from scratch a marketing function for a company that was not used to any marketing approach was a challenging task. It was a period when the international airlines were trying to develop a marketing-oriented approach and managers coming from consumer goods were the ideal resources to create a marketing culture where one hardly existed. In addition to the fast growth implied in the shift from a position of Senior Brand Manager to the one of Marketing Director being offered, I thought that such an opportunity would further widen my perspective by forcing me to work once again in a different culture and language. My knowledge of the Spanish idiom was rather basic, since I had been studying it through a tape course during my long drives to the workplace in my previous job. Since the language is a Latin-based one, and since I had studied Latin in school and could already speak Italian and French, it did not take me long to learn Spanish and be able to speak and write it fluently.

I fully enjoyed the years spent in Iberia: I loved the Spanish way of working hard but also partying very hard at night. I could not understand how my colleagues could party till three in the morning and start working at nine a.m. a few hours later, to start a feast at night again. After a few days I found out that they used to go home around seven in the evening and sleep for two hours or so. Around ten they were ready again for a round of *caña* and *tapas*,[5] and a late dinner between eleven and midnight. After that they would head for another drinking tour or in some discos till early morning. I was very lucky to have had in my first jobs very competent bosses who, in addition to

---

[4] Abbreviation for "Hotel, Restaurant, Catering."
[5] The *caña* is a draft beer (*cerveza*) and the *tapas* are a very typical Spanish small dish, at times made of canapés, at times with seafood or the delicious Spanish ham (*jamon iberico* or *jamon jabugo*).

being good in their job, were also excellent coaches and good human beings. Setting up a marketing department from scratch and creating a marketing culture would help me in my subsequent assignment in Italy and also in the creation of the new companies in Asia and Africa. In the first two postings I had had two Italian supervisors and a French one. In Iberia my direct superior was the "Delegado" or General Manager of the subsidiary, a fun-loving middle-aged Spanish manager, always very elegant with his Hermes tie and *pochette*,[6] with a deep knowledge of the company and an excellent sense of humor. Thanks to his guidance we managed to make Iberia Italia the largest subsidiary of the airline outside Spain, with one of the most respected marketing departments and a growing customer base. We expanded our number of business travelers through several actions, including a loyalty program conceived by us and designed for the managers' secretaries. We used the hub of Madrid to transport passengers from Italy to several Caribbean destinations and to Latin America, making Iberia the preferred airline for those routes. We evaluated and eventually started operating from a third airport in Italy, hence substantially increasing our customer base.

I had a three-year contract with Iberia: while this was coming to an end I was informally offered to join the central marketing department in Madrid. However, at the same time, I was also approached by a former colleague working for a consultancy firm engaged in a large restructuring work in the Italian Railways. It was a moment of transition for the Railways from a State company to a private one. Also, in this case, the challenge was to create a marketing culture where a technical one was predominant. From having been a mere public service company for centuries, the Italian Railways were pushed to become a more market oriented company by the pressure from the airlines' competition and the foreseen opening of the railway network to foreign firms. They were to become more competitive and independent also in view of a possible stock listing in future. I was hired as the Marketing and Sales Director of the Passengers Division and had the task of introducing new marketing tools, such as the railways website or new automated user-friendly vending machines, and to start infusing commercial know-how and skills among people who had no idea of what marketing or selling strategies could be. As a State company, the Railways could only hire via a complicated and bureaucratic process[7] that implied special exams conducted by State Boards. The only exception to this was for the top managers, who could instead be

---

[6] A small handkerchief kept in the jacket front pocket.
[7] This was called *concorso pubblico*, literally, "public contest."

hired directly from the market without any special procedure. A group of such managers had been taken on board in the months prior to my joining.

We had to literally carry along a huge wagon of almost a hundred and twenty thousand people who had no motivation whatsoever to perform, since they could not be sacked and their promotions were not linked to performances. The task was extremely tough. In thirteen hours of hard work every day, one would have produced maybe a tenth of the results usually obtained in a private company, where things happen in a linear way and are driven by objectives, performances and results. There were much too intricate working logics in the company, including those linked to the government and politicians, to allow a small group of external mangers to achieve acceptable results in a reasonable time frame. The price variable of the marketing mix could not be touched without the approval of the Ministry of Finance. Almost every day there would be politicians pressurizing us to obtain new stops of one of the high speed trains in some small villages so as to enlarge their local consensus and get a bunch of additional votes in the next elections. For those who were used to working in result-oriented private companies, this was a source of great frustration. A few years later, in India, when I went for the first time to the office of the Director General of Foreign Trade in New Delhi, I had a feeling of déjà vu: I realized that the office layout—dark and long corridors with very basic furnishing—and the bureaucratic attitude of the staff were not so dissimilar from what I had experienced in the Italian Railways. One episode made me understand that I would not have lasted long in that job. One day I was called to the office of one of my bosses, who, after talking about some other matters, told me in a paternalistic way: "I see a serious problem with you: You work too much and do not spend enough time lobbying in the corridors." That was true! I was not used to that kind of approach where contacts and networking rather than performances and results were the effective ways to advance in one's career. State companies followed different logics compared to those I was used to and I had to learn to work in a different environment if I wanted to grow in that world. But that was not really my intention, since after about one year I had already decided that I would go back to the private corporate world, having found that more rewarding and straight forward and therefore more in line with my working attitude. However, the experience in the railways had provided me with a very different perspective and exposure, one I could have gained only in similar state companies. The skills of handling the politicians' requests, responding to their interrogations in the parliament or negotiating with the Finance Ministry were part of a unique exposure I could have certainly not had in a private firm. It had also been a matter of pride for me to have had the opportunity to work towards the improvement of my country's infrastructure.

After about two years in the railways, I happened to see in an economic newspaper the advertisement of an undisclosed company searching candidates for General Manger positions in Asia; I decided to apply for the posts. I was called for the interviews after a few weeks at a consultant's office in Milan. Other interviews followed with the Group HR Head, the Group CEO and the former Group Managing Director, who was also the Chairman of the India subsidiary, having been one of the persons who had created the same. The selection process was successful, and, in the spring of 1998, I moved to Milan for my induction in Perfetti, in view of the future transfer to Asia soon after the summer.

2

ITALY AND INDIA: SO DIFFERENT AND SO SIMILAR[1]

Money, People, and Politics

What can a huge country—also defined as a subcontinent both for its physical size and demographic magnitude—a large multi-ethnic and multi-religion reality, have in common with a small boot-shaped strip of land located 6,000 kilometers apart, whose population is twenty times smaller, predominantly Catholic and from a singular ethnic group? We shall soon discover that, though it may appear difficult to believe, the two countries have many similarities and share a number of common traits only known to those who have had the opportunity of spending enough time in both.

Starting from the geography, we shall notice that both countries are peninsulas: one overlooks the Mediterranean Sea while the other rises above the Indian Ocean and the Arabian Sea. One lies in a central position in the south of Europe, the other in a central position in the south of Asia. Both have mountainous chains spanning over their northern regions. Consequently, substantial economic and socio-cultural differences between the north and the south co-exist in both countries.

Shifting to the political field, both nations have established similar forms of government: they are Parliamentary Republics with Bicameral Parliaments.

---

[1] A few excerpts of this chapter were published in an article entitled "India e Italia: un ponte tra due continenti" appearing in *Rivista della Civiltà Italiana*, Nr. 5–6 (Roma: Il Veltro, September–December 2007): 241–252.

Chapter 2: Italy and India: So Different and so Similar | 11

Coincidentally both became such in 1947. The two countries have a federalist vocation; in India there are states endowed with considerable autonomy from the Center, Union Territories and also states with separatist ambitions. What has been happening in the recent past about the possible creation of the new Telangana state prove that such secessionist aspirations are not a matter of the past. Italy too has Regions and other kinds of Local Autonomies, Special Statute Regions, Enclaves with territorial sovereignty situated inside its borders and even Regions with secessionist ambitions. Also in this case such ambitions seem to be progressively increasing and have brought about the formation of a party named the Lega Nord who would like to see the northern region—which they call "Padania"—separated and independent from the rest of the country. Despite being a minority party, this relatively new player[2] in Italian politics has had the power to cause the fall of more than one government. After independence,[3] India has seen limited changes in the parties ruling the country: a large majority party[4] with social democratic inclination has steadily ruled for almost four decades. Only towards the end of the last century were some other political parties able to conquer the power,[5] though with short-lived coalition governments suffering from instability. During the post-war period Italy had a similar political situation: there was one prevailing party[6] with initially center and, later, center-left orientations. Even here, especially during the 1970s and the 1980s, the coalition governments were short-lived; only in the last decades did a certain alternation appear, also in this case a bipolar one. Incidentally, the national flags of the two countries are quite similar: tricolors, one green, white and red, and the other green, white and orange.

Both peninsulas underwent various waves of domination by peoples coming from the north or the west; but none of the invading populations ever ruled over the whole territory within the borders proper to the current sovereign state. The domination left different inheritances: a variety of somatic traits and characteristics (in Italy) as well as of races and religions (in India). Probably it has also been because of such dominations and diversities that among the two populations highly creative bents, superior artistic taste and other shared traits have prevailed. Friendliness and hospitality are two of

---

[2] The Lega Nord party was founded in 1991 as a federation of several regional parties.
[3] India achieved independence from the British Empire on August 15, 1947.
[4] The National Congress Party, or just Congress.
[5] The BJP, a Hindu nationalist party, defeated the Congress and assumed power in 1996.
[6] Democrazia Cristiana was the name of the party, dissolved during the 1990s.

these: the poorest among Indian peasants would renounce his daily meal to provide his guest with a cup of tea; an Italian would do so with a cup of coffee. Strong sense of family life and tradition (recently on the wane in Italy) make Indian sons as dependent on their mothers as Italian sons or maybe even more; however, the idea of unity and significance of the family group has become, over time, less and less dominant in Italy. Here only a few decades ago different generations of one family used to share one roof: in India this is still the norm. Variety and elaborate preparations in regional cuisines are the source of an incredible diversity of food in both countries. Another consequence of past dominations, as well as of the above-mentioned creative bent of the two populations, is the richness of artistic heritages: well-known and celebrated in Italy, less known but equally amazing in India.

A few more soft facts allow Italian people to feel almost at home in India. Let us take, for instance, driving. In both countries the road rules are interpreted in a very flexible way. There is no concept of lane driving, speed limit or parking in the assigned spaces. The road signs are taken more as suggestions than compulsions. Parking on double or triple lanes is rather common; so is stopping in the middle of a crossroad at an orange signal and blocking the way for cars coming from other directions, hence leading to massive traffic jams. Even out of their vehicles people follow similar patterns of behavior while shopping; when in public offices they need to wait for their turn to pay or to get something done. Patiently and orderly queuing in a line is something just not conceivable, either for Italians or for Indians. Whoever has travelled in commuters' public trains in one of the countries knows very well that getting on or off them is always a struggle: more so in India, given the large number of people making use of them. Similarly, when a plane is about to land, Indian people seem to have the unstoppable urge of getting up to collect their belongings from the hat racks despite air crew warnings, so as to gain the first positions in the race to the closest door. The practice of "smart queuing" used to be at its peak in Italian post offices till the moment they were equipped with ticket mechanisms to space the queues. Frustrated by this, Italians now practice their queue-jumping in coffee bars, in the desperate attempt to have their espressos served (rigorously standing at the bar counter) in the shortest time possible. A similar show is witnessed daily in the Indian "booze" shops, particularly at the opening time (late morning) or during the after-office hours. The national sports (soccer for Italy and cricket for India) have in both countries the magic power of reuniting the whole nation, irrespective of social classes, castes or political affiliation. All possible internal conflicts disappear among Indians while watching the national cricket team playing against the arch-rival Pakistan. The same happens in Italy during an important mach played by the *Azzurri*.

Emerging India; Emergency in Italy

After the economic boom of the fifties Italy had reached a position of relevance in the global political scenario. In spite of its relatively modest territorial spread, it became the world's fifth industrial nation, with products and trademarks internationally renowned all over the planet. The country had virtually wiped off poverty and managed to feed the whole of its population, while exporting goods and talents to many countries. Even geo-politically it represented a most valued ally, given its strategic location in Europe's heartland yet bordering with the Soviet bloc. India, at that time, was instead considered the very home of spirituality and an exotic refuge for hippies; a huge nation outstanding mainly for its growing poverty; more famous for Bengal tigers, perennially itinerant holy men and Himalayan vistas, rather than for its factual economic or political weight on the international scene. Let us try to understand what has been happening in both countries in the recent years as well as to disclose the roots of their socio-economic evolution. A brief overall comparison will convey an idea of the current status of the countries.

Starting with India, we have already mentioned that, among the group of the emerging countries with international relevance, its current GDP growth rate is second only to the Chinese one, hovering around 8 percent during the last 10 years. Only recently[7] did the growth slow down to less than 7 percent for various reasons, including the Euro-zone crisis. Unlike other emerging nations this has been achieved without compromising freedom and democracy. The contradictions and problems typical of coalition governments, though, are very much present here, in a country that could achieve even higher development and credibility if led by a strong and stable government. The fundamentals of the Indian economy are steady: there are soaring currency reserves and growing export; the level of inflow of foreign investments has strongly increased during the new century, though not consistently year on year. While all sectors of the economy are developing, the one contributing for more than 50 percent to the Nation's GDP is the Services one. In the most recent Global Competitiveness Index 2011–2012 by the World Economic Forum,

---

[7] Financial Year 2011–2012.

India is ranked 56th out of 142 countries. From the provisional information of the last census of 2011[8] the Indian population has crossed the 1.2 billion mile-stone and is now growing at a rate in excess of 1.4 percent per year (1.64 average for the last decade): at this rate it is likely to overtake China and become the world's largest before 2030. India has now 17.5 percent of the world's population, the demographic characteristics of which are also unique: 31 percent of Indians are under 14 years of age; life expectancy remains below the age of 70. The Indians are therefore ensuring the reproduction of their people and the birth rate provides a large enough labor force capable to support those that are no more part of the same. Their population structure looks like a proper pyramid, with a steady base formed by hundreds of thousands. Literacy is quickly expanding, having now reached an average of 74 percent, though levels vary according to the different states.[9] Technical and business schools are mushrooming: every year tens of thousands of highly qualified graduates, with an excellent command over the English language, enter the work market. The political weight of India in the international scene keeps augmenting, thanks to several factors, not least a wise foreign policy based on a number of bilateral agreements, sometimes apparently contradictory but aimed at the ultimate goal of bringing benefits to the country. Massive economic growth allows financing higher military expenses, thus eventually strengthening the political position of the nation.

Unfortunately, when we examine similar sets of data for Italy, the situation appears very different. The Italian economy shows among the lowest performances among the European peer group. During the last ten years the average GDP growth for Italy was limited to about 1 percent. In the second quarter of 2011 the GDP growth in Germany had recorded 2.8 percent, in France 1.7 percent and in Italy only 0.8 percent.[10] Italy recorded a meagre 0.4 percent growth for the full year 2011, whereas the other two major Euro-economies

---

[8] The 2001 census enumerated a total of 1.03 billion people, whereas the 2011 census brings the number to 1.21 billion. Usually census numbers are approximated by defect, due to difficulties in the registering of people in such a large territory with many poor and illiterate inhabitants. See Chapter 3, "Size Growth Rate and Distribution of Population," page 5 on http://www.censusindia.gov.in/2011-prov-results/data_files/india/Final_PPT_2011_chapter3.pdf.

[9] Differences are remarkable among the states: in Kerala, south India, literacy is over 90 percent; in the eastern state of Bihar, which is the poorest, it just exceeds 60 percent.

[10] Source: European Central Bank, http://www.ecb.int/stats/prices/accounts/html/gdp_growth_yoy_2011-04.en.html.

Chapter 2: Italy and India: So Different and so Similar | 15

achieved a better growth, confirming the trend of the second quarter.[11] Till the first months of 2012 there was no clear and definite middle-to-long term plan in place to overcome the economy stagnation experienced in most recent years. The recently installed technocrat government led by Mr Monti[12] has offered at least some rays of hopes for an improvement of the situation. Economic fundamentals seem rather weak: the agricultural sector is suffering and so is the industrial one, which is mainly based on low technologies and therefore exposed to the emerging countries' competition. The huge debt burden has crossed 120 percent of the GDP in 2011 and caused extreme concern for its sustainability. Within the Euro-zone crisis, Italy seems to be at risk of default. The Italian population is getting old: birth rate is low and most new babies are born out of immigrant families who have recently become Italians. The demographic structure of the country has completely lost its pyramidal shape: the base is gradually lowering down and what would normally look like a pyramid will shortly resemble a piggy bank, the "belly" of which is moving higher and higher. The causes of such fall in births are various. Among these are a dramatic reduction in marriages, changes in married couples' life styles—where both members often work—and delayed access to labor market for young people, implying less economic resources and capabilities to support a family. Many of such traits are rather common in developed countries: what remains typically Italian is the delay of young people in leaving the parental home, resulting in late procreation. The improvement in life quality and the increase in life expectancy aggravate such situations, reducing the self-supporting cycle of the population.[13] Italy is growing older, but the youth that should support economically and morally the aging people is less and less capable to do so. Fertility rate amounts to about 1.3 children for each woman (vs. 2.68 of India). Gross birth-rate is below 0.9 births for every 1,000 inhabitants (22.2 in India), while death-rate is over 10 (6.4 in India). Ultimately, population is the wealth of countries since it constitutes the labor force, holds reproduction potential and contributes to supporting those too

---

[11] Source: CIA Fact Book 2012, https://www.cia.gov/library/publications/the-world-factbook/geos/gm.html (it and fr for the other countries). Germany closed at 2.7 percent growth whereas France closed at 1.7.

[12] The government took charge in November 2011. Mr Monti is an internationally respected economist who spent 10 years holding two of the most important portfolios of the European Commission.

[13] See G. Sacco, "Nessun bastone per la nostra vecchiaia," *Limes: Rivista Italiana di Geopolitica*, Nr. 2 (2006): 85–98.

old to be active. We could state that, as far as demographics are concerned, India and Italy have opposite problems, since the Indian population growth rate is excessive and the Italian one too low. In India, though, the urban birth rate doesn't keep pace with the rural one: this implies that it is especially the poorest and less educated strata which expand, a fact detrimental to a qualitative growth of the country. However, absolute numbers being so high, there will not be any shortage of educated people and, should the internal market be incapable to assimilate the excessive labor force, part of the same would potentially be ready to cross the national borders so as to become part of other countries that, being deficient in population (like Italy), would appreciate such inflows.

In Italy the education framework is also suffering at primary, secondary and higher levels. The share of gross domestic product invested in education between 2000 and 2005 has been around 4.5 percent, which is more than India's 4.1 percent, but also well below levels reached by bordering European countries (i.e., Austria 5.8, France 5.7 percent).[14] If besides comparing quantitative data we take into consideration quality, the gap would probably be even more glaring. The evolution of the Italian educational infrastructure has been marginal and not aligned with the major changes occurred in the last twenty years: consequently, the access to the first job is rather difficult for Italian students, who can hardly compete with their international counterparts.[15] Italian institutes with international standing are few; those internationally acclaimed are practically non-existent. In the last PISA[16] published by OECD in 2009, a good tool to assess the quality of education in different countries, Italy performance was statistically significantly below the OECD average. In the above-cited survey on international competitiveness, Italy resulted 43rd—a few positions higher but not too far away from India. If we look at the educational history of India we shall instead realize that since the 1950s, under the guidance of J. Nehru, India started to plan the future of its youth: a number of universities and applied sciences faculties sprung up in various Indian cities. The initiative was not just public, but private as well. Groups like Tata, one of the major industrial dynasties of the country,

---

[14] Source: Eurostat, http://ec.europa.eu/education/lifelong-learning-policy/doc/report08/invest_en.pdf.

[15] In fact statistics from ISTAT, the central institute for statistics in Italy, showed that in December 2010 the unemployment among young people in Italy touched 31 percent, increasing for five months in a row, as reported by TGCom, http://www.tgcom24.mediaset.it/economia/articoli/1035574/istat-a-dicembre-e-record-disoccupazione.shtml.

[16] OECD (2010), PISA 2009 Results: Executive Summary.

Chapter 2: Italy and India: So Different and so Similar | 17

founded training schools[17] that were soon to become points of reference in the scenario of the Indian education system. Later on, institutes for business education began to flourish; these would become, over time, more and more selective, and provide courses to compete with those of major American and European schools of management. Some of them created partnerships with foreign schools with the aim of encouraging exchanges of talents among different countries. Nowadays in India there are more than

> 380 Science Universities providing 200,000 engineers and more than 300,000 other graduates (disciplines like maths and physics, chemistry and biology)... A state like Punjab, not one of the most developed in the Indian Federation, counts 30 Engineering Colleges, 58 Management Universities and 50 Applied Sciences Faculties... 12 per cent of scientists in all American Faculties are Indian, as well as 36 per cent of NASA mathematicians.[18]

Last but not the least, the overall weight of the two countries in the world political scenario is going towards different directions: reducing in Italy, as a consequence of both a weakened economy and a somehow tentative and not strategically concerted foreign policy; increasing in India, thanks to a flourishing economy, wiser external policy and mounting geo-political relevance. While a few decades ago the comparison between the two nations would have led to different conclusions, today the situation appears much in favor of the emerging nation. While what we mentioned does not pretend to be an exhaustive analysis, a more in-depth study of the mentioned sectors would possibly suggest that the gap between the two countries is bound to increase.

A Bridge between Italy and India

Given the above scenario, future prospects would not appear too rosy for the "Bel Paese." However, comparisons between countries with different levels of economic and social development are not necessarily significant. The above parallel was meant merely to provide a frame of reference: most developed economies (at least the European ones) would probably end up losing in a direct comparison with any of the BRIC economies, especially with one of

---

[17] Among these is the Indian Institute of Science.
[18] See F. Rampini, *L'impero di Cindia* (Milan: Mondadori, 2006). The sentence has been translated into English from the original Italian.

the most promising among them.[19] We also mentioned that the growth for India has come down during 2011 and closed the FY 2011/12[20] short of 7 percent. A similar rate of growth has been forecasted by a government advisory panel for the FY 2012–2013, though some private economists' forecasts stand between 5 and 6 percent.[21] Unfortunately, at the beginning of 2012, a setback was caused by the long-awaited opening of the retail sector's majority holding to Foreign Direct Investors and the subsequent withdrawal of the measure after a few weeks, due to the pressure of some of the coalition parties as well as the opposition. Such back-tracking has certainly not enhanced the confidence of business people in the Indian Government, nor strengthened its image vis-à-vis world leaders and international investors. While in September 2012 the Government decided to again push the FDI in retail reconfirming the decision kept on hold for a few months and got it approved by the Parliament in December, there are still doubts about how the current ruling alliance will be able to sustain such a stance and to push other needed reforms. On the other hand, the first few months of the new technocrat government in Italy have drastically changed the standing of the nation among the financial institutions and international leaders, some of which publicly praised the actions of the newly appointed cabinet.[22] In as little as 60 days Mr Monti's cabinet was able to pass a tough austerity bill with higher taxes and public spending cuts aimed at eliminating the budget deficit by 2013 and a "monumental" pension reform, to the envy of neighboring France, passed after only three hours of strike. It has introduced reforms which should open competition among professional categories (eg., lawyers, notaries, and energy providers) and stimulate economic growth. Despite the mentioned unpopular measures, after the first few months of ruling, the approval rating for the Prime Minister among the Italians stood at a very high level.[23] Unfortunately, due to a change of stand

---

[19] See Stefano Pelle, *Understanding Emerging Markets: Building Business BRIC by Brick* (New Delhi: SAGE Response, 2007).
[20] India follows a Financial Year system beginning on April 1 and closing on March 31.
[21] See http://in.reuters.com/article/2012/08/17/india-economy-gdp-panel-idINDEE87G02 G20120817.
[22] So did Angela Merkel, the current German Chancellor, in January, as reported by Bloomberg on January 12, 2012, see http://www.bloomberg.com/news/2012-01-11/merkel-praises-italy-debt-cuts-as-monti-calls-for-recognition-of-progress.html; the praises continued also at the World Economic Forum meeting in Davos, held on January 25–29, 2012.
[23] See P. Spiegel and G. Dinmore, "The Wishes and Worries of a Parenthetic Revolutionary," *Financial Times*, Middle East, January 18, 2012, also available on http://www.ft.com/intl/cms/s/0/faaef4aa-4101-11e1-b521-00144feab49a.html#axzz2DQEgnRU5. According to Ipsos, a polling agency, Mr Monti's rating in January 2012 was 61 percent, more than double his predecessor's and well above the leader of the largest political party.

Chapter 2: Italy and India: So Different and so Similar | **19**

of one of the major parties which withdrew its support to the Government, Monti resigned in December 2012. He left the country in a much better condition than it was one year earlier when he had formed his Cabinet.

Considering the mentioned similarities between the countries, it should be possible to enhance not only socio-cultural exchanges but also economic cooperation between them. At the end of 2009, statistical data on trade related to the two countries saw still limited but encouragingly growing trade flows (see Figure 2.1).[24]

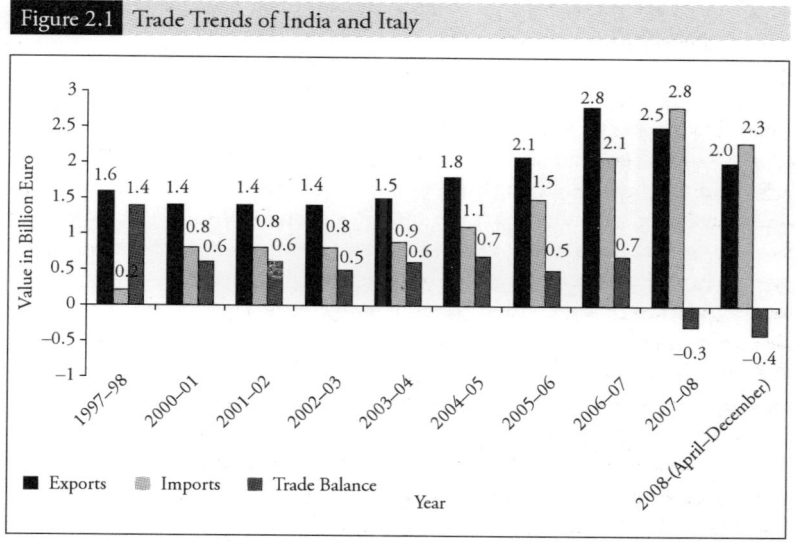

Figure 2.1 Trade Trends of India and Italy

Source: ICE calculations from Export-Import Databank, DGFT, Government of India.

It would seem as if Italy discovered the subcontinent only after 2005: the number of Italian press articles published since February 2005, when the President of the Italian Republic, Carlo Azeglio Ciampi, visited India, is certainly a multiple of those published over the whole previous decade. Further state visits carried out in the subsequent years, including a mission by the Italian Prime Minister R. Prodi accompanied by a large delegation of entrepreneurs and politicians, may be taken as proof of Italy's increasing interests for India.

---

[24] Italy–India Trade Relations by ICE, Italian Trade Commission, on http://www.ice.it/paesi/asia/india/upload/182/International%20Trade_23%20Oct%20for%20ICE.pdf.

In an interview published in an Indian weekly magazine in August 2006,[25] the then Italian Prime Minister remarks that India is bound to emerge as one of the main global actors and sketches out on some of the cooperation lines linking the two countries:

> There is room for unique cooperation between India and Italy. I found the Tata-Fiat agreement was simply whisky and soda—the right combination. India, more than Italy, has a mathematical-software culture. We have no Bangalore in Italy. But we put together excellent, small manufacturing industries. We are unable to do the same thing with software and services of this type. All these characteristics make India and Italy potentially complementary.

The cooperation between Tata—one of the largest Indian conglomerates, diversified in several sectors—and Fiat, now appearing well over the slump of a few years ago after the deal with Chrysler, is providing encouraging results and now also including sales of respective brands in various European and non-European countries. Even though Italian investments in India have been so far rather limited,[26] like Indian investments in Italy, the wave of entrepreneurs of both countries contacting potential partners—partly thanks to the mentioned state visits, partly coming from trips of entrepreneurial delegations organized through collaboration by Indian industrial associations (CII and FICCI) and Italian Confindustria—will no doubt create good business opportunities. Sectors of possible cooperation, as highlighted during the February 2007 Business Forum, happened during the above-mentioned Premier's delegation, were listed as food, metals, machines and electrical machinery supplies, chemicals and manmade fibres. Beyond these, Italian design and Indian handicraft—with its own skilled labor at much reduced costs—could join forces and develop, for example, some ventures in furniture and interior decorations with huge international potential. This way, the creative ability of both countries and the Indian technical craftsmanship could foster technological solutions, both in Information Technology and in precision instrumentation machinery, hardly imitable at an international level. Histories

---

[25] *Outlook*, "I Bet Many Times India Would Take Off. It Has," *Outlook*, August 21, 2006; see also http://vistidalontano.blogsfere.it/2006/08/prodi-e-il-cont.html.

[26] Italy ranked only 12th among the top investing countries in India from 2000 to 2009; see Italy–India Trade Relations by ICE, Italian Trade Commission, on http://www.ice.it/paesi/asia/india/upload/182/International%20Trade_23%20Oct%20for%20ICE.pdf.

of successful achievements by some Italian firms in India[27] and some Indian enterprises in Italy[28] are a valuable record, encouraging entrepreneurs of both countries to larger investments and wider cooperation efforts. Socio-cultural similarities, as already highlighted, have their role in facilitating personal interaction among natives of the countries. Human warmth of both peoples is one common trait, besides the already mentioned affinities due to millennia of historic and artistic cultural heritage. Ultimately, while Italy has an opportunity to be pulled along by one of most powerful engines of the world economy, thus gaining weight among the EU peers group, India may acquire know-how from a country that is seen as the icon of international design. This should prompt the two countries to collaborate at their best in the years to come, stimulating synergies and harvesting mutual gains, both in the economic field as well as in social areas, so as to raise a bridge connecting the quickly growing Asian continent to the mature European side. Such a bridge may create a real alternative to the American continent's supremacy in the last century.

---

[27] For example, Perfetti Van Melle or Piaggio.
[28] This is the case with Videocon, an Indian firm that set up a TV components' production plant in central Italy.

3

WELCOME TO INDIA

Landing in New Delhi

Two suitcases and the telephone numbers of two friends of friends: This was what I was carrying when I landed in India on October 22, 1998. What an irony in the fact that just a few years earlier, while boarding a plane from New Delhi to Rome, I had promised to myself not to go back to India, at least not until my retirement age. The circumstances were very different at that time. I had gone to visit Singapore and Kuala Lumpur for a holiday and had travelled with a frequent flyer reward ticket. I only had enough miles for a free ticket to India; so I decided to buy a ticket from there to my final Far-East destination and planned a stop-over in Delhi on my way back. Possibly due to the fact that I was particularly impressed by the green and tidy Singapore I had just visited for the first time, or perhaps because Kuala Lumpur sky scrapers had surprised me, my stop-over in the Indian capital was not among the most exciting experiences of that trip. The disappointment started from my arrival at night in an old and dirty airport, followed by the sadness and surprise of finding hundreds or people sleeping in the porch just outside the same. The scene was further aggravated later on by the stinking Ambassador car that took ten minutes to start and was driven by a peculiar individual with steel bracelets and a black turban on his head. These initial moments did not create an immediate chemistry between me and the country and the subsequent three days did not change much of my initial impression. The visit to a few dusty museums with artifacts without any description, seemingly just abandoned in dark halls; cows roaming around and eating any kind of garbage left in the streets; taxi drivers trying to cheat me in all possible manners, either charging a multiple of the due fare or taking me, by their initiative, to various shops to earn commissions from the retailers; finally the fact of staying not in a hotel, but in the house of an acquaintance who had kindly offered to host me, whose place was located just on the noisy Outer Ring road: All these circumstances made me reach the conclusion that India was not a country in my top list and I would have certainly waited many years (if ever) before planning another trip there.

And so it happened that less than ten years since such thought, I was to be posted just in that country. This time it would not have been a short three-day visit, but possibly a three-year stint. Looking back, I realized that this was an important lesson learned for me, teaching me that I should never say "never" again. At times I still wonder how I had come to the decision of leaving a very comfortable life in my own city; a well paid job 15 minutes away from my residence; a well furnished and owned apartment in an exclusive location in the Eternal City; a loving mother, four helpful brothers and a very large number of longtime friends and relatives. I had decided to leave all this to jump into a risky job for a company I hardly knew, in a country alien to me where I had no friends whatsoever. Over time I have given myself some rational explanations such as my love for traveling, my curiosity about new cultures, my wish to test what I could achieve, starting from scratch, of a completely new life in a different country. I have also thought that a close relationship with a girl who was a scholar in Sanskrit and researching the subcontinent had helped change my pre-conceived opinion about India. A certain role in my decision was played by my recruiters, who, during the hiring process, had offered to me the opportunity of a general management position in one of the four countries where the company had started operations or was about to, without disclosing which one. India was only one of the four, whereas the others (including Indonesia) were definitely more attractive to me; hence the risk of ending up in India was limited to 25 percent, still an acceptable percentage. My recruiters knew that India would have eventually been my destination, but they had also perceived that the country was my last choice and had smartly kept the other options open in order to ensure my joining. All the above are rational explanations. But, ultimately, somewhere it must have been written that I was to go to India, I was to spend many years there and learn to love the people, meet my wife and create the unbreakable bonding with the country that would completely change my life.

There I was in the autumn of 1998, landed in Delhi and proceeding towards my hotel. This time my company had organized a meet and greet for me at the airport, where the people sleeping on the floor had been replaced by a multitude clinging to a fence surrounding the arrival area. They were looking at the arriving *firang*s,[1] some with curiosity, some others with the hope of extorting easy money to complement their meager incomes. No Sardar with an old car this time but a rented car with a decently dressed driver taking me to a newly opened five-star hotel in proximity of the airport. The starting was definitely better compared to my previous experience! The smiling faces of the hotel staff gave me the first glimpse of the Indian hospitality deeply rooted in this people and contributing to make Indian hotels among the best in the world. Once alone in my room I realized that "it was really happening"; a new life was about to start and a whole new world was out there to be discovered. I had reached on a Saturday night and had intentionally planned to spend the Sunday relaxing in the hotel before starting work on Monday. That Sunday the weather was extremely pleasant, as it often happens in Delhi when the winter is approaching and the fog has not yet started. Coming from Milan, where at that time of the year the home heaters are already fully working and warm overcoats to go out are a must, the fact of spending the first day relaxing in a swimming pool, reading a book and munching exotic food was certainly an unexpected bonus. The initial impressions made a very positive mark on me, particularly since I had arrived with very low expectations. Learning from that experience over the years I made it a point to ensure that expatriates arriving in a country for the first time were greeted in the appropriate ways by the hosting companies under my responsibility. On the first day in India I also experienced one of the innumerable surprises I would have had during the years in India: climbing up and down on a high fence bordering the pool area, a few monkeys looked curiously at me and kept jumping around with no fear of the hotel staff, who would try chasing them away from the leftover food abandoned by some guests. I had read about the colorful and diverse population crowding the streets of India but I would have not expected to find such "guests" at the swimming pool of a five-star hotel.

Of Roads and Spirituality

The first day of work started with a long wait in the lobby of the hotel since my predecessor, who was to pick me up at 9:30 in the morning, showed up only one hour later. The trip to the office, located in the factory premises

---

[1] *Firang* is a term commonly used in north India for foreigners.

approximately 40 kilometers away from the hotel, gave me the opportunity to meet some specimens of the local population found in the streets. Not only cows, which I had already spotted in my first trip, but also horses, camels and even elephants were happily walking beside us. This was happening not in a small street of a village but on one of the most important highways of the whole country, the National Highway No. 8 (NH8), linking Delhi to Jaipur via the state of Haryana and later heading towards central west India. This highway was bound to become a source of knowledge, entertainment but also frustration for me. The hotel that was my home for the first few months in India was located on this road; so was our company's factory hosting the office, to which I would drive six out of seven days in a week; just a few meters off the highway was to be also the house I would select a few months later, and that would be my residence through the years spent in the country. Therefore, for 25 days in a month I would drive up and down the several kilometers to my office, observing the daily life going on along the road: The small shops starting up their business, at times with good success and results that would allow them to expand into larger spaces, renovate and place flashy boards to advertise; a few larger retailers starting operations with grand openings and being forced to shut down after a few months due to poor results or because their illegally built premises were demolished in order to leave space for the ever-expanding highway; farmers carrying on overloaded tractors their huge stacks of hay kept together by ropes that often would snap and let the goods flood the road; vans with huge quantities of cabbage so neatly stuck one to the other that would almost look like modern art sculptures; shepherds crossing the highway to take their flock from one field to another. During a specific time of the year religious pilgrims (called *Kavedi*s) would walk for hundreds of miles carrying the holy Ganges water to some shrines. For this event, happening once a year during the month of July, a special partition on the road would be created so as to leave a dedicated lane allowing a (relatively) safer walk.

As already mentioned, the highway we talk about is a national one, linking the National Capital Region (NCR) area to important cities and eventually to Mumbai. As it usually happens in emerging countries, infrastructures are continuously upgraded, though the works may take decades to be completed and by the time they are about to finish a further upgrade is already starting. Therefore the landscape along the NH8 kept on changing (and still does) with new lanes being added over time. This highway in particular crosses the area of Gurgaon, an upcoming city that, despite being in the state of Haryana, is today considered an extension of Delhi and represents a sort of new business district of the capital. When I arrived in India, Gurgaon was still a large and crowded semi-rural village a few miles away from Delhi: however, the old part of the town had progressively lost relevance in favor of the new Gurgaon, a conglomerate of high rise office towers and residential buildings which would soon host the offices of most of the multinational corporations creating large hubs in the country. Due to the massive development during the first years of the new century in that area, the highway had to be regularly widened and many long flyovers and bridges built to ease the traffic.[2] Nothing of this existed then, and only the first 10 kilometers or so of this road after Delhi's border would look like something similar to a highway. The balance distance to my office was a single-lane road where every alternate day a broken truck would be found in the middle of it blocking the circulation and forcing the commuting vehicles to find creative ways to overcome the obstacle. At times through side roads, other times through the fields, quite often with long diversions across the nearby villages. Thanks to such diversions I was first introduced to some glimpses of rural India. Initially I was saddened by the poverty I could see in such small villages: half naked little children in the street playing with old tires, wood pieces or whatever else they could use as a toy; women carrying huge weights on their heads and walking for long distances; a make-shift butcher shop with meat pieces left in the open and surrounded by hundreds of flies. Later on such sadness changed into a sort of sympathy, almost admiration for the dignity I started seeing among those simple people; the joy I would see in the eyes of the children playing with each other; the elegance I would find in the way women carried their colored and humble sarees even while engaged in heavy work. Little by little I realized that I was wrongly linking poverty with sadness, a mistake that people living in developed countries often make when they first visit some emerging countries and are confronted with poverty. The reality is that people can have just the money to survive and still be content and joyful. The belief that in today's world one cannot live a happy life without a television, a mobile phone or a car is fundamentally false. Even today, in 2012, thousands of villagers in India do not know what the internet is; millions of people in the globe do not have access to electricity, have never sat in a car, watched a television or used a cellular phone. Yet many of these people have fully satisfying lives revolving around more important and healthier habits and values other than the latest electronic gadgets.

---

[2] Eventually, by the year 2008, some stretches of the same highway had to become an access controlled toll road, though even today the access regulation leaves much to be desired, and the toll payment creates huge bottlenecks.

Another ever changing road which I would discover over the years was the Mehrauli-Gurgaon road (MG road). Curiously in other Indian cities there happens to be an MG road, but the initials have different meanings there.[3] This was the second major linking road between Delhi and Gurgaon but unlike the previously mentioned one, it was neither a national road nor a highway.[4] Starting from the NH8 in IFFCO Chowk, a crossing notorious for its frequent traffic jams, the road would cut across the new Gurgaon, run inside the marble market and continue with long straight stretches alternate to steep curves for several miles; it would continue along a few "farm house"[5] complexes—among which is the Chattarpur area hosting beautiful temples—reaching Andheria mor[6] and eventually the Kishanghar Mehrauli area, adjacent to Vasant Kunj and close to the Qutub Minar complex. This is one of the marvelous attractions of Delhi, a tall minaret constructed during the twelfth century and an example of Indo-Islamic Afghan architecture. Between the quoted landmarks the road crosses a vast green forest, also hosting an archeological park not much known and out of the normal tourist itinerary. So many names and places would not have much meaning for a common person, but instead evoke vibrant images to the Delhites[7] and to those who have had the opportunity to drive through the localities and visit the places. The initial part of the MG road is the stretch where the first mega-shopping malls had first appeared. The two pioneers were built in the first years of the new century and represented a stunning innovation for the local people. So famous had they become that during weekends dozens of tourist buses from the surrounding areas unloaded thousands of curious visitors who would spend the full day walking inside the several floors full of shops, restaurants

---

[3] For Instance, Mahatma Gandhi Road in Bangalore. Interestingly, even in Delhi there is a Mahatma Gandhi Marg, but it is only a segment of the Outer Ring Road, and it is not commonly called MG Road.
[4] In 2010 a proposal from the Ministry of Road and Transports to upgrade this road to an 8-lane highway was rejected by the Haryana Government; see *Hindustan Times* on http://www.hindustantimes.com/India-news/NorthIndia/No-national-highway-status-for-Mehrauli-Gurgaon-road/Article1-506171.aspx. Despite not having the official status of a highway today, this road looks very different from the one it was in the late 1990s. Most of it is already a six-lane high speed road, and the Metro pillars and elevated railway running in between the lanes have in some way reduced the charming appearance of a country road it used to have.
[5] Farm House is a characteristic local reference to villas with adjoining land. The denomination was introduced mainly for fiscal reasons—incentives given for farm use—rather than for any actual farming activity happening in the same.
[6] Literally meaning "dark corner."
[7] Word commonly used to indicate Delhi residents.

and other attractions. While this generated an incredible number of footfalls, these would not directly be translated into sales and revenues for the retailers, since most of the visitors would step in the mall to spend their time "window shopping" in a pleasant air-conditioned environment. The two original malls[8] had an extraordinary success: since they were built facing each other on the opposite sides of the road and without any connecting bridge or tunnel, hundreds of people kept on shuttling between the two of them crossing the high traffic MG road and creating safety and circulation problems. Thanks to the success of these malls several new ones started mushrooming in the same area. Most of them hosted the same retailers present in the two original ones, hence becoming unnecessary duplications for prospective shoppers, since the malls had all been built in the radius of less than a kilometer. When some builders started understanding that too many malls with the same outlets would not attract additional people, they tried to differentiate the positioning of the shopping centers by specializing in a given field (e.g., home furniture shopping). In the span of three years about ten mall projects had started in the same area: not all of them were eventually completed. Out of those finalized some started operating with large delays, since there were not enough retailers to be found ready to invest in expensive spaces. Overall, apart from the initial two malls only a few of the others had a reasonable success; some were complete failures and never took off; some others were inaugurated but became large liabilities for the stakeholders.

In and around the first two kilometers of the MG road in Gurgaon, a disproportionate number of high rise buildings were to be constructed, making this place the business hub of the large corporations who had entered India during those years or were already present but had shifted their offices away from the expensive and congested Connaught Place in central Delhi. Among these, our company decided to shift the corporate office from the factory in Manesar to the more convenient Gurgaon in 2001, and took some space in one of the first business complexes on MG road. Also this road has seen several changes over the year, even if not to the extent of the NH8. The stretch crossing the marble market was enlarged only in 2010, mainly to accommodate the confluence of another road linking this locality with the Sohna area. A few years earlier the pillars for the Metro project had started appearing, with consequent diversions of the main road lasting till the completion of the project in 2011. Other interventions to add lanes had been made since the year 2002. Partly because of the space needed for the

---

[8] Commonly called DT and MGF malls.

expansion and also due to the attention that the local government was giving to the developing important communication artery, the municipality was obliged to shut down numerous shops operating along the road. Such small stores had been there for several years and it was difficult to understand how nobody had ever found out that they were not legal. But even more surprising was when they decided to shut down a few large shopping malls also—named 1 MG and 2 MG—which hosted many fashionable apparel brands, and had become landmarks on the road. The project to build these must have taken several years and one of them had been in operation for a year or so. They were both finely decorated, externally and internally, and the overall investment to build them had certainly been substantial. However, all of a sudden, somebody decided that they were illegal. The retailers in the malls, who had heavily invested for the purchase and the decoration of their shops, were ousted within two days. Following a demolition drive happening in that period in other areas of Delhi also, the buildings were half demolished the day after all retailers had vacated them. Even today, after more than six years, the ruins of the buildings are left in the same state, abandoned and forgotten, offering an unusual post-war impression to those who drive by and with prejudice to the safety of people who might find their way inside the building.

Somewhere close to such semi-destroyed edifices I had to experience my first encounter with the parallel spiritual word coexisting with the very materialistic aspects of the daily life in a country in profound evolution. Through some acquaintance I had been told that in a small road not far from the Kishangarh area there was the house of a very powerful spiritual master—they called him Guruji—who received his devotees at given times during the week. Though such sessions were not opened to everybody, by mentioning the name of such acquaintance I was let into the house during one of those spiritual gatherings. In a long room, many people, maybe two hundred, all Indians, were sitting or kneeling in silence, occupying all the space available. A small corridor left in the middle of the hall led to a slightly elevated podium where the spiritual leader, dressed in white local clothes, was sitting facing the audience with his eyes shut. The attendees seemed to be in a sort of meditative status, interrupted at times by prayers in a language I was not familiar with. Every hour or so there was a short break when water was served for those who needed it and every two breaks some light snacks were also offered. During such breaks a few of the devotees, possibly those closest to Guruji, went to him either alone or with some people, spent short moments with him and then left the stage to others. When the evening was about to finish, all devotees were allowed to walk up to the podium, exchange a few words with

Guruji, get his blessing and move out. The overall experience was certainly unusual but extremely interesting.

Despite my difficulty in understanding the prayers and whatever was going on during the evening, as well as the pain of sitting for several hours on the floor in an uncomfortable position, I could feel that there was something special in that person, and that the hall emanated positive energy. When I walked to him at the end of the evening I was shortly introduced and just shook hands with him: he said a few words, in fluent English, stating that I could go there whenever I felt so and I thanked him for that. I was rather surprised by his good English as well as by his kind invitation. Later on I talked to some of the people who were there, and they told me that the short exchanges I had witnessed between him and the devotees were often requests for his help for various problems—health or other—they had. He would just listen to them, at times reassuring them, at other times saying nothing or just mentioning that he could not do much for the issues. Apparently many devotees had actually found major problems resolved after their visits, including fatal diseases having been healed. No rational and logical explanations could be given for such developments. At times, such sort of "miracles" may happen, thanks to the power of our own mind. Some call these events self-suggestion: our mind is so convinced that an event—in this case the intervention of a "holy" person—will help healing a disease that our whole body works with a renewed energy towards that objective. Having said so, some of the events narrated to me were very hard to explain rationally.

Of Friends and Celebrations

Going back to my first day of work, I distinctly recall arriving at the factory and finding some colorful decorations at the entrance reminding me of those one could find in Italy during Christmas time. I did not dare ask what they were, since I thought it might be a local custom to decorate factories and offices in such a manner. Only during the course of the day, while meeting the Human Resources in charge, did I come to know that those lights and adornments were part of the celebrations for Diwali, the festival of lights, possibly the most important Hindu festival of India,[9] which had happened just the previous week. I realized then that I had landed in India just the

---

[9] With the exception of the South, where possibly Onam is the most important festival. Diwali is also celebrated by other religions in India (e.g., Jains and Sikhs, though for different reasons associated with the dates) and is a National Holiday.

day after Diwali, and this was considered to be auspicious. The similarities to the Christmas decorations were due to the fact that Diwali is for most of India what Christmas is for most of Europe. Over the years I had the chance to celebrate many Deepavalis[10] in the country and understand much more in depth the spirit of the festival as well as the rites and customs linked to the same. One of the interesting moments of the week prior to Diwali was Dhanteras, the day when people were supposed to buy gold, silver or at least metal utensils. Since I kept forgetting about this custom, my very efficient secretary used to remind me by calling me on my mobile to ensure that I did not finish the day without the auspicious purchase. Another custom linked to this period of the year was the refurbishing of the houses to be completed soon before the mentioned celebrations. Despite my several inquiries I have never been able to get a clear answer about the reasons of such timing, but my rational explanation was that during those days people keep visiting houses of friends and relatives in order to exchange gifts: the renovation works were therefore carried out in preparation for such visits. Another possible reason more pertinent to the North of India is linked to seasonal factors: October is a month of still warm and pleasant weather there, with sunny days and temperatures comparable to the beginning of autumn in South Europe. This kind of moderate climate with low humidity allows carrying out work in the open and favors the drying of the freshly painted walls.

One of my favorite celebrations just a few days before the Diwali week used to be Dussehra, celebrating the victory of the Good on the Bad and the removal of the evil.[11] For the popular legend in this day Lord Rama defeated the devil Ravana, who had abducted Sita, Rama's wife, to Sri Lanka. I remember watching the celebrations for the first time in a large open space in Delhi where very tall effigies representing Ravana had been installed. Soon after the sunset the ceremony of setting fire to these had started amidst the increasingly loud music, the dances and the euphoria of the crowd happy to see the symbol of evil being burnt. The whole month leading to Diwali is dense with customs and rituals, which culminate with the lighting of the *diyas*,[12] supposed to stay

---

[10] Literally the meaning is "row of lamps" and is another word for Diwali used in other parts of Asia where the festival is also celebrated (e.g., Singapore and Malaysia).
[11] The celebration also coincides with the beginning of the harvesting season, which ends sometime after Diwali. For this it also carries the meaning of renovation, possibly also symbolized by the burning of the evil Ravana.
[12] Small celebratory candles mostly in terracotta containers. According to the Indian traditional legends the lighting of such candles is also associated with the return of Lord Rama after 14 years of exile.

lit during the whole night, marking the end of the celebrations. Together with candles the home lights also need to be left on with the objective of showing the way to the Goddess Laxmi, bringing prosperity and wealth for the following year. In fact Laxmi "pooja" is one of the most important acts of the whole festivity. Poojas are Hindu prayer rituals to some extent comparable to the Christian mass or the Islamic prayers in the mosque, with the difference that they do not necessarily happen on a given day (such as Sunday for the Mass or Friday for the main Islamic weekly prayer). They are performed on any day and for any occasion, do not have a fixed duration or fixed prayers and liturgies and can be very lengthy and articulated or extremely simple and short. Some people perform poojas everyday; some others attend them only for some particular occasions. Often a "Pandit," a sort of priest, leads the rituals: he decides about what to do, how to do and what to say. It so happens that some Pandits pronounce mantras or sing songs that most of the audience does not know or understand. He receives voluntary donations from the organizer of the pooja as well as from the participants. I remember my colleagues and friends telling me that a safe way to ensure that the ritual is performed within acceptable time limits (say 30 to 60 minutes) is to "bribe" the Pandit with a generous offer before he starts the performance: such initiative ensures that he does not need to prolong the rite in order to impress the audience with his skills and earn further donations.

While the two mentioned festivals mark the onset of the winter season, two other very characteristic occasions mark the end of it: Lohri and Holi. The first one is typical of North India, particularly Punjab, and should happen in the coldest day of the winter season: from that night on the weather would progressively improve till the onset of the summer, marked by Holi. I remember being invited to the celebrations in the house of a Sikh[13] family in New Friends colony in Delhi. The whole extended family took part to the get-together happening in their garden, where a large bonfire was lit. People were sitting around the fire while the hosts prepared delicious skewers on a barbecue. Given the rather low temperature, at times also close to 4/5 degrees towards the late hours of the evening, blankets and shawls were handed over to the guests, apart from generous offerings of spirits (often abundant in Punjabi parties) contributing not only to the warmth but also to the general happy mood of the night. The first of such celebrations I attended had found me unprepared both for the weather and for the conviviality. The daily temperature on a sunny day was in the low 20s centigrade and I had not anticipated

---

[13] One of the religions of India, particularly practiced in the north.

it to lower to the extent I was experiencing. Despite the shawls I borrowed, I did feel cold and was encouraged by friends to mitigate this feeling with the help of the drinks. Not realizing that the immediate relief of the drinks from the cold would have later on had side effects, I happily accepted their generous offers. The hangover in the morning after would act as deterrent for the "Punjabi parties" I would have otherwise attended in the future. Holi, the festival of colors, is one of the oldest celebratory customs in India: mention of the same were found on a stone inscription dating back to 300 BC found at Ramgarh in the province of Vindhya.[14] Different from Lhori, this festivity is widely spread across the country, though under different names. The legend says that the same Lord Krishna started the tradition by applying colors on his beloved Radha. To celebrate the occasion, people meet to "play" Holi in private homes but also in public places and on the streets. In fact it is very difficult to come back home with no damage on that day, be it to one's car, dress or hair. The tradition wants that colors in form of powder are applied on different parts of the body and dresses of people, and water is also poured to ensure that the same stick to the skin and provide an unusual rainbow effect, giving a funny look even to the utmost serious people. The celebrations usually happen among friends, but nobody is exempted, be he/she a member of the family, a work colleague or a complete stranger. In fact this is one of the rare occasions when the Indian society allows loosening of one's inhibitions in public. Also in this case, I associate some cherished experiences during the years in India with such festive occasions. After one of my first Holi celebrations, I ended up having to throw away all the clothes I was wearing, since they were irremediably stained. Next year onwards I ensured that I wore old clothes during the day, possibly white ones, where the mixed colors could stand out and transform a simple t-shirt into a work of art. Many years after my first, I celebrated Holi again with the person who would later on become my wife. This time she was the one to be caught unprepared by the consequences of the typical drink consumed during the occasion. Unaware of the deadly effect of the mix called *bhang*, containing intoxicating substances and offered as a refreshing milky drink, she consumed several glasses of this and I had to eventually take her home in a rather happy and confused state, where laughter and headaches alternated until the day after.

The first few weeks of my life in India were an immense learning experience. As planned, I used to spend long hours at work where I was progressively

---

[14] See "History of Holi" in http://www.holifestival.org/history-of-holi.html.

introduced to the complexity of managing a foreign company in an environment that was yet on his way to change and open up completely to foreign investments. The days were intense, full of events, meetings, discussions and decisions to be made. Once back in my hotel, exhausted by the amount of information processed during the day, I used to relax by reading, writing to friends and watching television, mainly the international news channels, which were one of my few links with the rest of the world. At that time the internet was not yet widely spread: the hotel did have a business center with internet connections, but the connecting speed was rather slow and costs were almost comparable to those of the international calls (called ISD). Incidentally, the use of short forms was one of the first peculiarities of the local writing jargon I noticed while, hungry to learn as much as possible about the new country where I was, I used to devour several local newspapers in a day. In an average press article one would have found dozens of short forms such as NCR, AIIMS, CII, DGFT, RBI and so on. To the lay person, unfamiliar with the local institutions and events, such initials (rarely explained in full forms) do not mean much and affect the comprehension of the text.

The fact that it took a few days for me to have a fully available vehicle with a driver, a few weeks to have a mobile phone and a few months to have a laptop, did initially limit my communication with the external world. During my second week in Delhi I thought that I should move my first steps towards a social life and decided to make good use of the two telephone numbers I had carried with myself from Italy. I called then the first contact on the short list, whose number had been given to me by a friend I had met in a music group in Milan. My own town is Rome, but I had moved to Milan when I joined my company, the headquarters of which was located there. When leaving that city I had mentioned to some friends that I would be relocating to India, and one of them happened to have lived for many years there during her school time. Only much later was I to discover that she was the daughter of a very influential Italian businessman linked to the ruling elite. She gave me the coordinates of a person she had known since those times, whose number I then dialed. Having established the contact we decided to meet in my hotel for a drink and so started my first friendship with an Indian person. Ravi was possibly an atypical Indian, having studied and worked in the USA for a few years and later returned to India. He was the only son, and had decided to come back to his native country so as to be closer to his aging parents. Having lived abroad also during his childhood, his frame of mind was much more open and progressive than that of an average local person of his age group. His way of looking at his country in an objective and detached way, mixed with the insights of being an Indian and having been brought up in an Indian upper-middle class family made of him a good mentor to coach me through my first steps within Indian society. Coincidentally we happened to be approximately the same age, both single and living in rather close locations, a non-marginal factor in a city like Delhi where distance and traffic can become a deterrent to meeting. He introduced me to a few of his friends, who over time became my good friends too. Thanks to him, I could start familiarizing with a cluster of relatively young Delhi professionals and their culture, families and daily life.

Delhi is a huge metropolis of several million people but for some aspects used to be like a small village. By segmenting among the well-off areas of residence in south Delhi, the circles of friends of a certain age group and with a given social background were not very many. Furthermore, at that time, the night life of the capital was limited to private parties or pubs, lounges or restaurants in the main five-star hotels one could count on the tips of his fingers. Inevitably when going to such outlets one would end up meeting the same people and spotting the same faces. Slowly I started understanding better the way that cluster of society thought and behaved, acquiring some of their idiomatic expression, comparing their mores and beliefs with those belonging to my culture and, when beneficial, adopting some of them.

One funny thing very common in such south Delhi crowd was the social need (almost a duty) of "showing one's face" in celebrations and parties. This would happen both in home parties and in public restaurants and clubs. The upper class fashionable members seemed to have the urge of hopping around get-togethers and "happening places" just for the sake of being seen there and maybe photographed by the local paparazzi so as to gain a visible portrait in the "Delhi Life" pages of the most popular local English language Newspaper.[15] The more the appearance on such pages, the higher the urge to perpetrate the hopping activity, the fringe benefits of which were invitations for the trendiest fashion shows, events and parties. The look in the pictures was to be always smart, casually smiling, and often sporting a drink; better if the beverage was the latest trendy one. Here I open a short parenthesis on the drinking habits of such part of the Indian society, whose drastic evolution I have noticed over the span of about 10 years. In the late 1990s, my Indian friends used to be heavy users of hard spirits (namely scotch by the gentleman and vodka mixes by the ladies). When the first imported beers started appearing some pioneers began occasionally to move towards them, while leaving the hard drinks for the latter part of the evening. Ladies moved towards the newly

---

[15] The Delhi tabloid insert in *The Times of India*.

launched readymade branded cocktail[16] and occasionally to some sweeter liquor. More recently drinking wine had become trendier among both men and women. This was also due to the fact that some Indian vineries had started operating and educating their targets, as well as the fact that custom duties on imported wine had been reduced. During the last parties I had hosted in Delhi, the ratio between scotch and wine had completely reversed, and by the end of the evening the empty wine bottles outnumbered by a ratio of one is to seven the scotch and vodka ones.

Back to the society I was discovering and still in the topic of drinking and eating habits, I recall the first party at somebody's place I attended after a few weeks I was in the country. My friend Ravi had picked me up from the hotel and driven me to a home where a party was being hosted by some friends of his. I had received a warm welcome by the host and the other guests present there, and had spent quite a long time talking to a person who had allegedly learned Italian in the past (obviously a far past) and wanted to show off whatever little he could remember of my native language. My glass had been refilled already a number of times and snacks had been served, but around 10:30 p.m. I started feeling rather hungry and went back to my friend asking if the evening was to be a cocktail party or a dinner. He had understood that there would be dinner but went to check again and confirmed. We kept on drinking and chatting for another hour or so, when I finally convinced him that we should leave and go to get a bite somewhere. With this idea we started the good bye round, but when we approached the host he categorically refused to let us go, insisting that we should have dinner and only then leave.

We were therefore stuck there with an empty stomach waiting for a dinner that arrived only towards 12:30 a.m. It was served as a buffet in the adjoining room, where we were advised to move. Surprisingly, by 1 a.m., everybody had quickly had his dinner, thanked the guest, and left the party, while I was still having the dessert. After we left, my friend explained to me that dinner is served very late in north Indian parties, since the main attraction for the participants is the drinking part, whereas the food is only a stomach-filler. During my years in Delhi I would have often attended parties where the dinner was usually served late in the evening, at times pushed to the early morning hours. The reason is indeed the fact that conviviality happens in the drinking act rather than in the eating one, and the meal is instead consumed quickly and often standing. This is very different from the European habits,

---

[16] Among these the Bacardi Breezers.

where people sit and chat while eating and meals can last as long as five or six hours.

Cars and Arts

My social life in Delhi improved sensibly once I had a car fully at my disposal. Since I would have inherited my predecessor's company car once he had officially left the company, in the interim I was given a rented car with a driver. This sounded already unusual to me, since in my country one would normally rent only the car. However, given the traffic and the peculiar Indian way of driving I agreed with the fact that a driver would have been useful. Those days the car market was quite regulated and protected from the international producers though with very high custom duties. Friends had told me surprising anecdotes about cars in the early 1980s, when the same were considered a rare and precious luxury. There were six months waiting lists between the placing of the order with full payment and the delivery of the car. The scene changed after the creation of a joint venture between the Japanese Suzuki and Maruti Udyog, which saw the first production in 1983. The Maruti 800 was the first car of the venture to be produced, based on the model of the Japanese producer. It was the only "modern" car at that point in time, since the competitors, the Ambassador produced by Hindustan motors and the Padmini, based on the Italian Fiat car 1100, were models dating back to 25 years earlier.

The first Maruti 800s were basic small cars, but a great novelty at the time they started appearing on Indian roads. Only much later, during the 1990s would they have been equipped with air conditioning systems. Those who have experienced summers in north India would wonder how it could be possible to drive around in cars without AC (nobody calls the air conditioning as such in India. Most likely many people do not even know that AC is the short form for air conditioning). Maruti-Suzuki cars soon became the highest selling in India: most families who could afford them would own at least one "800." At the opposite end of the market were the Mercedes that started appearing in India towards the mid-1990s. The price for the available models was extremely high, over two and a half times the price one would pay in Europe, making them the top end of the market, exclusively for the richest. Only when the regulations changed and foreign producers were allowed to import and assemble vehicles locally at reduced rates of duties, did prices start to drop and these cars became more accessible. Today, thanks to the changed foreign investment scenario, many foreign automotive producers have opened their factories in Tamil Nadu, not far from Chennai. The range of brands and models available in the market is therefore much wider and prices go from the equivalent of US$ 1,500 of the basic model of the Tata Nano,[17] to the several hundreds of thousands of the Rolls Royce.

Back to 1998, with a full time car and driver regularly available, including weekends, I became more enterprising and started exploring the city. While during the first few weeks I was so taken by what I saw around me that I did not even think about learning the roads; after some time I decided to pay attention to them in view of the fact that at some moment I would start driving myself. Coming from Europe, I was not used to the idea of having somebody with me throughout the day (or if required also at night) for seven days a week. I also did not find fair the fact that drivers would work for 15 hours a day, despite the fact that my colleagues had explained to me that the overtime hours were the most lucrative for the drivers who were happy to round up their salaries through these. However, drivers as anybody else had the right to be with their families, and I never liked to extend their work beyond reasonable timing. On top of this, I believed that only by driving myself would I finally have caught hold of the Delhi roads which seemed so complicated while being driven. In fact while in a chauffeur-driven car one uses the time to work, read or make calls.

During my first weekends, or rather Sundays, since I used to spend Saturdays at work, I went sightseeing the numerous monuments and historical sites of the capital. My guide book and camera always with me, every Sunday I would go from morning to evening to discover something new. Very soon I realized that the books and my drivers were not enough to do justice to the amazing amount of art and culture of Delhi, let alone the huge artistic heritage of India. I started then looking for a course that would help me get a better insight into the country's arts and cultures. It was during one of the exploratory trips to a new area of the city, South Extension, that I happened to step in the premises of the Alliance Française. Here I found on the pin board a typed sheet describing a program called "Window to the Indian Art," consisting of weekly lectures on several topics of the local arts and cultures. The outline of the course seemed interesting and the timing was compatible with my work schedule. Therefore I decided to attend a demonstrative free session to evaluate

---

[17] This car was introduced as the "1 lac" car, that is the car that could be bought with ₹100,000, at the time of the launch corresponding to approximately US$ 2,500. However the 1 lac price was thought as a promotional one for the lowest model and lasted for a limited period. Later on, with some minimal accessories the revised price was in the range of 1.4 lac, that is, about US$ 3,500.

if it made sense to enroll. I found the lecture so interesting that I decided to follow the whole program. The formula was very well thought since every session, lasting approximately 90 minutes, dealt with a specific theme linked to one of the visual or performing arts of the Indian panorama.

The course consisted of an introductory talk supported with slides and pictures, followed by a second part where artists would come on stage to perform some shows linked with the theme of the day. It was also conceived to be flexible so as to accommodate the schedule of the participants: if one had missed a session he could attend the same after 12 weeks, when it was repeated during the next cycle. Notes, glossary, and concept papers were distributed as an aid to the lectures and also to allow those who had missed a specific session to know about the contents of the same. Given that the number of participants was limited to 10–15, the meetings were interactive and, after the end of the performances, one would take the opportunity to talk to the artists and learn about their matters. I recall some of the lectures I had found particularly fascinating: one on the expression of space in Indo-Islamic art, complemented by a performance of Sufi musicians; another on the Ajanta caves, also touching upon elements of tantric paintings and providing fundamental concepts of Buddhism; a third one providing some basic concepts about Indian classical music. Many more topics were dealt with, among these being sculpture, dance, and painting. The creator and organizer of the course was a charming Indian lady, Navina, a PhD in Indian art and also an excellent *Kathak*[18] dancer. She was to become a very good friend over the years. To her I owe my introduction to the Indian arts and the lighting of the sparkle that pushed me to explore more and more of that fascinating country.

So engrossed had I become with Indian culture that during the subsequent months I attended a number of performances of Indian classical dance and music; I also bought a *tabla*[19] and had private lessons to learn to play the instrument for a few months. Navina used also to organize guided cultural walks in some of the most famous monuments in Delhi, such as the Purana Quila,[20] the Lodhi Gardens, Humayun's Tomb, and so on. Further to being extremely interesting, such walks were also occasions to meet people with similar interest and they became quite popular among the expatriate community at that point in time. Later on I remember discussing with her how the course

---

[18] It is one of the Indian classical dance styles.
[19] It is a musical instrument composed of two drums, very often used to accompany Indian classical dances and music.
[20] Literally the Old Fort.

could be integrated and better marketed so as to get to the next level and become a more profitable activity for her. This would also have ensured that more and more people could learn about the Indian arts, since I had found the exposure definitely enriching for me. Over a dinner after a performance held in a private home we chatted about the fact that Indian arts are so widely spread across the country that focusing only on the Delhi monuments was an avoidable limitation. The walks and visits should have been planned also out of the capital, so as to experience some of the most fascinating artistic destinations in the country. She took the suggestion seriously and organized after a few weeks the first of several cultural trips that would have taken us to visit old palaces, *haveli*s,[21] and museums across India.

A few months later, after the Indian arts period, I was to go back to my origins and get involved in a kind of music I felt definitely more familiar with. One night in December I had been invited to a western classical music performance in the Habitat Center, one of the theaters often used for performances in central Delhi. It was an evening with several performers, among which a 12 year-old boy who sang opera with the voice of a soprano! His performance was amazing and I thought I had to go and meet and congratulate him and his teacher. I have been in music for a large part of my life: I started studying classical piano at the age of 10, continued for many years and later on shifted to singing, initially in gospel and spiritual choirs. After a few years of choral singing I decided to study opera singing so as to work on my voice. I did so till I left Italy and moved to India. During the first months there I was too busy with my work to think about extra-curricular activities. However, that concert made me think about going back to playing and singing. When I met the teacher of the gifted boy I congratulated her and mentioned that I was a musician myself, albeit not professional, and here in India I was missing western classical music. She was very kind and invited me to be in touch, since she also wanted to do more in music but was struggling to find the right people to involve. That night I was to catch a plane to Italy for the Christmas holidays, but I promised to her that upon my return we would meet and try to organize something together.

And so it happened that we started meeting and working on a few musical programs. I had to get my voice back and she helped me in this. She gathered a group of people of different nationalities and we started working on some

---

[21] These are private mansions, generally with architectural or historical significance. Many of these belonged to the former Maharajas and Nawabs of India.

arias, both for solos and ensemble. After a few months of practice we were invited to a private home for our first performance, which was quite successful. Encouraged by the results we studied some more arias and eventually were invited to perform in the Hungarian Cultural Center. Also in that case the audience responded quite well and the gratifying musical trip started. We performed in several auditoriums and theaters, including Kamani Auditorium, possibly the most renowned space for musical and artistic performances in Delhi. We called ourselves the International Opera Ensemble, to denote our mixed origins and the passion for opera. I recall some very nice evenings, among which was one in Neemrana, an old fort in Rajasthan restructured and transformed into a hotel, in Rajasthan, just 90 minutes away from Delhi. We had a very successful performance in a moderately cold winter evening in the open amphitheater, surrounded by a wonderful scenario with old domes and candle lights. The after-concert was even more pleasant, since the audience as well as the hotel guests and the performers were invited to a gala dinner in the beautiful courtyard of the fort. After a delicious mix of Indian food and western drinks, the evening became very informal, and anyone who wanted to improvise was free to perform any kind of art he would have liked to. The get-together went on till late night and it was possibly one of my most pleasant memories of the musical trip in India.

The House in Rajokri and the House of Hope

After spending five months in a hotel the time had come for me to find a more permanent residence where to settle in. It was March 1999 and the summer was about to come. I had been warned about Delhi's "burning" hot season and I was intentioned to use the last weeks of pleasant weather to find a suitable house for myself. My company had arranged some appointments with estate agents. Those who have looked for a house in Delhi know that very often the estate brokers here are neither professional nor reliable. Interestingly, over the years, I got to meet people who called themselves estate agents, though their luxury cars and branded clothes did not seem to be those a common broker would use. I eventually realized that some people who did not have a regular job but were living out of the family money or other sources would use this tag to present themselves to the society with a business card. In some years they may manage to get one or two deals, none in a few others, but more than the money the "title" would provide them with a socially acceptable role.

Prior to starting visits with the brokers I thought I should first see a house suggested by a colleague who knew somebody owning a complex of "farm houses" and was willing to rent out some of them. They were in a locality in the vicinity of the border between Delhi and the state of Haryana, approximately one kilometer away from the NH8, about eight minutes' drive to the international airport and, in normal traffic conditions, thirty to downtown. Two houses in the complex were for rent: one larger, just at the entrance of the compound and bordering the road; the other more compact, 400 meters from the main gate, with a large and well-landscaped garden surrounded by fields and greenery. Both houses had good finishing, certainly above the average one could find in the market, as I had to realize in the subsequent weeks. The first one also had the luxury of having a grass tennis court, though not in very good conditions. The additional advantage of taking a house there was that the owners also lived in the compound: they would have been available for any possible complaint concerning the house and its maintenance. They were also offering to provide the main gate security for the whole compound at their own expenses. I was positively impressed by the place and instinctively thought that I would have liked to settle in one of those houses. I liked particularly the more compact one, for its beautiful garden and the tranquility emanating from it, being surrounded by nature and away from noisy Delhi. The only negative I could see in these places was the fact that they were slightly far from the center of the city and not immediately close to any shopping facility. However I also thought that I should visit more houses in order to have a more complete idea of what the market could offer. Therefore during the subsequent days I started exploring the options proposed by the agents.

Soon after the first visits I realized that it would have been difficult to find good standards of finishing. The rare houses with acceptable interiors had other problems (eg., location, small gardens and poor maintenance) that offset the positive points. By the end of the second week of house-hunting I had reached the conclusion that I might have to compromise on some of the requirements on my list. I thought then to go and take a second look at the houses I had first visited. Once there I experienced again a good feeling from the place. The parallel rows of Champa[22] trees framing the road leading to the main house; the large and well-landscaped lawns with up and downhill sections surrounding the house; the statues and small monuments spread in

---

[22] These are the Frangipane trees, quite common in India and, in general, in tropical climates.

the garden; the swimming pool surrounded by Neem trees[23] with a sunken bar and a small island hosting a beautiful frangipane on it; all this made me feel comfortable and at peace. So I made the decision to take the house. This had been vacant for some time and renovation works were to be done. The landlord mentioned that it would be a matter of two weeks or so and consequently we agreed for a hand-over at the beginning of April. However, when I visited the house again only two days before the agreed date I realized that quite a bit of small jobs had yet to be completed and my moving-in date would have to be postponed. Also, with the purpose of helping me set up the new house, my mother had come from Italy to visit me for the first time and had arrived just before the hand-over of the house. I had booked for her a hotel room mentioning to the reservations that I might have needed it for one or two nights, since we would have soon shifted to my new place. After the visit to the house I talked to them again and extended our stay for another week. Eventually my mother ended up completing her three weeks' stay in the same hotel.

That was my first impact with the Indian approach to deadlines. I realized over time that often the fact of not meeting deadlines was considered as normal, not really a problem or a sign of a lack of commitment or reliability. If I say that something would be ready by a certain day and it is not, but instead the deadline is shifted by one week or maybe one month, this is not a major problem and does not impact my overall image: I am still the same serious partner since what happened was due to some unpredictable circumstances; therefore I still count on the fact of doing business with you in the future. One may still understand such reasoning in case of one-off episodes when adverse circumstances are indeed out of one's control. Not so if the delay is the norm and the said uncontrollable facts are, for instance, the workers' not showing up for work, the responsible person having to attend the marriage of a cousin or some of the equipment not working properly. Such a way of thinking is maybe in some way linked to the Hindu religion and way of life. We know that such religion stresses the concept of destiny and the acceptance of what God (one of the hundreds gods Hindu followers believe in) may have reserved for an individual. However I have found the deadline problem also among non-Hindu believers, and hence it is not strictly a function of the credo. I thought I had found a partial explanation of the matter when I learned that

---

[23] The Neem tree is very well respected in India and it is believed also to have antiseptic and medicinal properties. Small pieces of branches of such trees are often used in India to brush teeth.

in the Hindi language, predominantly spoken across the nation except for the south, the word *kal* means yesterday but also tomorrow. Since languages do influence our way of life, this discovery enlightened me about the flexible interpretation of time I had often experienced in the country.

By the end of April I finally managed to get into the house. With the various works completed the place looked much better, though empty houses usually lack personality and warmth. Having left Italy with nothing but clothes I did not have much to personalize it. I had carried some more stuff from Italy back from my trips there and I had also started buying some small artifacts in the various places I had visited, but that first night my house had just the bare minimum to sleep in one of its rooms. Prior to that night my official entry into the house had started with a *pooja*, performed close to the fireplace in the drawing room by the company's "Pandit" and a few colleagues who had helped me find the place. This had been almost "imposed" on me by my team, though I have always been respectful of the local traditions and very often took part in the important religious celebrations together with them. The idea behind this rite was that my residence had to be a peaceful and lucky place for me to ensure that my work performances would also be good, and all of us could profit of the growth of our business.

Looking back I must admit that that pooja did work indeed, since I stayed in the house for over eight years and the results of our company have been extremely good ever since. It took a few months for me to furnish the house the way I wanted, getting some pieces in India, some other in the various countries where I used to travel. By the time I left the country I had to hire a 40 feet container to move my stuff. I have never regretted the decision to take that house and even today I miss my breakfasts in the verandah just outside the drawing room, where I would drink my morning tea for 10 months in a year, not rarely watching the peacocks walking in the garden or feeding the squirrels who dared coming close to me. When I moved from India the actual owners of the house,[24] based in Dubai, became very good friends of mine. Even today when we meet they refer to that house as if it was still my place. In fact they had built the place for themselves, but eventually never ended up living there and I had been the person who had stayed there the longest.

---

[24] All houses in the complex were handled by the landlord we used to deal with; however, some of them belonged to his brother-in-law, who had requested his sister and the husband to look after his properties,

When I moved into the house the HR manager of my company arranged the domestic help for me. He lined up the interviews with my future staff on his own initiative. I was stunned when I realized that, in his opinion, I would need quite a number of people to handle the place: apart from the main caretaker, there should be some gardeners as well as security people. On top of this I would need also a cook, not only for myself but also for entertainment occasions. It was almost a team of a small company we were about to hire. I was rather reluctant to this, since in Italy we are not used to having that much of domestic help. Even more hesitant and almost irritated was I when, the same day I had got into the house, the caretaker arrived at my place with his small suitcase. The idea of having a person full time in my place was against my concept of privacy. However, with the system of the servant quarters, I later realized that the living in domestic help was quite useful and comfortable. I also had concerns about the cost of such a large staff: however, when given the total monthly bill for them, I realized that it was more or less equivalent to the cost of one full-time maid in Italy. This is one of the major fringe benefits one can get when living in emerging countries.

The cook used to work for me in the evening and cooked for the whole management team in the office at lunch time. Over the years he was trained by my mother, who visited me several times, and by some other occasional Italian visitors, who taught him several recipes. After over eight years of cooking he had become good in Italian food but his Indian dishes, in which the level of spices had sensibly gone down to suit my palate, had lost a bit of authenticity, as a few Indian friends had the occasion to point out. I did have a driver also: he used to drive for the rent a car company I had utilized during my first months and I had found him extremely efficient, sincere, reliable, and hard working. Hence I had proposed to him to become my personal driver. Not without hesitation, due to the fact that his tips would have gone down drastically going from a "tourist" driving job to the one I was offering, he did join. He proved to be one of the best helps I had in India and became such an integral part of my days that I considered him as part of the family rather than a driver. When I met him in 1999 he had just had a daughter: I have seen her and her brother growing up and becoming adults, and after so many years I do feel that it is also my obligation to ensure that they have a good future.

I also had to develop similar feelings for the family of my caretaker: in this case I saw him getting married, followed his children's birth and growth, his concerns about his sister's marriage, and other matters he used to tell me and seek my advice about. Both of them are people I fully trust and their sincerity and commitment towards me and my family are far beyond what one may find in an employer-employee relation. Another member had to soon become part of the Rajokri family: it was a smallish grey puppy found roaming around our complex on a foggy and cold winter day. He was alone and lost in the middle of the road just in front of our complex and my driver, knowing that I was thinking of adopting a dog, brought him inside. When I walked out ready to go to office I saw my staff around this little cute doggy, who had been given some milk and was happily finishing it. It was love at first sight and since then he has been with me. I named him Lucky, for the good luck that had allowed him to escape an almost certain tragic end on the road along our complex. However, since the name Lucky sounded too western, to do justice to his pure Indian (stray) breed I also thought to add some other common Indian names: his full name was hence decreed as Lucky Kumar Singh. He has been ever since a loyal companion of my days in India. I used to travel often but, even when I was not yet married, there was always somebody to greet me when I reached home; and there was always somebody at my place to take good care of him. Today he is still with me in my house in Goa and has become the major attraction for my children during our holidays there.

My house and my staff gave me the opportunity to receive guests quite often, in informal get-togethers as well as in more formal receptions. During the good season[25] the house was the meeting place of several friends who would join me for lunch or drop in for a coffee. We would then continue the afternoon with competitive volley ball matches in my garden, followed by a dive in the swimming pool, where we would relax with drinks and snacks. At times we would end the evening together in a movie theater or in some restaurants in town. Sunday morning was instead devoted to the tennis. I would go and play in a small tennis club close to Vasant Vihar,[26] where after a warm up session, I would play a few games with my coach who would make me run and sweat and inevitably beat me without appeal. When the weather allowed it I would ride to the tennis courts on my bike, a 1965 Royal Enfield completely refurbished, with a huge tank, a double seat and two large leather bags. I loved the sound of that bike, but I hated the fact that it was so hard to start it. At times it would stop at a signal and there was no way I could start it again. So I used to call my driver to rescue me and he would arrive and start the bike with the first kick. I found that extremely frustrating, but

---

[25] October to March is the season with pleasant weather in Delhi. April to June are extremely hot months and July to September is the monsoon season.
[26] An area of south Delhi considered rather posh where usually expatriates live.

later realized that one had to grow up with those machines to handle them in the proper way. When I left India I was planning to take the bike with me. However I could not find the original papers and so had to send my driver with a copy of the same to a police station in Uttar Pradesh where supposedly my bike registration had been made. He was to get a duplicate of them but instead risked to be jailed when the police realized that the papers had been faked and the bike had never been registered there. When I confronted the person who had sold me the bike he denied having faked the paper, but eventually accepted to take the bike back at almost the original sales price when I threatened through a lawyer to file a legal case against him.

Once at a party in a friend's place I was introduced to a couple of unusual Italians who had been living in India for a few years. The husband had a degree in economics and the wife had also studied economics, though had not eventually graduated. They had been in India already for two years and were part of a charitable NGO taking care of children, mainly small girls, without parents or with parents who could not look after them. At that moment their organization was still relatively small, had about 30 children and was operating out of a house in Gurgaon. The Italian family had left their country soon after the birth of their second daughter in a sort of missionary posting. They were sponsored by an Italian Catholic organization that was also one of the partners in this charitable venture called Asha Niwas, or House of Hope. The other partner was an American Catholic organization, whose nuns were running the home.

While talking to them that evening I tried to understand what had pushed a middle class family with two small children to leave their job and their country in order to go and work for a small organization with very basic infrastructural support and hardly any comfort in a far away country. I never had a definite answer to this question, but I guessed it must be something inside that drives such decisions: to some extent something similar to what pushed me to move to India and start a completely new life. In my case though I knew I would have a gratifying career and salary package and possibly live a very comfortable life, whereas in their case it would have been much more difficult. Maybe they were such thoughts and also the similar choice we all had made that led me to befriend them and get to know more about their activity. Later on I went to visit Asha Niwas and I discovered that the home was just two kilometers away from my office in Gurgaon. This made my visits there convenient and so I started going to see them and spend time with the children quite regularly. Even if I had only half an hour free I would drop by, bring some of our company's sweets or some other goodies for the kids and talk to them, play with them, and try giving them love, something they clearly missed and needed. Not that my Italian friends or the nuns who were handling the place would not give them love and affection: they were excellent educators as well as almost substitute parents. But kids who have had very difficult lives, often brought up without one or both parents do need as much love as they can find from everyone around them. I realized that they really longed to be stroked or hugged, kept on one's lap or just wanted their hands held. Physical contact and human warmth were as vital to them as light to plants. The great thing out of this was that this closeness would give immense joy to me too.

After about one year of my regular visits, the main Sister and I decided that I could maybe sponsor one or two children, granting them a better education and developing a special relationship with them. And so I thought of taking care of a little girl of about four years, whose smile I particularly liked; she had already become closer to me than the others. Her exact age was not known: hence we decided together with the Sister to formalize a date of birth so that she could have the papers necessary to enroll in the school. During the years such a relationship developed into almost father-to-daughter rapport. When possible I would go and pick her up at school, talk to the teachers, attend the school's special occasions. I would take her home with a few other children during the weekend and play with them in my pool, teach them swimming, give them lunch, and then take them back to their home. It was a fantastic opportunity to see them enjoying our Sundays together and sharing my place with kids who, in their extremely troubled previous family situations, would have not had the chance of eating regularly, let alone swimming in a private swimming pool.

After a few years, the Italian friends had to go back to Italy. Even after their departure the principal nun, Sister Beena, kept on working towards expanding the scope of the initiative; increasing the number of children to whom they could offer a more comfortable living and above all chances of a much better life; finding sources of funding, but always in a discrete way. She was (and still is) a true parent, teacher and counseling friend to the elder girls, careful to maintain an iron fist for their discipline in a velvet glove. She managed eventually in 2010 to buy some land where a larger house could be built, so as to host and reunite almost 80 girls who had been scattered in several parts of the country. I tried helping them also by spreading the news of Asha Niwas among the Italian community: a few more friends decided to sponsor some of the children. Some Italian companies started organizing fund-raising initiatives for them; even the Italian Embassy was involved in this and annually offered some very welcome aide. At a certain point in time I even thought to try and understand if I could legally adopt my little girl, but my unmarried state at that moment would have made this almost impossible to happen. The idea was also to make sure that she could stay in that home without being claimed by some alleged relatives who might disrupt her stable life and education. Such claims had already been made in several other cases and had been rather a defeat for the Sisters and a source of sadness when all news of the kids taken back by their guardians had been lost. In such extremely poor families one would have not known what could happen to the children, especially if girls.

To avoid such eventuality for "my child," Sister Beena managed to find a way to become a sort of legal guardian for her. Today she is a grown-up girl, just a few years away from completing her school. Though my move from India has affected the frequency of our meetings, we are regularly in touch thanks to my frequent visits to India or over the phone. I am very grateful to the friends who created the link with such a home, as well as to the Sister who has been the driving force behind the initiative.

4

WORKING IN INDIA

Indian Talent

When I landed in India, in addition to my two suitcases, I also had a baggage of stereotypes and prejudices carried from my previous trip there. My knowledge of the country was superficial and acquired mainly through books. With such background I did not have very high expectations about the professionalism of the local management team and in general of the staff of the local company. I had to change my mind soon though, thanks to the intense interaction I had with them during my first weeks of work. In fact, to the merit of my predecessor who had hired most of them, I had found a very capable team in place in the various departments, and the functional heads were all skilled professionals with adequate experience, remarkable functional knowledge and very vocal ambitions. My direct reports, all locals except one expatriate from Italy, displayed very clear ideas about their tasks and were certainly comparable, if not a notch above in some cases, to the colleagues I had interacted with during my first months in the headquarters. I had been hired to become expatriate, but training requirements and organizational issues had kept me in Lainate[1] for a few months. Here I had also heard stories that had warned me about the way of working in the Indian subsidiary.

Some of them were due to misunderstanding and cultural intelligence issues; some others to a sub-optimal flow of communications between Italy and India. While being personally there I could eventually learn the point of view of the local company and work on sorting out such misunderstandings,

---

[1] A locality in the proximity of Milan, where Perfetti Van Melle has its Italian headquarters.

creating at time wrong impressions and lack of trust at both ends. It would have taken years to drastically reduce some of the issues and create a smooth and transparent communication flow between the local company and Italy. Some of the problems were caused by lack of information, some others by scarce knowledge of the different ways of working; in many cases the "ego" was a stumbling block. I had to learn that among the Indian colleagues this last was rather developed, even more at the highest level of the local organization. Not infrequently I had to intervene to resolve disputes among the heads of departments caused just by mundane arguments or "power games." While I fully respected the functional competencies of my direct reports, I realized during my first year in the company that some of them did have serious scope for improvement in teamwork and interpersonal relationships. Such issues would have needed addressing since the beginning of their stint in the company but apparently had not been properly handled and over the years they had increased instead of getting corrected. To facilitate the teamwork I created a system of regular meetings of the whole management team, initially in the office premises, later on also in different locations in the country, typically over two days, when we would also have occasions of informal interaction and relaxation. It was nothing particularly new or innovative, but had not been previously done in our company, or if at all, not in the most appropriate way. The importance of such meetings and at times short trips was in the opportunity for everybody to speak in a more open way in a "neutral" environment other than the office one, where the roles and hierarchy were more established and people were used to more formal behavior. Spending a few days together and interacting also in unusual situations (e.g., in games or sports) would have disclosed some sides of the colleagues' personalities not shown during office hours. I recall one of them telling me in a joking way: "how can I go back to office and fight or abuse my colleague now that we have been taking a sauna together?"

During one of the first off-site visits I had the opportunity of going, together with the team, to visit one of the most venerated temples of the whole country, the one in Tirupathi, in the state of Andhra Pradesh. Unfortunately, being a foreigner and not a Hindu believer, I could not complete the visit till the inside part of the temple, the *sanctum sanctorum*, normally located in the heart of the building and hosting the holiest shrine. The place was incredibly crowded and, apart from the spiritual experience, it was apparently a huge source of business. I was told that the annual donations were accounted in millions of dollars and the small-time traders all around the temple had clients throughout the day. I also took the opportunity to watch for the first time the typical way of making and pouring out coffee in south

India, as well as tasting it. Strangely enough, I found its taste not too different from the Italian "caffellatte," a mixture of espresso and hot milk. In the same trip I also had my first typical south Indian breakfast: *idli* and *sambar*.[2] In addition to providing the team the opportunity to connect with colleagues, such occasions also gave me further insights about my direct reports, as well as glimpses of Indian culture. In another similar occasion, unaware of the local sensitivity about relationships between men and women, I committed one of the rare cultural blunders during my career in India. The whole team and I had held a meeting in a town and had come back to the hotel where we all were staying. Coincidentally, in the same town that day, the wedding of a friend's relative was happening, which I had promised to participate in. A friend had arrived from the airport and needed to change her clothes and I spontaneously offered her the use of my room to do so. I took her to the room passing by the colleagues' rooms and some of them saw me entering my room with her. Though they also saw both of us getting out of the same room after twenty minutes dressed for the wedding, this story became quite a piece of news in the company. Nobody told me directly about it and I had to learn of the matter only many months later, when I was discussing about the India business in Italy with my direct boss. With a mixture of envy and embarrassment he mentioned to me that he had heard rumors about me as a sort of "Italian playboy" in the country, and this had been very much talked about in the local company. At that time I was single and within those twenty minutes in the room we would not have had the time to do anything else but change our clothes. Despite this I realized that I should have been more aware of my acts in front of my team.

During the years prior to my taking over, some of the departments had been working almost in isolation, caring about their specific objectives rather than the common ones of the company. This was happening particularly in some of the functions, where the heads thought they were the undisputed and unquestionable "owners" of their departments and hardly tolerated any interference from colleagues. The issue was even more accentuated in one department whose head, strongly in the trust of the headquarters, thought that he could get along with anything, at times even questioning the authority of his boss, let alone his colleagues. After many such instances had created serious problems in the way of working and some team members had told me in confidence that they could not deliver in such conditions, we had to take some

---

[2] *Idli* is a sort of steamed dish made of rice and *sambar* is a lentil and vegetable soup to be eaten together with Idli or Dosa, another typical south Indian preparation.

corrective actions. At times it is better losing a very good performer rather than letting this one upset the work and the spirit of the whole team. Over the years new team members replaced the more problematic personalities and the working environment improved dramatically. The competitiveness at the managerial level was beyond that sound level that stimulated better results from the individuals. Some individuals would have not hesitated in putting down their colleagues, though indirectly, in order to achieve the goals in their agenda. While trying to understand why such a behavior was rather common I thought that it may be caused by the strong competitiveness that dominates the Indian education system. At primary level the number of good schools in the country is limited and, since the moment of the admissions, students have to fight to ensure the best results that will open their way for the access to the next level of education. Since the system of marking is not in absolute but in relative terms, in order to excel a student needs to perform better than his peers. Only those with scores well above 90 percent will have the chance to get into the best colleges and higher education institutes.

One of the programs we had created in our company in order to get the best potential resources from the management institutes was the Management Trainee one. We would go to the campuses as soon as the placement period started, or even before the opening of this (e.g., day zero), present our company and our programs and try enrolling the best students in these. Our offering consisted of two years, alternating periods of training in different functions with others of actual work, initially supervised by a tutor and later with more independent charges. By the end of the period the young boys/girls would have been absorbed into the company staff at the first managerial level. We created such a program initially for the Sales and Marketing functions, but later extend it to other departments too. We would have every year a batch of six to eight students enrolled in it. Some other multinationals used to run similar schemes, which became extremely popular at the beginning of the year 2000. Over the subsequent years the job market in India became more and more heated and the initial compensation offered to the students from the campuses grew disproportionately high, with the risk of destabilizing the whole salary structure of the companies. The Management Trainees had to be absorbed in the existing organization at the completion of the period, but with very high initial salaries they would not fit anymore into the compensation package of the level they would join. To avoid such discrepancy the overall compensation structure of the organization would have to be revised. Furthermore, the increased demand for such fresh resources caused more frequent poaching by other companies even before the two years were completed. The risk was that such a scheme would push up salaries while not ensuring the inflow of fresh resources, which would be trained for a few months and then leave us to join other companies offering them much higher compensations. Also for this reason we suspended the program for a few years to start it again later. However, we had formed a pool of high potential resources and those who stayed in our organization would grow fast and add value to our business for many years.

We also used to recruit new talents through the summer internship scheme. Campuses require that their students in the MBA program attend periods in companies during summer breaks. Normally such internships would last for eight weeks and would give students the opportunity of having a window into the job world, and the companies of having a few projects executed at low cost and at the same time get to know possible future employees. After the periods we would give a tentative job offer to the best performers: this would ensure that, once they finished their MBA a few months later, they could already have a job and we could count on fresh high potential resources before other companies could give the students alternative offers.

A fundamental belief I have always had in the relationship with my direct reports is that I need to fully trust them so that I can delegate to them as much as they can take. From their side they need to keep on reinforcing this trust and discharge their duties according to the agreed objectives and values. If for any reason that trust is lost it becomes very difficult to me to acquire it again. I am convinced that being straightforward and empowering people gets the better out of them, provided that they reciprocate the transparency and take full responsibility of their actions. While it took some time to eventually succeed in this, I was clear in my mind that I had to create an open culture, where people were free to talk, propose and disagree, though with supported reasons to do so. My people had to grow with me, and their direct reports had to be groomed to be able to take higher responsibility and eventually replace them. The presence of managers who did not believe in an open environment and kept basing their authority on hierarchy and fear rather than on results and trust delayed this process, which could be accomplished only once some of these managers had left the company. The grooming of one's successor however has often been a difficult task for many managers, and still in recent years we have had difficulties in implementing a culture of training and structured succession planning.

One of the interesting findings I could notice already in the first year was the marked difference of attitude and skills between managerial levels and lower staff levels or workers in the shop floor. While the former were in general ambitious, motivated, hard working, and rather open minded, the low level staff and many of the factory workers would often show lack of ambition and pride in their work, a lax attitude, and inconsistent behavior and performances. This was not only the case for our company: I had the opportunity of sharing this observation with friends in other firms and they would confirm that such gap was rather common throughout industries and corporations in the Indian market. One of the explanations I had given myself for this was the different level of education, international exposure, and training among the different strata and classes of the society reflected in the companies. The least educated would show much more the "resigned" attitude typical of the Hindu caste system, whereas the more educated would be able to discern and interpret their beliefs in a progressive way that would positively impact their work attitude. The training received, particularly if in state-of-the-art management institutes (local and international), in foreign (or successful Indian) companies and the exposure to a progressively opening culture and to international traveling created the hedge for the higher managerial levels.

A useful tool to better understand the Indian talent is the cultural dimensions analysis carried out by Geert Hofstede (see Figure 4.1).[3] In the 1970s, this researcher studied the cultural differences among many countries and created a grid of cultural dimensions (initially four, later integrated with a fifth one) that characterize the culture of the countries studied. Though this is rather dated now,[4] it still offers good insights into the attitude in the work place in this country. I shall compare India with Italy so as to have a benchmark that will help interpret the numbers quoted. We shall start with the Power Distance (PD), the extent to which the less powerful members of organizations and institutions (like the family) accept and expect that power is distributed unequally. India's score for this is 77,[5] a rather high score compared to that of Italy, which scores 50 in the same dimension. This high score would imply that in organizations, hierarchy is very much accentuated and accepted. If this is coupled with a medium-to-high score of the dimension called Uncertainty Avoidance (UA)—dealing with the acceptance of uncertainty and ambiguity—the combination would possibly bring the members of the organization to believe that the apex of the same holds undisputable power. In India, the UA is at a medium/low kind of level, with a score of 40.

---

[3] He is a Dutch social psychologist and anthropologist, pioneer in researches on cultural groups. He worked for IBM and administered over 100,000 questionnaires to IBM Managers in over 30 countries. Later on, when he resigned from IBM and started teaching in IMEDE Lausanne, he administered the questionnaires to his students. In 1980, he published his book *Culture's Consequences*, where the results of his analysis were presented.

[4] The study dates back to over 30 years ago.

[5] The scale goes from 0 to 100.

Despite a moderate score in UA I recall having found very often Indian companies were the leader was considered unquestionable, particularly when his personality would also favor such an attitude from his subordinates.

Looking at the dimension of Individualism (ID), as opposite to Collectivism, defined as the degree to which individuals are integrated into groups, we find that India scores 48. While the number is in the medium range, in a society that was historically divided into groups (the castes) and such groups are still very much present and important, despite discriminations based on the same are constitutionally banned,[6] one would have expected even lower scores; more so when we consider the nature of the Indian joint family—generally large but very cohesive—with parents, children, cousins, and uncles (not necessary related) all living under the same roof. In such an environment the emphasis is certainly more on the group than on the individual. Maybe as a reaction to this, those who manage to achieve a certain degree of individual recognition (as it may happen to managers in a company) fight hard to maintain this also at the expenses of their colleagues: this may partly explain the issues of teamwork in my initial team I have previously mentioned. Looking at the predominant role of men in Indian society, one would expect the dimension called Masculinity (MS), which refers to the distribution of roles between the genders, to be very prominent. But also in this case India's score is 56, only in the higher side of the medium range. This does not reflect the actual organizational structures in India, where women rarely achieve top corporate positions or appear in the boards of directors.[7] However, such a score may explain the hidden power of women, who appear to be in the backstage due to the traditional role they are requested to perform in society, whereas in reality they have a larger role than the one publicly shown. In these two dimensions Italy has comparatively much higher scores, since in ID it shows 76, and in MS, 70. Both such scores are reflective of the reality of Italy of a few years ago: possibly a more recent study may reveal that particularly the MS would have decreased nowadays.

India has a growing number of expatriates, brought from the opening of many sectors to Foreign Direct Investment after the liberalization in 1991. While till the end of the 1990s, when I had arrived in the country, expatriates were still relatively few, during the latest years the opening of large hubs of multinationals in India has sharply increased their number. I have noticed

---

[6] See Article 15 of the Indian Constitution.

[7] There are, though, examples of women heading important companies in India, such as Chanda Kochchar of the ICICI Bank, or Naina Lal Kidwai, country head of the HSBC Bank.

Figure 4.1 Geert Hofstede Cultural Dimensions—India and Italy

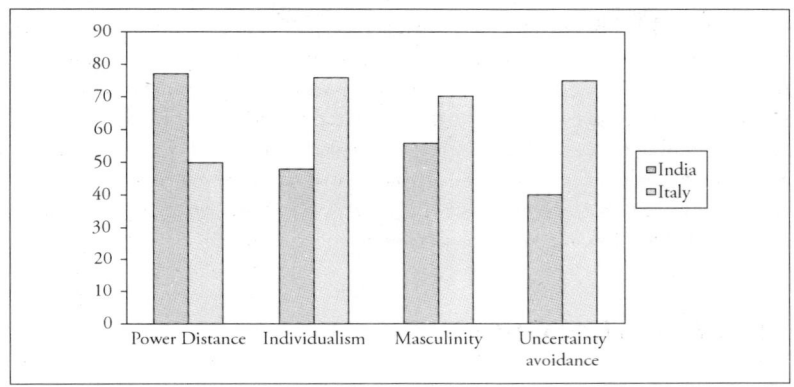

Source: http://geert-hofstede.com/italy.html; http://geert-hofstede.com/india.html.

that the reaction of expatriates to posting in India could be completely opposite: they could freak out within six months and leave the country or they could start loving it and try to extend their posting for as long as possible. I must say that the late 1990s were more difficult years for expatriates in India than the current ones. At that time infrastructures were definitely worse, bureaucracy and corruption higher, and even personal life was more restricted, given the limited availability of entertainment as well as of foreign goods. I do recall returning from my trips to Italy with suitcases full of pasta, olive oil and Parmesan cheese, whereas today I would certainly not need to bring back such items, since they are now widely available in the market.

The relationship between local staff and expatriate is not always very easy. Since the latter often represent the headquarters to the local subsidiaries, they are respected but at times also looked at suspiciously. I have noticed that when an expatriate is the head of the organization his authority is normally not questioned. On the other hand when he/she is part of the middle management his/her life in the company is definitely more complicated. Issues are often due to lack of cross-cultural understanding but also at times to the gap of compensation between expatriates and local resources: the latter may resent that their expatriate colleagues may be younger, less experienced, and yet better paid. However, once again such issues were more common in the past, when the expatriates' number was limited and they had more visibility in organizations. Even the compensation gap is today much lower, since in India during the last years local salaries have significantly gone up. At a managerial level they are now very much comparable to those in Europe or in the USA. At lower levels, though, blue and white collars still have much lower salaries compared to their Western peers. However even this is bound to change: already during 2011 the Indian labor market, particularly in the manufacturing sector, has experienced a spike in the importance and power of the Unions.[8] If such trend is confirmed in the years to come, salaries will sensibly rise also at workers' levels, even in this case bridging the gap between some other East Asian countries, and maybe later on also with the West, where the economic continued slow-down is keeping salaries relatively stable.

The *Chalta Hay* Attitude

The amazing performances of the Indian economy in the last 20 years seem hardly compatible with a very common attitude one encounters while working and living in India. I mentioned in the previous chapter about the unreliability of the suppliers or service providers in general when they give a word or commit to a deadline. Similarly, the attention to detail seems to be a very rare virtue in India. I had experienced this while I was trying to find a house as well as during the work carried out to refurbish the place I eventually selected. In the various houses I had visited I would find that the windows would not close properly; the color of the glass on the left side would not be matching that of the right one; the window sills would be crooked, or their corners asymmetrically cut. I could point out dozens of such details, but apparently the landlords would not even notice them.

When work was going on in my future residence I would point out that a certain wall was not well painted and request that it be painted again. The day after I would come back and find that it had only been touched up and not fully re-painted, so that the patches of new paint were visible. I would thus mention that they had to do the work again and the day after I would

---

[8] An example of this: in autumn 2011 a several-weeks'-long confrontation between the Unions and the management of the Maruti Suzuki Company in Manesar, started as a rebellion against the alleged collaboration of the Unions with the Company which had previously fired a few workers and refused to hire them back. This had led to a 33 days lock-out that was resolved with an agreement between Unions and the Company, considered by many workers too penalizing for them. On October 7 about 2,000 workers launched a strike and occupied the Manesar factory. This strike soon prompted sympathy strikes by over 10,000 workers in several auto-related companies in the Gurgaon-Manesar industrial belt.

come back to find that their newly painted wall had a different color. When I asked the reason for this they would reply that the original paint was over and they had bought the same color of another brand, which happened to have a slightly different shade. The same work that could have been done once and for all in a few hours would have to be done over and over again and eventually take one full week. Later on, while purchasing furniture for the house I would have received the delivery one or two days after the agreed date and would find scratches on the pieces, missing items (e.g., drawer keys) or other minor problems (e.g., locks not working). Most of the time when I pointed out such imperfections to the shop owner he would look at me almost surprised so as to say "how would you expect to have a perfect job done? This is India!" That is exactly what is commonly called the *chalta hay* (anything goes) attitude. I remember that one of the innumerable times I got stuck in a traffic jam I observed some workers painting a zebra crossing. The way they were doing that would be the exact explanation of the above mentioned attitude: using half broken paint brushes and paint tins possibly recovered from some other previous work, they were painting here and there, not paying any attention to the lines to be followed. Since they were painting over an existing layer of paint and the surface had not been previously cleaned or prepared, some of the zebras were darker, some lighter; most of the lines were not at all straight; leaves and other objects lying on the road had also been painted. After the work was finished, the objects stuck to the floor (and the new paint layer on them) would have soon been removed by passing cars. Patches of old paint with the shape of the objects would have then appeared and a freshly done job would have looked already old and shabby in a matter of some days.

Initially I had thought that the humble origins of the people doing these jobs were the cause of such an approximate way of executing them: one could not expect high standard of precision and details from people who have very low education and are used to living in very basic places (often in slums), surrounded by garbage. But later I realized that the attitude was spread also at higher levels of the society, among the middle class and even among very educated people. In fact normally the workers have supervisors, and the supervisors have some other people checking the jobs done. The owners of the shops where I had bought my furniture were often educated people. Despite this they just would not notice the faults I could see; or possibly they would see them but just accept the same without bothering to correct them. This is indeed the key of the matter: the low threshold of acceptance of sub-optimal work. Possibly this is due to the fact that Indian society tolerates mediocrity. In order to understand why this happens, one would need to look at the past and find the root causes. Firstly we must state that India is a very tolerant nation: the fact that many of the world religions have found a home here and their believers live together without major problems, barring a few rare incidents, is a proof of this. Another evidence of this is the fact that in a country where over 80 percent of the population is Hindu, the political leader of the current ruling coalition is a person of Catholic faith (and Italian origins), who has made space for a Sikh to become the Prime Minister. The latter was appointed by a Muslim President, Dr Abdul Kalam, who was the highest State Authority of India at that time. All this could not have happened in an intolerant country. A few authors attribute the wide acceptance of mediocrity to British colonialism in India: in a hundred years the British would have succeeded in creating an Indian elite patterned after them. This would have caused imitativeness instead of search for creativity and excellence.

When people think they cannot be as good as someone else and spend all their energies trying to be like someone else, they usually end up being much less than what they can be. A nation that internalizes a sense of inferiority begins to accept inferior standards for itself.[9]

While this could be part of the explanation, I would not agree with the creativity part: Indian arts have been rich in creative talents, both in the past as well as in the present. In India there are among the best advertising agencies in the world, whose talents have been several times part of the judging committees in many international advertising festivals, including the Cannes one. The vast production coming every year from Bollywood confirms that both visual and performing arts are strengths and not weaknesses of this nation. While there are criticisms about some Indian movies productions having copied or at least taken inspiration from the Hollywood original ones, most of the movies are so rooted in Indian culture that they could not have been conceived anywhere else in the world. One more cause of the acceptance of mediocrity could be the environment where Indian people live and operate. It is known that bureaucracy, nepotism, and corruption pervade the lives of Indians. On top of all this also the many legally sanctioned reservations[10] for specific categories contribute to limiting the potential of the unprivileged individuals. With such premises the initiative of the common man is often frustrated, contacts become more important than merit and the incentive to excel is heavily affected. This would explain the fact that Indians who emigrated

---

[9] P. K. Varma, *Being Indian* (New Delhi: Penguin, 2004), p. 134.
[10] Be these for small scale industries or for some "scheduled castes" or "scheduled tribes."

and left the domestic environment to work in places where recognition and achievements come from hard work with a direct link between merit and return have become prominent researchers and successful innovators.

An additional factor contributing to explaining the *chalta hay* way of living could be found in the concept of *moksha*, or liberation from suffering, the ultimate goal of man and a pillar of the Hindu religion. This is linked to the conviction of the existence of a higher level of reality, beyond the empirical one of our world. Due to this the human experience is pervaded by uncertainties and men have to bear the "inescapable conflicts and incomprehensible afflictions of fate."[11] Therefore if everything is eventually part of a larger design there is no point in trying hard to excel in material matters. This concept is combined with that of *dharma* (moral duty, right action), which is the tool to achieve the ultimate goal: people who believe in this know that what is important for their spiritual progress is not what they do but how they act in conformity with their *dharma*. The implication of this is that one could be a rich industrialist, a plumber or a janitor: his spiritual progress will not be measured by his success but instead by his consistency with his *dharma*. Also, such a way of thinking could depress one's ambition and affect the work attitude. However, the flip side of this is that despite the worst of circumstances one could be facing at a certain point in time, if there is an unknown order there is always a hope that things will improve in the future, be this future the next month, the next year, or the next life. This is possibly what keeps people who live in miserable conditions and work 15 hours a day, seven days a week going. "The Indian mind then tends to convert even the slightest ray of hope into a blaze of light."[12]

I have come across quite often over the years in India a recurring word related to the practical sphere, but also to some extent linked with the above-mentioned attitude. The term *jugaad* is specifically north Indian but has some corresponding words also in other Indian languages.[13] Literally the word means something like fixing, but it is widely used in several situations. I recall having walked in one of our factories to find unusual devices hanging from a certain machine: it could be a rubber band tied to a brush to keep it down, or some scotch tape on a disk to avoid the scratching of some parts. The operators had run into an unforeseen problem and had devised a temporary

---

[11] See Sudhir Kakar and Katharina Kakar, *The Indians* (New Delhi: Penguin-Viking, 2007), p. 182.
[12] Ibid., p. 183.
[13] For instance, *bandobosto kora* in Bengali and *setting kiya* in Mumbai slang.

solution to sort it out, a *jugaad*. The idea behind this is that "one cannot fix all the problems, but can make it work." While this may seem just a word like so many others, there are at least two reasons why I am mentioning it in the current context. The first one is that the *jugaad* is a culture and not only a word. This way of acting is so rooted in Indian life that it has lost its original temporary meaning and has become a permanent solution, though sub-optimal. This is the link I see between this concept and the *chalta hay* attitude: once again Indians manage to do things in one way or another, but then the temporary fix becomes the final result, and the quality of the same is certainly not up to the mark. The second reason that makes such a word interesting is that it shows how resourceful and creative Indian people can be when they face unpredicted issues.

At times it may seem that things are not going to happen, but at the last minute everything falls in place, almost magically, very often thanks to such *jugaad*s. This happens in Bollywood movies but also in real life, for instance when getting ready for an event or a party. The Commonwealth Games held in New Delhi in 2010 have been an extraordinary example of this: less than one week before the starting of the same a few countries had almost decided to withdraw their teams, due to the infrastructural works being far behind schedule; however at the last minute everything was made ready, and the games could be held smoothly. The opening ceremony of the same gained even worldwide appreciation. I often happened to tell friends and colleagues who asked me how it was working in India that there everything is difficult but nothing is impossible: the difficulty at times comes from the *chalta hay* attitude, the solutions from some creative *jugaad*s.

The Inspector *Raj*

The almost 100 years of British domination in India are commonly called the *Raj* or the reign. The independence in 1947 and the creation of the Indian National Congress party started an era in which economic policies were aimed at achieving self-sufficiency, possibly as a reaction to the long foreign domination. Jawaharlal Nehru, the nation's first Prime Minister, was certainly very close to Mahatma Gandhi, who had been preaching the necessity of *swadeshi*[14] throughout the Indian independence movement. Nehru embraced this concept and established a sort of centrally-planned economy, also defined

---

[14] The word is a Hindi as well as a Bengali word and could be translated as self-sufficiency.

as "mixed economy"; he also tried ensuring that the nation became proud of its ability to survive on its own sources. The following statement attributed to him would summarize such sentiment of pride: "a second-rate Indian good is superior to a first-rate foreign product."[15] He established state ownership and import-substitution industrialization in hopes of developing the nation's internal capacity. However, India's socialistic planning failed to develop a strong economy and efficient institutions: even the self sufficiency preached by Gandhiji[16] happened only in the food sector.[17] A side effect of this was that red tape and corruption flourished. The state bureaucracy became known as the "License Raj" since all business activities required licenses and this created fertile ground for widespread bribes and political kickbacks. One of the examples often quoted was that of a fertilizer factory continuing in operation for years without ever producing any fertilizer.[18]

Many Asian nations during the 1970s and the 1980s saw strong rates of growth; India—which, also due to such an introverted political economy and consequent heavy bureaucratism—saw the rate of growth of its economy stabilizing around an average 3 percent per year until 1990; this was deridingly called the "Hindu rate of growth." It is well known that after the liberalization and the opening of the economy in 1991 many of the licenses were abolished, though restrictions were maintained in many sectors. One of these was, for instance, a segment of the sugar confectionery, the sugar boiled candies, which was a Small Scale Industry reserved one till a recent amendment. Our company had to cope with such restriction and was forced to find alternate sources of business within the sugar confectionery industry as well as creative ways to have at least a minimal presence in the reserved sector. While the liberalization did not stop but in some way mitigated the "license raj," large powers were left in the hands of the so called inspectors, deputed to check on many aspects of various industries. Such roles, typically covered by middle bureaucrats with relatively low qualifications and salaries, had however, large scope for discretionary decisions, hence a strong capacity to harass individuals

---

[15] Source: Sandeep Ahuja et al., *Economic Reform in India: Task Force Report*, January 2006, PPHA-50900: International Policy Practicum 2005, Professor Charles Wheelan, Harris School of Public Policy, University of Chicago.
[16] The *-ji* suffix after the name of a person is used as a form of respect.
[17] As a result of the "Green Revolution," India increased its yield per unit of farm land and in 1978–79 achieved self-sufficiency in food, producing over 130 million tons of food grain. On the other hand, the currency crisis that obliged India to open the economy in 1991 was a result of this seeking self-sufficiency.
[18] See note 15 for the source.

and firms at various levels. A picturesque example of the license/inspector raj was in the telephone sector. One state company handled single handedly the same and the fixed landlines were a rarity in the households. The national telephone company's employees were therefore important personalities, since they could "put a word" to accelerate the process of obtaining a telephone line, typically a matter of months if not years, or grant maintenance interventions within reasonable times. In the late 1990s, when the mobile communication industry appeared, the same employees lost power and favor of their friends and became ordinary people to their huge disillusion.

Our company had started pre-operational activities in 1993 and had been subject to similar issues as far as telephone lines were concerned. I had not yet joined the company then but I was told later than when we were building our factory we had started using as office a space that was to become our laboratory. In this there was a wireless telephone line installed, which rarely used to work. Even when it did, the line would be too feeble to be heard across. We used to make complaints to the concerned authorities who would depute inspectors at their will to check what went wrong and how. They would take their sweet time to understand the issue and then ask somebody in the maintenance wing to set matters right. But often after a very short time the line would go bad again. Despite this we remained liable to pay the bill for the usage (minimum fixed charge) every time, which in itself was a considerable amount. Many times it had been hinted to us that a faster and more effective fixing could have happened in case the inspectors had been pleased by us. Such a wireless line was still in function even after I had joined and, at times, remained our only working line. By that moment (1998) we had obtained several landlines to serve our factory and offices. However, due to our location on the NH8 and the continuous work happening on the same, the landline wires were regularly uprooted or damaged, making the mobile line the only option for us to continue the business. Luckily a certain relief came from the fact that at that time cellular phones were already in use, though only a limited set of people (even among our staff) used to own a handset or operate with it. Also in this case we continued to be charged for the full service of the landlines, despite their being out of order for long periods during the year. Still in telecommunications, I was told by my colleagues an anecdote of the early 1990s, about an inspector deputed to carry out a pre-installation survey for a fax machine. The same had let us know that he desired to be picked up with a car of an adequate level so as to be able to come for the inspection. Once in our premises it was clear that, apart from the small payment for the license fee, he was expecting also some additional favors.

Chapter 4: Working in India | 65

Telecommunications were not the only problematic area we had to face. In our industry, and in general for the food processing and distributing industry, the most feared authorities were considered to be the infamous food inspectors. They used to lift samples very often in view of the profit they could manage to extract out of the complaint they would file. We had innumerable issues of samples collected resulting in having failed for one or another parameter. A very easily attackable issue for our liquid-filled gums was the moisture content. There was a limitation of 3.5 percent of total moisture permitted in the gum, failing which the sample was considered adulterated. However such a limit had been stated for normal gums and not liquid-filled ones, which did not exist at the moment of the law coming into effect. The illogical issue behind the legislation,[19] dating back to 1956, was that, irrespective of the fact that an adulterated sample was harmful or not, the inspector had the power to open a criminal case against the producer, threatening to send behind bars all the Board of Directors of the same.

A few states were notorious for their single-minded and hungry inspectors: among these was Kerala. Such officers used to have a very good network and often it would happen that, after the lifting of one sample in a certain town, a few more were later picked up by other inspectors in other towns. A colleague of mine remembered that once in three days' time nine samples of our products were picked up at a go by different inspectors. Some of those were so shrewd that before expressing their demands they would forcibly take possession of the mobile phones of the people meeting with them to avoid possible recording. While our general strategy was to make clear that our internal systems and audit functions would not have allowed any kind of side payments and most of the time this would be eventually understood, at times the threat or the delays caused by such greedy inspectors were so damaging that we had to take drastic actions. For instance it so happened that we had to make a complaint to the police against a Chief Medical Officer who was deliberately delaying the issuance of a license to us at Gurgaon. The special investigation team in the Anti-Corruption Bureau of the Haryana Police laid a trap and he was eventually taken in to jail. The use of such confrontational approach a few times led to retaliation cases being filed even against me as the ultimate responsible of the company and some of these took years to be sorted out. In fact I remember going to Chandigarh to meet personally the

---

[19] Prevention of Food Adulteration was the name of the law amended in the late 2000s but not yet fully in effect at the moment we write.

Pollution Control authority in charge for a matter linked to our Effluent Treatment Plant (ETP) and explain to him the unreasonable behavior of one of their inspectors. Interestingly in the area we had our factory we were one of the first companies to have set up a proper ETP, but for some unfortunate reasons we were also one of the most frequent targets of the inspectors. The fact that we were a foreign multinational company with a plant very visible just off a busy highway certainly contributed to such unwanted attention. In some other instances I had to go personally to Mumbai to inform a judge about other unjustified attacks on one of our products which translated into threats to our whole Board of Directors.

I have many times experienced that direct interaction with the top officials and bureaucrats was almost always the best way out in tricky cases, since they were normally educated and understanding people who would positively react to a genuine plea for justice. Once, just during the visit of our Top Management from Italy, some police people landed in our office carrying an arrest warrant in my name as the MD of the company. Our Legal Department, always very careful and used to handling such difficult circumstances, stated that I was not in the office and immediately rushed to understand the cause of such warrant. This time however it turned out to be a genuine mistake from the Metrology authority side, which apparently had sent to us several notices on some products having missing expiry dates and allegedly had not received our replies: when we showed the proof that these had been duly submitted the case was immediately dropped.

All this takes us to wondering why corruption is so spread in India; not that other countries in Asia or in general other emerging countries have not had corruption; but some of them have found ways and manners to at least drastically reduce it, whereas India has not yet done much in this direction. The real question to ask would be if there is a political will to stop corruption. It does not seem to be a priority either for the Central Government or for the states to do so: at least this was the case till the recent developments brought forward by the social activist Anna Hazare. This last started in 2011 a strong campaign against corruption in the contest of the approval and modification of an anti-corruption law (Lokpal Bill). His continued protest and rallies seem to at least have increased the awareness of the problem that the widespread briberies represent. On the other hand the average Indian person does not see corruption in a completely negative way: in fact he thinks that it is even useful when he can grease some mechanisms to obtain what he wants. Not so when somebody pretends to be bribed against the will of the person who has to pay. People in India have been brought up in a society where bribes are part of the system; for the man in the street they are something he has to cope with; for the entrepreneur part of the costs of doing business. Drivers find it normal to pay a policeman hundred rupees instead of paying a fine of one thousand; for the small traders, particularly the street ones, it is an accepted practice to pay some pocket money in order to be allowed to operate: in fact in the large Metros every year millions of dollars of bribes are paid by street vendors to be able to continue their activity. Companies find creative ways to create unaccounted funds that can be used to bribe at the appropriate moments. It is believed that black money accounts for a large percentage of the economy of the country. Why is corruption so much part of the system that it seems almost impossible to stop? One of the reasons is certainly the low pay of the civil servants and more in general of public employees. When people hardly get the necessary means to lead a decent life and ensure the education of their children, they start looking for sources of income besides their meager salaries, particularly if their position allows them to make relatively easy money at low risk. And this is the other major problem that helps corruption proliferate.

In countries like China corrupt officers are jailed for long years or, at times, even executed. In India until recently corrupt civil servants rarely got sacked, let alone sent to jail. This reinforces the idea that there is no political will to stop corruption: also because many politicians count on it in order to finance their re-election or even just to accumulate huge funds to be sent in some fiscal havens. Transparency International, a global organization leading the fight against corruption, measures the corruption perception level of the public sector in 178 countries. From the year 2005, when India was ranked at the 88th place, to the year 2009, when the country was ranked 84th, the four positions' jump seemed to tell a story of progress and tackling of the issue. However, in 2010 the country slipped again to the 87th place and the subsequent year even lower to the 95th position. This was due to a few major scandals including the 2G ones, leaked to the media in 2010 but concerning facts of 2008. In what became one of the major scams of the last years, the Telecom Ministry[20] sold 2G spectrum mobile telephone frequency licenses at prices much lower than the market rates, causing severe losses to the exchequer and major gains to those involved in the matter. The whole story had a large resonance for the number of politicians and high level corporate people

---

[20] The Ministry was headed at that moment by A. Raja, part of the DMK, one of the parties allied to the Congress in the ruling coalition.

involved, but also because it affected heavily the image of the government, including the Prime Minister;[21] thus it caused the deterioration of the mentioned perceived corruption index. A further possible reason for the high level of corruption in the country is the fact there is not much of notion of universal human nature in Indian culture, but rather a strong context-sensitivity that makes everything relative to when and where it happens.[22] Therefore for the specific case of briberies, they are not perceived as something generally bad and immoral, though they may become such in a certain context. The recent hiked awareness by the above-mentioned activist has possibly struck a chord because it has succeeded in making people understand that the generalized corruption directly or indirectly damages their own interests, even if they are not those materially involved in the bribery. To some extent Mr Hazare has managed to generalize the negative moral connotation of corruption, and has been able to do so also thanks to the support of young people with an evolving culture and the media, who are becoming more and more a driving force of Indian democracy.

---

[21] The opposition alleged that both Prime Minister Manmohan Singh and Finance Minister P. Chidambaram lied when they stated that they were not aware about what had happened and hence were not responsible for the facts. Furthermore, the government came under attack because the prosecution of the involved civil servant was kept pending for many months.

[22] See note 11 for source.

5

THE PERFETTI VAN MELLE INDIA SUCCESS

How It All Began

About twenty years ago a member of the Perfetti family landed in New Delhi. He had his room booked in the Oberoi hotel and had planned his visit with a clear objective in his mind: expanding the company's business to one of the Asian countries with most potential that had just opened its economy to foreign investments. Through contacts he had been given the name of an Indian boutique consulting firm which specialized in helping foreign investors start their business in the country. After the third day in Delhi he had been shown several plots of land; a few days later, before catching his plane back to Italy, he had already decided to buy one of those plots and start a green field venture in India.

At that moment the Perfetti Company was still predominantly an Italian set-up that just a few years earlier had started its internationalization process with the opening of some subsidiaries in south Europe. India was to be the foray into the emerging Asian countries and the project of creating a manufacturing location here was parallel to a similar project being undertaken in China. A few months after that visit, the plot of land was bought from nine farmers, each one owning small portions of it. The individual owners had different expectations; hardly any of them spoke English. The deal was eventually concluded, thanks to the mentioned consultant and the first employee of Perfetti India Private Limited, the local subsidiary just created, which had in the meantime recruited a few members of the leadership team. Once the deed was signed and sealed, the various procedures to obtain the change of land use from agricultural to industrial were started and the process of designing the factory initiated. The deal was finalized in November 1992; the conversion into industrial land was a process not at all easy then (it continues to be a very tricky process even now). Eventually, the CLU (Change of Land Use) was obtained, also thanks to some connection found between Perfetti's consultant and some Ministerial Secretary, and in February 1993, the work for building the factory started. The person in charge of the project was an Italian engineer, who would have later become the first Managing Director of the company, though his stint in that position would have lasted only some months due to health problems.

During the early years of the Perfetti Group's international expansion the knowhow was mainly concentrated in the Italian headquarters and progressively being transferred to the subsidiaries: hence the first team who was to lead the company in India was formed by a majority of Italians, but for the Head of Corporate Affairs/Finance and the Head of Sales. Later on a local HR Head was also hired. In my years in India I was told of interesting anecdotes that had happened during the inception period. Among these the fact that some long sweeping brushes were imported from Italy since the expatriate management team took pity on the local sweepers who cleaned the floor with their backs bent using the typical hand brooms still used in India,[1] made of a bunch of grass. The Italians were not used to seeing people cleaning in that position and they thought they should procure for them long brooms and mops that would allow them to work in a more erect position. When these tools finally arrived numerous, the Italians handed them over to the concerned people hoping to see them cleaning in a more comfortable posture. However after a few days the cleaners were once again sweeping with their backs bent and the Italians were left wondering what had happened to the imported brooms. After a more careful look they realized that the Italian sweeps were actually being used, but their poles had been broken so as to allow the workers to clean the way they had always done! Another anecdote I heard was concerning a mishap caused by the Italian team because of their craving for authentic Espresso coffee. In order to ensure their daily supply of it, which at that time was very hard to find in India, they decided to import, together with a container of ingredients for the gum, also an Italian-made coffee machine with several kilograms of coffee beans. When the container arrived, a zealous custom inspector did manage to find the crate containing

---

[1] Such half sweep is called *jhadoo* in Hindi.

Chapter 5:   The Perfetti Van Melle India Success | 71

the coffee and the machine in a container full of gum materials. The bill of lading did not mention the items, which possibly represented a marginal part of the container load, but the scrupulous officer decided that the goods' declaration was wrong and the container had to be sent back to Italy with consequent delays and extra costs.

The construction of the factory lasted for approximately 15 months. There was hardly anything around that land at that time and even to obtain the power connection the company's team had to find creative solutions. Getting an electrical connection used to be rather difficult at that time: given the high sanction needed for the factory, the expectations at the electricity sub-station in charge were quite high. Only after months of discussions and networking, Perfetti managed to get the sanction: however, the state of Haryana seemed to have not enough money to connect the load to the Busbar close to the land. The company was then forced to buy and install on its own initiative and expenses the electric poles to link a distance of several miles from the local power sub-station to the factory plot. The production lines' installation and commissioning overlapped with the last construction stage and the first trial runs happened around May of 1994. The first invoices, partly manually written, were issued in July of the same year and so the adventure of Perfetti in India eventually started. The first products to be sold were some gums that had had a large success in the home country. But then the first market problems started. The strategy used by the company was centered on the standardization of products and communication[2] and specifically the extension of the products and communication mix used with success in the home country. The formats initially produced and marketed were similar to those utilized in Italy, namely stick pack of five pieces each—both for Big Babol, a bubble gum, and Center Fresh, a liquid-filled chewing gum. Such packs were sold in display boxes of 24 pieces at a (consumer) price of ₹7 each (hence ₹168 for display boxes). The price was way above the market prices from two different perspectives: local gums were sold at ₹0.5 each—Re 1 for the "premium" ones—and they were mainly sold in mono pieces. Formats like those initially introduced by Perfetti were unaffordable both for the retailers and for consumers. The former were used to buy displays of 100/150 pieces of much cheaper products, for a total expense of ₹75 to 150 (at consumer price). Perfetti used to sell the displays for ₹168 (at consumer price), hence with an

---

[2] Such strategy is called Double Extension in academic theory; see M. Kotabe and K. Helsen, *Global Marketing Management* (New York: John Wiley & Sons, 2007).

out-of-pocket for retailers up to over two times that of the local competitors. Only restricted elites among Indian consumers could afford spending ₹7 for a pack of gums, particularly since the core target here was children and not young adults, like in Italy. The communication used was a standardized one: Italian commercials were dubbed in English and aired. Even the communication mix did not really work well, since there was a kind of disconnect between the Italian commercials and the average Indian public. If the reason to enter the Indian market was mainly the large number of potential consumers, given the country's huge population, the initial marketing mix was possibly not coherent with such objective. There was scope for learning also in the formulations of the products. After a few weeks since the liquid-filled gums were in the market, the first complaints surfaced about the fact that products had started leaking: the syrup inside was coming out of the gum making the product look messy and the wrapper sticky. Here the problem was caused by much hotter and humid climatic conditions compared to the European ones, whereas the products' recipe of the home country had not been changed much. Soon the management realized that a complete revision of the marketing mix was necessary and studies began to improve the formulation and create a tropical recipe that could withstand the local climate. Pricing was perceived to be an extremely important variable and actions were taken to create an offer more appealing also to masses. To the five-pieces stick pack, the price of which was brought down from ₹7 to 6,[3] were also added single-piece offers for both the brands: gums were individually wrapped and sold at the price of ₹1.5 per piece.

The new formulation helped minimize the leakage problem but after a few months of sales and the products still moving slowly off the shelves it was clear that even the reduced price represented too high a premium compared to that of local competitors, despite the gap in the product's overall quality. A price reduction was then planned and the single pieces were eventually priced at ₹1, in line with the premium local competitors with national presence, though still at double the price of some regional ones. In order to be able to maintain profitability at this price level it had been necessary to indigenize as many ingredients of the raw and packing materials as possible. Later on also the communication was modified and locally produced, with Indian talent and plots more familiar to the local public. The additional change that triggered a major increase in sales was the tie up with the National Cricket Team

---

[3] Later on, a further revision to the price was implemented, and the price was brought down to ₹5, a level at which it stayed for several years.

in a deal that saw one of the two brands becoming the official gum of the India team. Cricket is an extremely popular sport in India, a national passion; the whole nation watches the matches dreaming to meet their idols or at least watch them playing live. During a World Cricket Cup the millions of Indians who watched their team players munching Center Fresh gums and the wrappers glittering on the cricket pitch made a huge impact on the brand's sales, its popularity drastically increased and the sales had a major hike. From that moment onwards the company sales would have seen a few years of strong growth, with production hardly managing to supply the requested sales volumes and the supporting functions catching up to handle the increasing size of operations. Based on the good success of the gums it was decided to enter the candy segments also. Even in this case the existing market was large but with an average level of quality. There were many regional players, particularly strong in the southern and western parts of the country, but hardly any national one.

Part of this segment, the hard boiled candies, was reserved for small scale industries:[4] due to this restriction Perfetti could have not been able to take advantage of the market opportunity in this segment. However, thanks to the entrepreneurial attitude of the local team, the company found smart ways to circle around such a reservation and managed anyway to enter some of the segments of the hard boiled industry. Thanks to its high milk and fat content, Alpenliebe, the main international caramel brand of the Group, could in fact be launched in 1995 as a "proprietary toffee," a category for which the reservation did not apply. The toffee was produced with an innovative deposited technology—not yet available among local producers—giving the product a superior texture; it was packed in an individually sealed pillow packs, a new form of packaging—unseen in the market at that point in time—granting a superior climate resistance and hygiene compared to the commonly used twist wrap. The launch was an immediate success and sales grew steeply to make Alpenliebe one of the pillar brands for Perfetti India. Two years later another candy (Chlormint) was launched as an *Ayurvedic*[5] medicine. Selling the lozenge under such route implied increased complexity in manufacturing and selling (need to obtain a specific license for ayurvedic products; provide

---

[4] The hard boiled candy sector in India was reserved to Small Scale Industries with limited capital and investments (> US$ 250,000). This was a major limiting factor, since the cap on the investment would have not allowed building a state-of-the-art production plant for such candies.

[5] Ayurveda is the ancient medicinal art of India, based on natural ingredients.

a dedicated manufacturing space, etc.) but allowed the company to reinforce its presence in the hard boiled segment in spite of the reservation.

The First Crisis and the Re-launch Years

Three years of continuous growth had given the company the confidence of being able to conquer a large share of the market while driving the development of the same. Like in most operating companies of the Perfetti Group, in India also, the Sales and Marketing functions had the leading role in taking the firm towards the achievement of its objectives. In a country like India, were the distribution is extremely fragmented and the number of retail outlets is counted in millions, the distribution variable constitutes a vital element of the marketing mix. Perfetti decided to create its own distribution network so as to avoid relying on external parties; the company intended developing a tailor-made infrastructure for the needs of their own specific category of products. This implied a relatively longer time to create the network of distributors and their own sales force, but would have turned out to be one of the critical success factors in the medium-long term. However, in 1998, the fourth full year of operation, complacency due to the positive sales results, some short term-oriented distribution policies as well as an IPR issue on the main brand caused a setback, leading to a reduction in the annual sales turnover of the local company.

Complacency is a very common mistake among successful companies. The feelings that the position gained is un-attackable and the reputation of the company allows it to sell anything in the market are rather dangerous symptoms of future problems which may eventually lead to market share and sales loss. The other two issues concerned Big Babol, one of the two gum brands originally launched. A very aggressive sales promotion during the first quarter of the year had led to overstocking of distributors, who had bought large volumes of the promoted brand. However the quantities purchased were much higher than those demanded by consumers, and for the subsequent three months the distributors were overstocked and bought less and less from the company. The reiterated mistake of the sales force was to try and force sales to distributors rather than allowing the pipeline to dry up before starting to sell again. This created a vicious circle that ended up with retailers and distributors not wanting to purchase anymore for almost two full months. Such facts happened during the Indian summer, and the products stagnant in the warehouses started deteriorating also due to the climatic conditions. Therefore, not only would distributors not buy, but they also started returning the products and claiming their money back, requests to which the company often would not agree. Hence, on top of temporary reduction in sales consequent to the above described situation, the company's reputation got affected vis-à-vis the distributors, who felt cheated for having been pushed to buy products not moving out and not returnable to the producer. Some of them left the company and caused further sales loss. Several months after the initial promotion, the company had to eventually take back large quantities of products lying in the depots and damaged by the long permanence in extremely hot weather conditions.

That year the problems seemed to be piling up. During the second part of the year, when the crisis caused by the overstocking was about to be resolved, an episode linked to IPR forced the company to stop the sales of the brand Big Babol for almost three weeks. The matter started with "The Big Bubble Gum," a brand belonging to a domestic rival company, trying to make inroads by confusing gum consumers with the brand name similarity. Perfetti cautioned the domestic manufacturer through a legal notice in the form of "Cease and Desist." The rival filed a legal suit before a district court. Despite a gentlemans agreement between the Managing Directors of the two companies, following which Perfetti withdrew the legal notice, the rival continued with the legal suit, obtaining a court injunction order against Perfetti not to manufacture, sell and distribute Big Babol. It took Perfetti 20 days to vacate the orders, and, in a moment when the pipeline was lean due to what had happened in the first part of the year, this translated in actual sales loss. The episode proves that in emerging countries like India, even apparently clear cut court cases may be tricky. At times, this is due to the influence of networking, or even bribery, which has the power of diverting the right course of justice. From what I have seen or heard, episodes of corruption are not rare in lower courts, less frequent at higher levels of the judiciary system and possibly not reaching the highest level. In the case just mentioned, it took almost a decade for the court proceedings to see an end. Eventually, the brand Big Babol won the case. In the meantime it had gained a large share of the market whereas the rival brand (and its producer) has almost disappeared.[6] Several years of litigation had caused high legal costs, attention diverted from the business and at times lost opportunities.

---

[6] We have heard that the same rival company, who even in other instances tried to attack Perfetti on other legal grounds, possibly hoping to make money with amicable settlements, has had several commercial and legal troubles in the recent years.

All the above matters caused the arrest of the previous years' positive growth trend amidst a loss of confidence inside the company and among its partners. The year closed with a 12 percent reduction of the sales turnover compared to the previous one: considering the very high rate of growth recorded during the initial years, the results were quite a change of direction and caused strong concern in the company as well as at headquarters level. Crises often happen to be the right times to look back and re-discuss some assumptions given for granted. This was the case also for Perfetti India: the process of analyzing what had gone wrong and taking the necessary steps to ensure that learning became the base for a revamped business model was also facilitated by the fact that by the end of that year I had joined the company and would soon take over the MD role. I had the advantage of being able to look at the past with an objective perspective, since I was new and could not be much influenced by the past. The subsequent year was therefore a year of transition, when we started rebuilding the credibility of the company, both internally and externally. The sales systems were reinforced so as to avoid again having episodes of volumes dumped on distributors to artificially inflate sales and achieve targets in spite of the real demand. Marketing became more aware of the mid-term dangers of aggressive promotions and started better planning and monitoring of the same. The other supporting functions progressively acquired a stronger role with better checks and balances vs. the previous undisputed leading role of the Sales and Marketing departments. For instance the Finance department gained a much stronger role in handling the sales accountants, who had previously been managed by the Sales department also due to their operating out of the four sales branch offices in the territory.

The Big Babol episode had shown the necessity of building several pillar brands that could reduce the dependency of the company upon one major brand. The launch of the brand Chlormint as an ayurvedic lozenge in 1997 had been a step in this direction, and was meant to expand Perfetti's presence in the candy segment. However its launch had not been supported with advertising and the sales volumes had been reasonable but not very high. We managed to obtain from the headquarters the sanction to advertise Chlormint and develop a local communication for the same. We worked with our local agency and came up with a path-breaking advertising that, after over 10 years from its first appearance, it is still remembered[7] and quoted among the most

---

[7] See, for instance, *Brand Equity*, insert of *The Economic Times*, February 15, 2012, "When The Chips are Down," by Ravi Balakrishnan, where this ad is mentioned.

impactful of the category. It featured a local *paanwala*,[8] who becomes quite irritated with a customer inquiring about Chlormint usage up to the point of dunking him into a bucket of water while yelling a pay off that would have become extremely popular.[9] We also introduced new variants under existing brands with the double objective of capitalizing on an existing and known brand name to introduce new products. This would add critical mass to the brands already in the market and also generate synergies in communication by advertising the range or selectively supporting one of the variants under the same brand. One of the innovative variants introduced during these years was a sub-brand[10] called Center Shock, a liquid-filled fruit flavor gum coated with a thin layer of acid. When popped into one's mouth the acid coating would give a very sour taste, rather hard to cope with: however, in a few seconds, the initial "shock" would leave space to a much sweeter taste coming from the filling and the gum itself.

Apart from the product formulation, quite unique in the market, what worked well was the overall positioning of the brand: "the electric gum." To reinforce such proposition we tied up with a show that was very popular among the youth in that period named "Who Dares Wins" and anchored by a very funny Australian guy. The anchorman and his whole troupe had immediately liked our idea of challenging consumers to chew our sour product and had agreed to shoot a few episodes in some colleges and other spots where young people used to gather. The challenge consisted of chewing the highest possible number of Center Shock gums within a minute while keeping all the products chewed inside the mouth throughout the available time. The show itself was hilarious with the participants sporting all kind of facial expressions each time they popped a gum in their mouth and the showman commenting on their efforts, while their friends all around encouraged them by shouting and laughing. A very unique advertising film completed the mix. This featured a barber in a typical old shop in a small Indian town who, upon the request of a very special hair style by a young client, thanks to a sudden inspiration, places a Center Shock inside his mouth. A few moments after receiving this, the youngster starts shaking in a continuous crescendo that would result in

---

[8] Typical street vendors selling *paan*, a very popular natural breath freshener made with a piece of betel nut with spreads of spices wrapped into a leaf. It is usually chewed and later on thrown away once the flavor is over; however there are people who swallow the whole mixture.
[9] *Dobara mat poochhna* was the Hindi version, meaning "do not ask again."
[10] Part of the extended Center Fresh family.

his hair taking the desired pointy style. The base line of the ad was *Hilake rakh de*, which would literally mean "will shake you up." The overall mix was a thundering success and in the span of three weeks, sales shot up at a rate that nobody had foreseen, causing severe out-of-stocks and becoming the marketing case of the moment. Such a large success benefited the whole "Center" brand as well as the overall company. In this case, and also in others later on, we did notice that the effects of the communication on one variant of a same brand also benefited the others and the overall brand image in general.

Within our company during these years we reinforced our organizational structure in many departments and particularly in the sales, marketing and finance. We also worked on a better definition of roles and internal policies; we put in place the management trainee scheme and the teamwork activities mentioned in the previous chapter. The idea was to ensure that the overall ecosystem could grow from a small sized company with basic structures and policies to a more organized one which could support the fast development of the sales. We also created a specific Supply Chain department clubbing the purchase and logistic functions, initially handled partly by the Technical function and partly by the Sales. In general, we laid the foundation of a stronger organization ready to face the increased level of competition and the new challenges of a market in fast evolution.

North Meets South and Rural India

The beginning of the new century was to further enhance the growth of Perfetti India, not only organically but also through the absorption of another entity. The Perfetti Group had for a long time shares in the Van Melle Group, a Dutch conglomerate listed on the Dutch stock market and owner of internationally reputed brands such as Mentos and Fruittella. Towards the final part of the 1990s, this Group was considering its possible next steps to grow internationally in a more competitive market environment. After surveying possible alliances they eventually accepted the offer from one of their shareholders and longtime business partner, Perfetti, to take over the company and merge it into one larger conglomerate. This happened early in the year 2001 and, a few months later, once at central level all financial transactions had been settled, the two companies started merging their local operations all over the world. Van Melle had recently opened a local subsidiary in India. They had built and just inaugurated it at the time of the take-over a manufacturing unit in the south of India, close to Chennai. The company had started distributing their brands regionally in the south and the west of

India, initially with imported products, later on with those produced in the newly opened plant. Even in their case, as it had happened in 1994 for Perfetti, they had had problems of product stability due to the climatic conditions and had been forced to withdraw some of the products initially launched to substitute them with newly formulated ones that would not melt during the hot season. Both for the product portfolios and for the location of the respective factories, the take-over of the local Van Melle subsidiary from Perfetti India was a win-win situation.

For the young Van Melle subsidiary, which was struggling to achieve a national distribution with a limited product portfolio, it would have meant a sudden major leap in the presence of their products throughout the country. They would have also benefited from the consolidated experience in the country of Perfetti, both in operations and in R&D. For Perfetti, which historically had a very strong presence in the northern and eastern region, the acquisition of new distributors in the southern and western regions would have integrated the existing network. Furthermore the new brands, chewy candies with international awareness and status, were complementary to those already existing in the Perfetti portfolio, consisting of gums and hard boiled candies perceived as local rather than as international brands. The location of the newly acquired plant in the south would add a second manufacturing pole located at the opposite side of the country vs. the Perfetti plant in the north, with obvious logistic advantages. The whole process of merging the two entities was an enriching experience for me and for my team and helped me get to know much better the southern culture, very different from the one I had been exposed to while living in Delhi. India has multiple cultures in every region, possibly every state. In the north, Punjabis are very different from Kashmiris or other north-eastern people such as the Nagas or Manipuris. In the south, Keralites would feel offended if assimilated into one with Tamilians (and possibly vice-versa).

While dealing with teams mainly from a northern and a southern state I could find major differences among the regional cultures. Starting from the workers in the factories, one would have immediately noticed the different attitudes in the Manesar (north) plant against the Chennai (south) one. This was also due to the fact that the average education level of the shop floor members in Chennai was higher than that in Manesar, reflecting also the major difference in literacy between the south and the north. While the *jugaad* fixing was very common in the north, the Chennai factory would have a much better maintenance of the machines. The semi-finished product would be kept in different trays scattered around the production hall in the north; it would be instead temporarily stored in the demarcated area with the trays' colors varying according to the product type in the south. The meals break would see a flow of workers moving as kettle towards the canteen in Manesar while an ordered queue lined up at the food counter in Chennai. Changing rooms in the southern factory would be distinctively cleaner and better maintained than those in the northern one, though upkeep was also a function of the different age of the two plants. Also in terms of white collars and managers, the southern ones would be of lesser words and low profile, whereas the northern ones would be more vocal and ready to show off their latest car or gadget. Such differences could have led to a difficult integration of the two teams, had adequate actions not been taken. To encourage the interaction between the people at a plant level we decided to relocate one of the production lines of hard candies to the south: this meant that several people from the Perfetti factory would have spent a few months in the Van Melle plant to accomplish the task; a group of Van Melle operators would have spent time in the Perfetti factory to see the line running and get the adequate training. After this initial period we offered some of the technicians in the two factories to swap roles, and, surprisingly, most of them accepted.

Such moves did create a much better understanding among the teams, who would eventually not look at each other as strangers or almost rivals, but more and more as one team. At an operations level we analyzed the vendors providing the main raw and packing materials in the two set-ups and realized that often there were considerable price advantages to buy from one supplier for the whole country, in spite of the differential logistic cost. Sugar, for instance, had a differential of almost ₹2 between the northern and southern suppliers: hence we started buying more in the south and shipping to the north. Though such change would have created logistical extra-costs, the overall gain net of the additional freight would still justify the move: furthermore this would create more competition among suppliers, give us a stronger negotiating power and eventually lower prices. The highest advantage came certainly from the integration of the sales teams and distribution networks. Apart from the already mentioned higher coverage, the Perfetti Van Melle combined sales structure had a wider brand portfolio to sell and a growing number of SKUs. This helped us gain clout with the retailers but had the potential to cannibalize the sales of the slower products. In fact the typology of retailers selling confectionery in India has limited capital resources and low purchasing power. A sales call attempting to sell a large number of brands in such small retailers would end up in a zero-sum game, hence limiting the Company's potential to sell the whole range and grow by introducing new brands. A system to overcome such distribution limitation was then engineered. The Brand portfolio was split into two product groups, each assigned to a division. For instance, a certain area would have had two set of distributors, each carrying different brands and visiting retailers in different days of the week, so as to allow the limited daily working capital of the specific retailer to be allocated over the full range of PVM brands. This opened the way to the introduction of new products without the consequent cannibalization of sales of the existing ones.

During these years we also started developing products specifically for the Indian market: some of these remained limited to the local market, whereas some others were liked and demanded by our sister subsidiaries that started producing and selling them in their markets.[11] Such a model proved to be very effective and led, later on, to the creation of a third division, or set of distributors, when several new products were launched. Also, thanks to such change, we became (and still remain today) the sugar confectionery company with the largest brand portfolio in the country and our total sales more than doubled in four years, even without considering the recently acquired Van Melle brands. Our distribution model had to become a benchmark for all our competitors, many of which tried replicating the same over the years but did not manage to achieve comparable results. From the organizational point of view we tried keeping all employees of the merged companies, hence avoiding any redundancy trimming. The Van Melle structure was not very large, and consequently, we managed to accommodate their employees in the merged entity at different levels of the newly restructured organization. The Van Melle Management Team members were fully integrated in the new set up: not all of them remained with us over the years, but those who stayed had the opportunity to grow and cover important roles in the Indian company as well as in other sister subsidiaries. Due to the fact that Van Melle had operations in many countries where Perfetti already had a set up, many similar integrations were to be carried out throughout the continents: however, the India case was considered possibly the smoothest take-over of the whole Group.

Once the new organizational structure had stabilized and our market positions consolidated, we started looking at ways and manners to sustain the growth rate of the previous years in a growing but competitive market. While our presence was quite spread across the country, we realized that our strength was mainly in the larger towns and the big metropolitan areas. There was hence scope to go deeper into the connective tissue of rural India, which

---

[11] Among the local ones which remained only in India was Chattarpatar, a spicy candy with tamarind and black pepper flavor. Among those who became regional brands were Cofitos, launched in that period and Creamfillz and Mangofillz launched a few years later.

represented a huge untapped potential for us. To provide a clearer idea of such potential I would quote the words of a renowned author and scholar C. K. Prahalad. "Companies assume that people with low incomes have little to spend.... While individual incomes may be low the aggregate buying power of poor communities is actually quite large."[12] To the lay person, India is perceived as a poor country, with a nominal per capita income little over US$ 1,200:[13] the poorest part of a poor country may appear to have no market potential, but the reality is very different. In fact rural India represents alone almost 12 percent of the entire world population. While people living in such rural parts may, as an average, be poorer than their urban counterparts, in 2010 sources[14] mentioned that 41 million credit cards had been issued in rural India, and 22 million only in the urban part. More specifically, about the sugar confectionery category, well over 30 percent of the sales of this industry come from rural India, and the percentage is increasing year upon year. The total number of households in rural India is close to 140 million, spread in almost 640,000 villages. Such few figures contribute to give a clearer picture of the huge potential of this part of the country.

PVM started studying this market in 2005 through some first field experiments. A little later we carried out some extensive consumer and trade researches as well as direct engagement activities with consumers. We needed to address all the elements of doing business: the right product and SKU mix, the best distribution option—eventually decided to be through Super Stockist network, a Hub and Spoke model—and the most appropriate structure to manage this network. The villages would be reached through van operations. To communicate with such consumers we would increase our advertising investments on the national broadcaster channels[15] for the TV and on All India Radio. To be closer to consumers we participated in various *melas*[16] and planned extensive school visits with a specifically developed School Contact Program. The rural operation started as a trial grew exponentially in the span

---

[12] C. K. Prahalad and A. Hammond, "Serving the World's Poor, Profitably," *Harvard Business Review on Emerging Markets*, pp. 45–69.

[13] Source: *The Economic Times* on http://articles.economictimes.indiatimes.com/2011-05-31/news/29604458_1_capita-income-national-income-economy-at-current-prices. PPP Estimates from the CIA Factbook rank the per capita GDP in 2011 at around US$ 3,000.

[14] Ruchi Katyar, "Rural Marketing: Challenges, Opportunities and Strategies," May 26, 2010. Available online at http://www.coolavenues.com/mba-journal/marketing/rural-marketing-challenges-opportunities-strategies.

[15] The National Channel is called *Doordarshan*, commonly called DD.

[16] Local fairs.

of a few years and reached an annual average weight of more than 20 percent of the total company's sales in 2011; in some of the regions it represents today almost 30 percent of the business. In five years we added over 6,000 sub-distributors to our already extended distribution network and reached out to an additional 5,000 towns and about two million outlets. The new channel strongly contributed to maintaining the compounded annual growth rate in the region of 20 percent during those years. Also, thanks to the rural drive as opposite to many multinationals who limit their presence to the top tier, PVMI has been able to compete in all four tiers of the market structure of emerging countries as defined by some scholars,[17] including the bottom of the pyramid, where regional and local brands normally have the lion share.

Fiscal Incentives and Masala Munching

We mentioned that the quantum jump of the sales of Perfetti India happened when the mono pieces were introduced at the prevailing market prices of ₹1 for the gums and ₹0.5 for the candies. This had happened in 1995. Since then the market prices have not changed for the two segments of confectionery, despite costs of raw and packing materials growing year after year. At times the annual inflation recorded rates as high as 11 percent, but none of the market players ever dared to increase the price of their core mono piece products. The reason for such reluctance in increasing prices was the coinage. The smallest coin available was the ₹0.25, not anymore easily found after the turning of the century. Therefore, the minimum possible increase for a candy would have meant doubling the price from ₹0.5 to 1. Similarly in the gum segment, the minimum feasible price increase would have brought the products to ₹1.5, hence increasing it by 50 percent. The known price sensitivity of the demand in the country was the stumbling block preventing companies to increase prices. Over the years PVM had taken continuous actions (egs, weight reduction, alternative packaging materials, larger secondary packaging formats, etc.) in order to limit the margin erosions, but over 10 years of unchanged prices started taking a serious toll on profitability. Other multinational companies[18] operating in India had exploited the route of availing

---

[17] See T. Khanna and K. G. Palepu "Building World Class Companies in Developing Countries," *Harvard Business Review on Emerging Markets* (2008), pp. 131–151.
[18] One of these had been Unilever, previously known in India as Hindustan Lever Limited (HLL), for many years the largest FMCG company in the country.

of the fiscal incentives offered to investors by some less developed states seeking industrialization and employment.

In order to find solutions to the problem of decreasing profitability, an initial proposal of setting up a plant in a fiscal friendly area had been presented to PVM shareholders already in 2004, but at that moment it was decided to keep it on hold. A more detailed proposal was presented again at the beginning of 2006 and was eventually approved. A third factory was to be built in a location about 400 kilometers north east of New Delhi, in the state of Uttaranchal.[19] Such a project in the initial plans had foreseen only a small plant with three production lines, providing important savings on account of direct and indirect taxation for the company. The deadline to be in production in order to obtain the fiscal benefits was the first half of 2007. We did meet the deadline but the same was later extended and also provided the opportunity to expand the capacity of the existing plants in the territory of the state. We decided then to enlarge the factory by building an additional floor and to maximize the production capacity. Eventually the scope of the project had become four folds the initial one: 12 lines were installed in the plant, which became PVMI's largest one in the country. Thanks to such expansion, the fiscal saving became more and more important, making a clear difference to the company's bottom line and consequently to the capacity of re-investing both in fixed assets as well as in promotional support. This allowed us to beef-up our advertising and promotion budgets so as to support a number of new launches in existing and new segments of the confectionery market. One of these was the éclairs segment, historically shared between Cadbury and Nestle, where we made an entry at the end of 2010. Later on we also launched a pectin-based jelly product, a new segment not only for PVMI but also for the local market. We had studied this opportunity for a long time with a gelatin based product, but the problem in using gelatin, which is usually of beef or pork origin, was that one would end up upsetting either the Hindu or the Muslim part of the Indian population.

With the perspective of getting out of the price point trap that had created so many limitations for us we started investigating possible opportunities of diversification. The thought was also guided by the finding that other confectionery players in India had presence in other higher margin categories and this helped their overall ability to manage the lower profitability sugar confectionery sector. It certainly made good business sense to leverage PVMI market strength and distribution network to exploit the opportunities in

---

[19] The state was later renamed Uttarakhand.

the growing Indian market. After evaluating several new markets (egs, oral hygiene, biscuits) we presented a recommendation to enter the savory snacks segment. The reasons behind the choice of this were multiple: the snack market was (and still is) one of the highest growing markets in the food category;[20] at the moment of our study there were not too many organized players in the business.[21] The nature of the category allowed experimenting and rebounding from possible mistakes, also because the initial fixed assets investment was reasonable. Our recommendation was approved and, in 2010, we ordered the machinery and started creating space in the Manesar factory, completely separated from the sugar confectionery production, dedicated to the project. In parallel we initiated the development of the products by evaluating several shapes, recipes and seasoning. The Indian snack market was estimated to be a one billion Euros' market in 2010, with an annual volume in excess of 300,000 tons and almost 40 percent growth rate. However, well over one third of this market was what is defined as traditional Indian snacks, a low margin segment with relatively slower growth where we did not intend venturing. Another 35 percent was the potato wafer segment, which appeared to us too complex for the implications on its supply chain linked to the procurement of the raw materials. Hence we decided our focus to be the extruded segment,[22] representing approximately 25 percent of the overall market and with the highest growth, well above 50 percent. The snacks project was a very important development, since no other operating company in the PVM world had tried a diversification strategy and India was to be the first one to lead into this new adventure.

While the group has a deep knowledge of the sugar confectionery market and its R&D expertise has made it known for its fast innovation and time to market, there was no knowhow about the savory snacks and everything had to be started from scratch. By the beginning of 2011 the factory was ready and the first product trials started. Since in the meantime many more competitors had entered the market, we needed to come up with unique products in order to increase our chances of success. Several innovative products were developed in cooperation with our machinery supplier, who happened to be a long time vendor of equipments for the Group and was extremely helpful for the initial stage of the project. Among eight products short-listed we

---

[20] During the years 2008–2011, the market grew at rates higher than 30 percent per year.
[21] The competitive scene changed during the subsequent years with several other players entering the market.
[22] This segment also included a sub-segment called "Bridge."

eventually zeroed in on three and started a market test with two of them. The first product tested was a ring shaped one we called *Golz*, in two varieties of seasoning, "full masala" and "happy tomato." We also tested a small *somosa*[23] we called *Fofos*, with similar masala seasoning but baked, not fried. The test happened initially in two states (later extended to a third one) in the north and the south of the country and lasted for six months.

After reading the results and taking the corrective actions from the learning of the same we decided to launch nationally only the *Golz* in four variants, in November 2011. The results of the launch were quite encouraging: we developed a very different communication for these products, to some extent divisive but certainly impactful. A few articles on the press talked about this, one in particular in rather negative terms, many more acclaiming the same for its uniqueness and fun. Later on, during 2012, a different product named *Disk*s was introduced in four flavor variants: also thanks to this, the snack business started gaining momentum.

Based on the large benefits of the factory in the fiscal friendly state, and thanks to the continuous growth of the sales and the need to generate additional production capacity, in 2011 we started evaluating the opportunity of

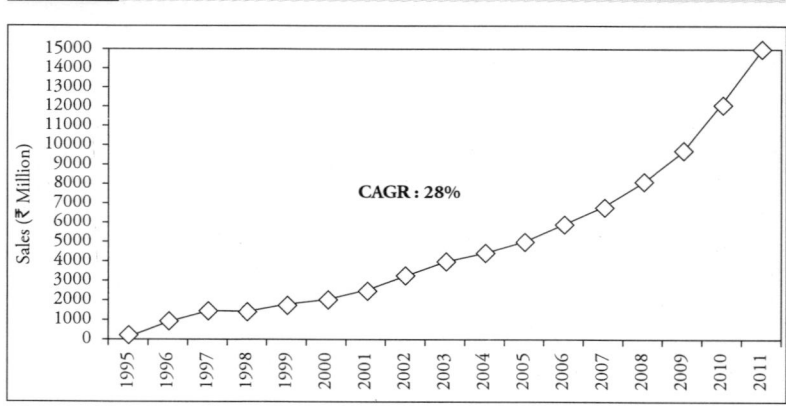

Figure 5.1 Perfetti Van Melle India: Sales trend 1995–2011 (Value in Million ₹)

Source: Author.

---

[23] *Somosa* or *samosa* is a very typical savory snack, usually served as appetizer or as mid day snack, fried and stuffed with vegetables or meat.

Chapter 5: The Perfetti Van Melle India Success | 87

a new factory in another state offering fiscal incentives. In this case the idea was not only to exploit such incentives but also to gain logistic advantages by building a plant catering to an area of the country that today is serviced from plants located far away.

Today Perfetti Van Melle India, further to being the second largest company for volumes sold in PVM Group, is the undisputed market leader in the local sugar confectionery market, with a share close to 25 percent. It dominates the gum segment, where its market share is 58 percent.[24] It is also the company with the widest product portfolio, with volumes still growing in two digits and an extremely wide distribution. Nielsen estimates that PVM India products are present in over 3.4 million outlets in the country. PVM India has a network of more than 4,000 distributors and almost 8,000 sub-distributors and super-stockists. We estimate that every week our sales people visit over one million retailers and that every day we sell more than 70 million pieces: in a fortnight an equivalent number to the whole Indian population eats at least one of PVMI's products. The company has been several times listed among the fastest growing companies in India and has received a high number of recognition for its operations[25] in several fields, such as technical and technological. I have personally had the honor of receiving in 2005 the National Award for Energy Conservation from the hands of the then President of India, A. P. J. Abdul Kalam.

The reasons of our success have possibly been multiple. The entry in India soon after the opening of the country to foreign investments gave PVMI a first mover advantage that helped building entry barriers. Furthermore the progressive foray in various segments of the sugar confectionery market with a brand building long term perspective contributed to reinforcing and consolidating the advantage over the years. Other international players entered the market together with Perfetti but for various reasons (egs, limited product portfolio, sub-optimal strategies) were not able to achieve similar results. When Perfetti entered the Indian market the average quality of the existing products was rather low. However, the company had chosen since inception to follow the home country quality standards for his local products. Local ingredients were used only when adequate quality vendors had been identified, so as to never compromise on the quality of the finished product.[26] This, as

---

[24] Nielsen Retail Audit, YTD December 2011.
[25] Among these some received during 2010 are: National Award for Food Safety received from the Confederation of India Industries and the CIO 100 awards India on Using Virtualization Technology.
[26] All the local manufacturing facilities of PVMI have obtained ISO and HACCP certification.

well as the continuous innovation, contributed to the perceived uniqueness of PVM's products in the market and the building of a superior quality perception among the trade and consumers. We were the first to introduce candies produced with a new technology and packed in individually sealed pillow packs that guarantee a better protection to the product. Perfetti introduced the first liquid-filled gum in the market; created breakthrough promotional activities; set up new distribution models; challenged the conventional way of advertising confectionery products.[27] Our Marketing department has been extremely active and has strongly contributed to make our brand household names. The creativity and uniqueness of our advertising has been recognized in India as well as abroad. In the period from 2005 to 2011, PVMI received an average of 22 Marketing and Communication awards per year, with a peak of 43 awards received in 2007, where we won silver and bronze awards also at the Cannes festival.

In spite of our high quality and brand building investments our products were (and still are) priced at market prices and not at a premium: the importance of this in a price-sensitive market as the Indian one was understood after a few months from the launch. Some of PVMI's competitors insisted for several years on the international standardization approach, both in the product format and in the communication. Even with heavy above and below the line promotional support they did not succeed in making significant inroad among the consumers. On the other hand PVMI managed to gain a high image while engaging the local consumers and speaking their language. Even with promotional support relatively limited vs. some competitors more focused on few specific segments of the industries, Perfetti Van Melle brands have always been recognized as part of the India everyday life and almost perceived as "super local brands." This culturally intelligent approach was followed both in the market and inside our organization: the company realized how important it was to understand its own people, rely and invest in them. The number of expatriates was limited to a number one could count on one hand and little over a decade of operations the company had its first local Managing Director. Its competent and loyal management team grew with the company and vastly contributed to its success.

---

[27] One of the various innovations in this field was the use of celebrities for advertising the confectionery products. We were the first to utilize a famous Indian actress, Kajol, as a testimonial for one of our candy brands, Alpenliebe.

6

CONQUERING SOUTH ASIA

Exporting in the Subcontinent

After the first few successful years of operation in India, Perfetti started receiving some requests for its products from distributors in the surrounding countries. The tie-up with the Indian cricket team proved extremely powerful not only for India: the whole Indian sub-continent is crazy for the sport and religiously follows the matches happening in the region. Consumers of the surrounding countries had watched the matches of the Indian team and seen them chewing Perfetti's gums: they had learned about the same from our advertising during the broadcasting and wanted to try them. Apart from the satellite nations such as Nepal and Bhutan, where our products had already found their way most likely through the wholesale channel, several requests from Sri Lanka and Bangladesh started coming; hence we decided to initiate export there. The first occasional shipments happened around 1998 but initially the operations did not seem to have a future. The production for export was not considered a priority and the shipping deadlines were often not met. The documentation to be produced both in India and in the country where the products were sent was rather complex and time consuming. One would risk spending time and money in producing, packing and shipping a container load of products to see it stuck at the customs for weeks due to some administrative quibble. In the worst of cases the goods would reach their destination but would not be cleared by the local customs authorities, hence having to be shipped back. Therefore, during the first few years, we could only tactically export a few containers to the mentioned countries but did not plan a serious presence in their markets.

However, with the Indian operations stabilizing and having developed a better internal know-how and infrastructure we thought that there could be larger scope for establishing more organized export operations towards the surrounding countries. So we started looking for more professional distribution partners in the countries and selected those we thought could help us build sustainable business. We agreed with them on some mid-term objectives for the business and worked out an adequate marketing mix to become a significant player in the market. The operations became better organized, with regular orders and clearer internal procedures, and, in the span of a few months, we established the first platform to build on for possible future results. When we eventually created a dedicated position to head this nascent business we really experienced a sustained growth against the ups and downs of the previous years; the sales results slowly but steadily became more significant. In business, as also in most other activities, one needs to devote time and resources to drive a quantum leap in results: activities carried out with marginal attention and sporadic managerial attention are bound to remain limited in scope and results.[1]

We were in the first years of the new century and we started perceiving that there should be a way to replicate the India success story in the whole sub-continent. With this new perspective we decided to study the export markets with a longer term horizon in view of the future possibility of investing in such countries and building the brands that had become household names in neighboring India. By that time we had in Perfetti India a strong infrastructure in terms of Marketing, R&D, and Supply Chain that could support possible entries in other countries also. We had the advantage of the spill-over of the India advertising into such countries, thanks to the spread of satellite channels. We had also built production capacities so as to avoid destabilizing interruptions of supplies to export markets. In fact we had just concluded the integration with the recently acquired Van Melle, which had given us an increased brand portfolio and a factory located close to a port, ideal for export. It was time to venture into the rest of south Asia and build new success stories here.

---

[1] A very interesting book highlighting the importance of focus and efforts in successful ventures is *Outliers*. See M. Gladwell, *Outliers* (London: Allen Lane, 2008). In this inspiring book the author quotes that a unified pattern of successful individuals is the focus and hard work behind their activity, usually requiring a minimum threshold of 10,000 hours of hard work.

The Bangla Opportunity

Bangladesh is, among the large countries, the one with the highest density of population in the world. The total population exceeds 160 million, being thus higher than Russia, though it has a territory well over hundred times larger than that of Bangladesh. The country is bordered on all sides by India and the Bay of Bengal, except for a short boundary line shared with Myanmar. The current borders were created in 1947, the year of Indian independence, which also marked the partition between India and the then newly-created State of Pakistan. This used to have a Western and Eastern part, divided by 1,600 kilometers of Indian territory. The Eastern side of Pakistan was the poorer part, and its inhabitants felt they were neglected by the dominant Western side. This led to the liberation war in 1971: the Eastern side, supported by the Indian army, won the war and declared its independence by forming the new nation State of Bangladesh.

However, the new-born state was not to have a lasting political stability and for the subsequent 20 years, several coups and political turmoils, as well as natural disasters, limited the economic development of the country. Coincidentally also for Bangladesh as for India the year 1991 marked a turning point with the restoration of democracy that helped social and economic progress. Maybe due to their passionate and emotional nature, for the Bangla people politics have always played an important role in the country and they are all pervasive. People love to talk about politics and even the lowest individual in the social ladder will have clear ideas about his political orientation, supporting one of the two major parties that have dominated the scene since independence. Starting with the help during the 1971 war India has often acted as an elder brother to this nation, which has accepted this role, taking inspiration and at times fully replicating many of the laws and regulations of India. In fact the language, culture, and food habits of Bangladesh and the neighboring West Bengal are still very similar and people of the two areas have many more common characteristics.

Perfetti started evaluating more seriously the opportunity of a structured presence in this country only at the turn of the century. We had found a distributor who had started selling some of our brands but, at the same time, was also marketing part of the assortment of a competitor, further to being also in many more business lines such as paper production and watches. For some time the association with him was good enough to create a base on which we could build, but over the years we had realized that we would not be able to agree on a long term plan, since our products were not his main focus and he had shorter term objectives for our business. A deeper study of the market had shown to us that there was only one major local competitor who could have been capable of hindering our growth, whereas no international confectionery player used to have operations in the country. The local rival was quite a diversified group and its main focus was not sugar confectionery. The market was not very developed and the per capita consumption was still relatively low, but the vast, growing, and young population represented a huge potential for our products.

With the objective of creating internal competition for our partner and stimulating him to focus more on the range of our products and a smaller territory, we hired a second distributor for a specific area. While the experience and results from the second importer/distributor were not outstanding, they served, however, the purpose of improving our original distributor's throughput and our overall sales results. A further positive consequence of our move was the fact that later on, when we agreed to stop our cooperation with the second distributor, we directly took over the area he had been handling by creating our own sales and distribution structure. After the initial teething period in this area we saw much better results compared to those coming from the third party's distribution. Such results, as well as the disproportionate increase of the custom duties on our products, gave us the courage to propose a local manufacturing in the country. The proposal was kept on hold for almost one year, since it was thought that starting a green field project in such a complex and relatively unstable country could be risky.

In order to reassure our shareholders we discussed a deal with Nestlé, whose representative for the region was a person known to me. They would lease to us a part of their factory in the outskirts of Dhaka for a few years and we would also buy from them part of the common services like steam for our utilities, security, and food for the workers. It was a mutually convenient deal since their local factory was at that moment under-utilized: by renting out part of the vacant space and unused utilities they would recover part of their depreciation and overhead expenses. From our perspective we would avoid the risk of an initial fixed investment in land, building, and utilities and would also avail of the help of a company as Nestlé for matters such as security and Industrial Relations, for which a local know-how is necessary. We would also have had the time to better evaluate the country for a possible investment after a few years. With this perspective we managed to ensure the approval from the shareholders: we then incorporated the local company, signed the lease and made the necessary works to equip the empty factory for our production. We started our first line approximately six months later. Once the news that we had inaugurated the factory was in the market, our distributor informed us that he intended to terminate our agreement since he expected that soon we would communicate to him the intention to fully take over the distribution in the country. Though at that moment we were still planning to continue with him for some time, such a development forced us to accelerate our plans and in less than three months we hired our own sales force, opened two depots and appointed our distribution network. The experience of directly handling the area of the second distributor became so very helpful in helping us set up our own distribution infrastructure. The Bangladesh adventure then started as a sort of brown field project from the industrial point of view; from the sales angle the distribution had gradually evolved from an indirect model through one main partner to a direct one fully handled by us.

The product portfolio initially included only candies. Here we did not have the limitations of the legal reservation for small scale industries encountered in India. Also here, as in India, the scarce presence of modern trade and the even lower purchasing power of the population obliged companies to sell in small units. For PVM this meant selling almost exclusively mono-pieces. Interestingly in this country both candies and gums had the same price, one Bangladeshi taka, roughly corresponding at that moment to one and a half times the candy market price in India, but only to about 75 percent of the corresponding gum price. Apart from the locally produced products we kept selling some imported products, the profitability of which was however hindered by high custom duties. While the first results were encouraging and after a few months we enlarged our candies range, during the second year we thought that we needed to complete our product portfolio also with a locally produced gum. Since it would have been risky—and not sustainable in the mid term—to introduce a product similar to the ones existing in the market at the prevailing market price, we decided to go with a differentiation strategy. We launched a liquid-filled gum, bigger than the existing competitors[2] at a price that was double the one of the local gums. The product was marketed under the Center Fresh brand, an established success in neighboring India and partly known locally thanks to the advertising spill-over and parallel import from wholesalers; it was supported by an advertising commercial adapted from a European one and also through PR activities.

It was by all means a bold move, but we realized that a sustainable business could not be created without a profitable base and we decided this time to

---

[2] The weight at the moment of the launch was 5 grams vs. the average of 4 grams of the existing competitive products.

be price makers rather than price takers. Our bet proved right and local consumers showed themselves to be ready to pay a premium price for a unique product and a completely different chewing experience. The very good results obtained and the exhaustion of production space in the rented factory provided the momentum to obtain an approval for our own factory: in order to select the land we visited over a hundred sites and finally found an adequate one just a few kilometers away from our previous plant in the Nestle factory. We bought the land and completed the building in 10 months,[3] so as to be able to have a stop and go into production by the moment of the expiration of the contract with Nestle. In the new plant we had much more space available and we added new lines in order to minimize the costly import of finished/semi-finished products.

During the subsequent years we kept introducing innovative products and variants. As we had done for the gums, we also introduced a soft filling candy priced at double the prevailing one: also, in this case, the uniqueness of the product ensured that sales could achieve the expected results. In two years from the start-up of the new factory our existing lines were almost fully utilized and we had to invest in new capacity. In five years of local operations we had multiplied the value of our sales by 7.5, had become the undisputed market leader in gums with about 50 percent share of the market and gained an overall market share in the vicinity of 20 percent. Though our main competitor had been in the market for decades and could leverage a very strong and diversified set-up, the overall sales value of their confectionery operations was not very different from ours, and the gap was being progressively minimized. The profitability break had been achieved even earlier than the date projected in the initial business plan and soon we had to start looking for additional land to further expand our local production. We had managed to replicate the India success story also in another large country in the sub-continent.

Tigers and Monks

The other market where we had actively started exporting was Sri Lanka. This island, located just a few miles off the south-west coast of India, has a total population of about 20,000,000 people, though with per capita income of the same was higher than all other countries in south Asia. The number

---

[3] The plant was inaugurated in June 2009.

of inhabitants is hence comparable to one of the large Indian metropolises, and approximately one eighth of that of Bangladesh. Such a small country was certainly not a strategic priority for us and our initial plan was to keep on exporting from India so as to gain and maintain a relevant presence here. However also in this case, the custom duties of about 30 percent had been progressively increased to the level of almost 90 percent. Also in this country most of the confectionery products were sold in individual pieces, but the modern trade was comparatively more developed than in the rest of the region and this allowed having a non negligible part of the volumes in multiple piece formats.[4] In order to better understand the context of the country we need to step back and provide a brief historical background.

Buddhism has had a strong influence on the culture of the country, having been followed in the island for over 2,000 years.[5] The recent story of Sri Lanka after its independence in 1948 is linked to socio-political issues among the main ethnic groups inhabiting the country: the Sinhalese, over 70 percent of the population, and the Tamils, hailing from the nearby state of Tamil Nadu in south India, representing about 10 percent of the total. The introduction in 1956 of the *Sinhala Only Act* that replaced English by introducing Sinhala as the official language of the country failed to give explicit recognition to the Tamil language. Since then the Tamil community felt neglected and oppressed. Such feeling translated into the demand of a separate Nation State, which had to be at the origin of decades of civil war. The insurgency started in 1983, driven by the Liberation Tigers of Tamil Eelam, better known as LTTE or Tamil Tigers. It is somewhat surprising that one of the few countries in the world where almost 70 percent of the population embraces Buddhism, a faith preaching peace, kindness, and friendliness, has given birth to one of the most violent rebel groups, the LTTE. These rebels became notorious for its creation of guerrilla techniques such as suicide bombing, later adopted by many terrorist groups in other parts of the world. To some people it was also quite surprising that Buddhist monks seemed to support the government in the war with the militants.[6] The conflict continued on and off for almost two

---

[4] In sugar confectionery the multiple piece formats are usually stick packs, flip-top boxes, blister packs, bottled, and pouches.
[5] According to Sinhalese tradition, Buddhism took root in Sri Lanka soon after the arrival of Asoka's son, the monk Mahinda. Source: *Encyclopedia Britannica* online, http://www.britannica.com/EBchecked/topic/83184/Buddhism.
[6] Those interested in understanding better the positions of the monks in the matter may read the article in the following link: http://www.lankaweb.com/news/items/2010/01/09/have-the-buddhist-monks-of-sri-lanka-faulted-by-supporting-the-government-to-defeat-the-ltte/.

decades till in 2002 a ceasefire was signed and for a few years the country dwelled in peace.

During such years PVM, whose export to this country had achieved interesting levels, had seen its margins eroded by the increased duties, particularly high for finished products. Our imported products were sold at market prices[7] and this had brought the margins down to almost zero. At that point in time the decision was either to stop the export and abandon the market or to consider a local manufacturing base. Though the potential profit pool was not large we decided to venture into a limited investment in a small plant that would allow us to compete locally while ensuring that our presence was maintained without major prejudice to the overall bottom line. The decision was facilitated by the relative political stability of the previous two years and the efforts of the government to attract foreign investments. Furthermore there were no international sugar confectionery players with local manufacturing units in the country;[8] we thus thought that we should be the first. The approval to proceed with direct investment was given by the end of 2005; we started looking for adequate land plots or even existing buildings during the first months of 2006; we found a plot conveniently located in the spring of the same year and took it in a long term rent; having completed all necessary permits and licences we started building the factory. The same was completed by the second quarter of 2007.

Unfortunately during the course of 2006 the ceasefire with the Tamil Tigers had come to an end and the conflict had started again. The increased military expenses led the government to further increase taxes. The war took its toll on the economy, with a drastic fall of tourism, a major source of income for the country, soaring inflation and a strong devaluation of the local currency. By the moment we started production in 2007 the assumptions of our business plan were completely changed and we had to redefine the marketing mix on the basis of a new set of parameters. We started producing locally some of the products we had already been importing. For others we imported the semi-finished products in bulk and packed them locally: despite this, due to changed circumstances we were forced to re-launch some of the products at an increased price:[9] to partly justify the higher price we also increased the weight of those

---

[7] The prevailing prices for the mono-pieces were SLR 1 for candies and 2 for gums. Multiple pieces formats such as stick packs were sold at prices going from SLR 10 up to 20.
[8] Nestlé had a large set up but did not produce confectionery here. Cadbury had licensed one of their brands to be marketed locally, but its production was outsourced.
[9] This was the case for Mentos candy, which was re-launched at SLR 2 for 2.7 grams, vs. the previous SLR 1 for 2.2 grams.

products. Also in this market we started producing locally our liquid-filled gums and launched them at a premium vs. the prevailing market price.[10] Like in Bangladesh also here our distribution agreement with the main importer/distributors came to an end soon after the starting of our local manufacturing and we had to set up our own distribution network rather quickly.

The task of establishing not only a new manufacturing but also a new sales and distribution network in the span of a few months in a country with a civil war in progress was rather challenging and this was reflected in our sales results that suffered for some time. Differently from the rest of the subcontinent, Sri Lanka has a very specific distribution model where distributors use vans to carry the products and a team of three people—a driver, a salesman, and a cash collector—is employed in the process. This has several implications: first, the distribution costs are much higher compared to those sustained in countries where distributors operate through bicycle or motorbikes units with only one person performing all the functions; second, the distributors need to have stronger financial muscles due to higher working capitals required and expect a higher profit margins in return of the increased exposure; third, the number of available distributors in the market is limited, making their recruitment more complicated. On top of this, moving around with vans gives lower flexibility for reaching smaller outlets located in narrow streets, thus limiting the scope of the distribution penetration.

Over the years we also tried to introduce a cheaper distribution model by substituting motorized three wheelers to vans and reducing the number of people involved in the sales calls. However, we encountered strong resistance from the sales people who thought that moving in a three wheeler would negatively affect their image in the market. We even tried experimenting with a motorcycle, but the concept was completely refused by our distributors and sales force. Eventually we did manage though to bring down the costs through a combination of order bookings and reduced sales staff, but the overall sales expenses remained the highest in the region. We also decided that we would service the modern trade directly, without the intermediation of the distributors. This allowed us a faster reaction time, a better negotiating power and, not least, reductions in costs. Thanks to the relatively high number of supermarkets in the country and to our focussed efforts in this channel we were able to sell here a reasonable percentage of multiple unit formats, much higher compared to the percentage sold in the neighboring countries. The emphasis on such formats as well as on the higher margin

---

[10] Price for the gum mono-piece we launched was SLR 3 vs. the prevailing market price of SLR 2 for the traditional bubble gums.

gums and the mentioned cost saving actions, combined with further efforts from the supply chain point of view allowed us to achieve the break-even in this case earlier than the initial business plan.

Here the result was even more satisfactory considering the deteriorated cost scenario and business climate brought by the new start of the conflict. Since the second part of 2009, when the insurgents were finally defeated and peace was restored, the overall business environment had improved sensibly. During the subsequent years the economy—pulled by the revived tourism and export—improved sensibly, the inflation came down, and some of the taxes were reduced. All this helped us expand our distribution reach, introduce new variants and eventually achieve better results. While the overall market share gained in this market was slightly lower than the one achieved in Bangladesh, here we also became market leaders in the gum segment and among the first three players in the candy segment. Given the relatively small size of the markets, the size of our business was limited; however, we managed to achieve our objective of maintaining a significant presence in the country with operating profits.

Trying to summarize the lessons learned in these two countries we can certainly say that our strategy of entering the markets with innovative and premium products in the gum segment has worked well. Had we chosen to be priced at the prevailing market prices we would have never been able to achieve and maintain profitable operations. The shift from a third party distribution to our own network has been difficult in the initial period but has paid back over the years. This has allowed us a much larger flexibility in quickly modifying our strategies when necessary and pushing our brands through in a capillary distribution that might not have been achieved otherwise. Time to market has proven to be extremely important: following our move in both markets other competitors have also increased their price and launched products similar to ours, but we had in the meantime gained an advantage that was difficult to bridge. Also in these markets, like in India, our efforts to be as close as possible to the consumers in our way of marketing our brands have helped us to be accepted and recognized as "super local brands." This has been possible mainly thanks to the contribution of our local talent, who guided us through the process of studying and meeting consumer needs. Incidentally, I must say, that people in the two countries have shown very different behavioral attitudes: emotional, passionate, extroverted, and very hard working the Bangladeshis; more detached, introverted, and relatively laid back–as often happens in the islands' cultures—the Sri Lankan, possibly also influenced by the prevailing religion. Needless to repeat once again that a statement concerning the nature of people is a necessary generalization and may not hold true in many cases.

Attacking Pakistan

Among the south Asian countries Pakistan is the second most populous with about 180 million people, almost nine times the Sri Lankan population; it is however the weakest market for PVM. This is due to several reasons. First, its political instability does not make it attractive for a possible direct investment. Second, its sugar confectionery market has been historically crowded, with a mixed presence of strong local players and international ones. Third, the low average price level of this market squeezing the profit margins create high entry barriers. Furthermore, in spite of the proximity of the country to India, historical rivalries have kept the two markets insulated, with no possibility of direct trade in most sectors until very recent developments. In fact trade does happen between the countries but mainly through Dubai, that function as a re-export hub were goods coming from one country are repacked—at times relabelled—to be later forwarded to the other one. As already mentioned earlier in this chapter, Pakistan was born in 1947, when India gained independence and a new nation state made of Western and Eastern Pakistan was formed. It took almost 10 years for the country to adopt a constitution in 1956 and declare itself an Islamic Republic, but two years later a coup stalled the civilian law. Since then various internal conflicts, army repressions and wars with neighboring India created continuous instability, with the exception of some rare periods of relative calm and civilian law.[11] Even recently the assassination in December 2007 of Benazir Bhutto, whose political dynasty lasted for several generations and mirrored the history of violence, corruption, and division of the country, brought to power the controversial personality of Asif Ali Zardari, Benazir's husband, and perpetrated the chaotic political scenario of this troubled nation. Since his taking over the Presidential seat in 2008 the country's economy has deteriorated sensibly, with a drastic slow down of the GDP to a level of around 2–3 percent, double digit inflation, declining tax revenues, and worsening current account balance.[12]

Possibly this has happened also because of the global financial crisis and the reduction of textile exports to the economically depressed West, representing a large source of revenues for the country. Another reason adding to the nation's budget deficit are the costly military campaigns in Swat and South

---

[11] One of these was soon after the loss of East Pakistan, between 1972 and 1977, under the rule of Zulfikar Ali Bhutto.
[12] During the years 2005–07 the average GDP growth was ~6.5 percent and the average inflation (CPI) about 8 percent.

Waziristan aimed at gaining control of the territory where strong local tribesmen do not recognize the central government. A few of such territories are said to be the sanctuary of international terrorism, where many potential or established terrorists are trained and find refuge. Military expenses are going up also to partly match the increased defense budget of the arch-rival neighbor India. In 1998, a few months after India's second nuclear test, Pakistan detonated five nuclear devices, entering the rows of the few countries in the world who have successfully developed and tested nuclear bombs. The country is believed to be increasing its nuclear arsenal as fast as it can, to the point that it would be close to becoming the fourth largest nuclear power after the USA, Russia, and China.[13] Despite all the economic and political problems the current government has been in office at the moment we write for the last four years and may become the first in Pakistan's history to have served a full five-year term. Only in June 2012 had a sentence from the highest court sanctioned the demise of the Prime Minister, who had been substituted without prejudice to the rest of the cabinet.

When entering a market, PVM often starts with tactical exports, becoming later on more organized and systematic: when the business achieves an interesting threshold a strategic evaluation of the market is made so as to decide on a possible investment. In the case of Pakistan, we were in the first stage till 2008. Since then, also thanks to the setting up of factories in Sri Lanka and Bangladesh that could become a good export platform to that country, our study of the market has gone more in depth and so has our focus from a sales perspective. In fact also in this country import duties are rather high and vary depending on the country of origin, but imports from Bangladesh avail of a preferential duty agreement for which the custom duty is reduced to 5 percent;[14] from Sri Lanka the duty is fully waived off. As in all south Asia markets, as well as in many other emerging ones, products in the local sugar confectionery market are mainly sold in mono-pieces to the individual consumers, and such pieces are priced on fixed price-points. The price-points in Pakistan are nominally the same of those in India, PKR 1 for the gums and 0.5 for the candies. However, the value of one rupee in Pakistan is equivalent to approximately ₹0.53 in India: this makes the prices in Pakistan much lower than those in India when compared for instance to US dollar terms.

---

[13] As reported in "Pakistan's Nuclear Weapons, a Deterrent against India, but Also United States?" in *Afghan Journal*, http://blogs.reuters.com/afghanistan/2011/04/09/pakistans-nuclear-weapons-a-deterrent-against-india-but-also-united-states/.

[14] This compares to > 50 percent of custom duty for import from Indonesia or 22 percent from China, with which Pakistan has also preferential agreements.

In addition to this, the average weight of the products is higher in Pakistan,[15] making the price per gram even lower. Therefore in such a market, producers tend to have low margins and need very high volumes to generate a decent overall profitability.

PVM has been associated with an importer/distributor for many years in this country. The same used to distribute both Perfetti and Van Melle products well before the takeover. Due to the price-point constraint as well as the portfolio of the other products they have been distributing, PVM used to sell only multiple units formats, with Mentos and Fruit-tella being the main brands.[16] Incidentally we have noticed that the brand Fruit-tella used to have much higher sales in towns with the prevailing Muslim population in India: I have never been able to find a reason to this, but the fact that the brand is our highest selling one in Pakistan, an Islamic country, did not come as a surprise. When we started focusing more on the country, we clearly realized that to be present in the mass market we had to start selling in mono-pieces too. In order to do so the factories in south Asia were the ideal sourcing base. Though the Sri Lanka plant would have been the ideal one, both for the location and for the zero duty preferential agreement, the fact that in this factory there were only few production lines and the higher cost of production due to higher costs of materials in the country made us shift most of the volumes to Bangladesh.

With continuous efforts also in driving the distributors towards smaller outlets also selling mono-piece formats, we saw the percentage of sales coming from such formats grow from an average of 2–3 percent in the previous years to 10 percent and later 15 percent of the total sales. Considering that in the same period the total volumes grew at a rate of 25 percent year on year, the mono-pieces volume was multiplied by six compared to the initial years: this contributed to spreading the awareness of our brands also to the general public rather than limiting the same only to the highest socio-economic clusters. The presence of a dedicated sales resource in the country helped achieve such results. Even today, when compared to the rest of the south Asia countries, our operations in Pakistan are very small, but the growth experienced during the most recent years has triggered a higher interest in the market and built the base for further possible developments.

---

[15] The average weight of a candy used to be four grams in Pakistan and three in India. Recently producers have started reducing the weights for obvious pressure on margins.

[16] Such brands used to be originally "chewy candies," i.e., candies with a bite similar to gums. Later on under such brands were launched also other kind of products, such as hard boiled candies and jellies for Fruit-tella and gums for Mentos.

A major change may occur now that the trade relationship with India evolves. After the slump caused by the Mumbai terrorist attack in November 2008 that killed more than 170 people and was planned and carried out by Pakistanis,[17] a dialogue between the countries had resumed and in November 2011 Pakistan granted India's exports most-favoured-nation status, reciprocating what India had already done 15 years earlier. Thanks to this the ban on import from India may be lifted for several items, as many as 1,209 in a first list that will be effective by the end of 2012.[18] Luckily confectionery is not included in the negative list and soon we should be able to offer the Pakistani market the wide range of products sold in India and make them available there with minimal lead times and transportation costs. This could provide a strong impetus to PVM presence and share in the market and a platform to rapidly develop the current business as well as new opportunities.

---

[17] See *The Economist*, "State of Vulnerability," *The Economist*, February 11, 2012. Also available online at http://www.economist.com/node/21546888.
[18] See "Islamabad to Push for More Concessions in Trade with India," *Gulf News*, Dubai Edition, March 2, 2012.

7

AN INDO-ITALIAN WEDDING

Marriage in India

There is perhaps no better way to understand the culture of India than studying what revolves around marriages in this country. Traditions, values, social customs, and obligations and, not least, economics, are what make this event an essential step in the life of the individual and a paramount occurrence for his/her family. In fact, more than a relationship between individuals, marriage in India is an alliance between families. In pages and pages of the sections dedicated to classified matrimonial advertisements in many Indian newspapers the most common messages start with the words "Alliance is sought ...." The content that follows is usually about the characteristics of the bride/groom sought and those of the advertiser. Caste, religion, educational qualifications, and earning capabilities are announced, at times together with physical characteristics of the seeker and requirements for the partner to be, to the extent of stating also a tentative request for the dowry. While in contemporary India things are changing, the role of the family's role in the event is extremely important even today and arranged marriages still represent the norm in rural India and a majority of urban areas.

What may sound surprising to people from Western societies is that many of the young people do accept such traditions even nowadays, the same being a way of getting relieved from the burden and anxiety of having to find the right mate. The arranged marriage is also a way of re-stating the importance of the parental relationship: India is still a society where the ties between children and parents (at times even relatives) are stronger that those between husband and wife. Parents and relatives have more experience and networks of contacts and are thus more likely to find the right match for their children: if the choice was left to these they would have a more limited pool of candidates among which to choose and may be more prone to mistakes due to emotional factors and temporary infatuation. I do remember that, during my first years in India, I was stunned to learn that almost the totality of my senior manager colleagues had had arranged marriages. This concept is rather alien to modern Western societies, particularly in north America and central/northern Europe where individualism has become a widely spread value and the "responsibility" of the children's personal life is often relinquished by the parents as soon as the youngsters leave the parental house. In some European countries[1] children are encouraged to go and live on their own soon after secondary education; since then their personal choices depend only on their own will. In such countries, very rarely would parents have a say in the selection of their child's life partner, let alone going all out to find it for him/her.

After many years spent in India not only do I understand the logic behind it but I also have eventually come to appreciate the positive sides of the arranged marriage, particularly in the context of the Indian society. Such a system has at least one major advantage against so-called "love marriages": that is the fact of sensibly lowering the expectations of both the partners. Often, problems in marriages are caused by the high level of expectations that bride and groom have from each other: the role of the perfect husband who is an excellent father, lover, companion, and bread-earner is not an easy one to perform and can put quite some pressure on a person's shoulders, with consequent negative repercussions on the marital life. The opposite for the wife is also true, particularly in today's society where women are more and more expected to have their own work and independence, on top of taking care of their husbands and children.[2] In a marriage where the partner is chosen by the family, though more and more with the consent and approval of the future partner, the level of expectation from the future concubine will naturally be lower, whereas the mutual acceptance and tolerance for his/her at times sub-optimal personality or way of behaving will instead be higher.

An additional important positive factor I find in the arranged marriage is the fact that partners tend to discover each other over the years—at times during their whole life together—and the process may keep the excitement of the

---

[1] France is an example of such countries; the UK and the Scandinavian countries also have similar customs.
[2] This holds particularly true for Western societies: however, the task of taking care of children is more and more shared between the two parents.

relationship alive as well as eventually leading to a stronger bond between the couple. While the partial knowledge of each other at the time of the wedding may be considered negative, the effort in sorting out possible issues coming up when the relationship becomes more consolidated will possibly be stronger than in the case of love marriages. The fact that in such marriages families are highly involved does help, since the children try hard not to disappoint them even at the cost of enduring difficult situations in order to salvage the relationship with the partner and between the families. Overall, arranged marriages are much more pondered choices compared to unions born from emotions. Such feelings may last for a few years and then fade away, leaving two very different individuals alone with themselves during difficulties and without a strong supporting system like the extended Indian family. In fact in the Indian traditional society love marriage often happens against the will of one or both of the families; in some extreme cases the couple *in fieri* is forced to elope to fulfil their will; in some others they go ahead and get married but the link with their families is weakened or even severed. Anybody who has seen Bollywood[3] movies is familiar with such situations.

As mentioned earlier, Indian marriages are also matters of money. The organization of the wedding event itself implies a non-marginal investment, usually borne by the family of the bride. While different religious groups across the country have different customs and rites, the arrangements for the occasion are usually made for a large number of guests, with celebrations lasting for several days. The organization includes efforts and expenses starting from the printing and delivery of invitations, accommodation for the guests, the banquets, decorating the places where the feasts are to happen, and gifts for the groom's party. Such arrangements are also made with the objective of enhancing the status of the bride's family. But one of the main economic burdens on this is perhaps the dowry to be given from the bride's family to the newly created one, or at times even to the groom's family. In old times this was considered a woman's wealth, due to the daughter who had no claim on her natal family's real estate.[4] It would typically include jewelry and household goods that a bride could keep throughout her life and possibly sell during times of economic difficulties. More recently the dowry has become more of cash payments and goods for the bridegroom and his family. Perhaps such a custom has been conceived as a compensation for the fact that the groom's family will keep on having a role in the welfare of the newly created family; this is still

---

[3] A word used for the Indian film industry base in Bombay.
[4] See US Library of Congress, *The Indian Marriage*, http://countrystudies.us/india/86.htm.

true particularly in northern and central India where, once wedded, the girl leaves her family and starts living in the boy's parental house. In contrast, in some of the communities of south India,[5] the boy leaves his family and settles in the bride's parental house; in this case the above-mentioned justification of the dowry may not apply. The fact that more often in south India marriages happen among the circle of relatives and that some of the southern societies have matriarchal systems, may partly explain why in such cases the boy is to join the girl's family, hence ensuring "protection" of the bride. A consequence of this is a less spread custom of dowries.

The economic burden of the wedding of one or more daughters in India is very rooted and its weight heavily felt among families, often to the extent of causing the heinous aberration of infanticides for new-born females, an atrocity still practiced today in rural India. Matters of dowry are also causes of abuse and mistreatment of a bride by the groom and his family, particularly when the wife has settled in the husband's marital home. Despite the existence of anti-dowry laws, which remain mostly ignored, unmet demands for excessive dowries have caused incidents among families and even "accidental" deaths of brides. Unfortunately such mishaps are not something of the past, but instead a widespread problem even today. A shocking article recently appearing in a popular newspaper in India reported that "in 2010, there were 8,391 cases of dowry death in the country. That works out to a shocking one death every hour approximately. Bride-burning is on the increase—just a decade ago, in 2000, there were 6,995 cases."[6] It is hard to think that such incredible facts may still happen in a nation considered to be among the most tolerant, with a rapidly rising economic and scientific progress, and with the brightest minds in the world.

A Single's Life in Delhi

I spent the largest part of my thirties in India. During most of these years I was not married, and I lived a comfortable life as a happy single in the Indian capital. The first years in India were mainly focused on my work, which did not leave to me much time to think about a possible family life; over time

---

[5] This is for instance the case of the Kerala Muslim communities.
[6] See S. Varma, "Dowry Death: One Bride Burnt every Hour," *The Times of India*, January 27, 2012. Available at http://articles.timesofindia.indiatimes.com/2012-01-27/india/30670050_1_dowry-death-harassment-and-cruelty-section-498a.

I had the opportunity to develop a good network of friends and acquaintances that kept my spare time busy. It did take some time to do so, and I must admit that the initial period as a single man in India was not particularly easy. Since men usually marry in their twenties there or at least used to do so during those years, the fact that I was approaching the second part of my thirties and was not yet married awakened the curiosity of my colleagues and occasional friends. Maybe because I was their boss my workfellows never asked about the reasons behind my being unmarried. For some time they might have even thought that I did not like women, though I have been told that my look and behavior does not leave many doubts about my sexual preferences. Later on, a few facts described earlier in these pages had removed such doubt form their minds, but I did perceive some puzzlement in the fact that apparently I was not interested in getting married, despite my growing older. Had they been more exposed to European societies they would have quickly found out that in many such countries people tend to get married in their late thirties, not later; yet in Asian and Indian culture I was considered a sort of rare animal.

Traditional Hinduism recognizes four main stages of a man's life, which could actually be classified as three plus one.[7] The first three come from the life-affirming Vedic side of Hinduism, the first one being a sort of preparation to life; the forth implies the rejection of life and preparation to death. The last one is the ascetic stage (*sannyasa*), where in exchange for the attainment of *moksha*[8] the material life and the attachment to the same are rejected. The first three stages are that of the Student, the Householder, and the Retired. The second stage (*grihasta*) starts when the celibate (*brahmacharya*) student one ends, around the age of 25: it is marked by marriage and the taking-on of responsibilities for sustenance and support of the family. According to different interpretations of the texts, such stage ends either at the age of 42 or 50, depending on the length of estimated human life.[9]

If we look at how the lives of Indian people are structured even today, the ages just mentioned reflect more or less the phases of life of an average person and they are not dissimilar to those written in the traditional Hindu texts, at least for the first stages. Students in fact finish college around the age of 22

---

[7] See "The Three Stages of Life." Available at http://uwacadweb.uwyo.edu/religionet/er/hinduism/hslife.htm.
[8] See Chapter 4, The *chalta hay* attitude.
[9] If a life span of 100 years is considered then the four stages are of 25 years each. If a life span of 84 years is taken than the four stages would be approximately of 21 years each.

and get married in their twenties (though the marriage age has been recently going up); the official retirement age is still fixed at 58. According to the Hindu vision and also modern Indian standards, I had abundantly crossed the threshold age to start a family and was dangerously going towards the retirement stage with the risk of completely skipping the *grihasta* phase. This implied that Indian people of my age normally had family and children in their primary (or even secondary) school: hence the styles of our lives were very different and the chance of socializing in my age group not too high. Therefore the Indian friends I used to more frequently meet were all a few years younger than me. On the other hand within the expatriate community, not particularly large during the 1990s in Delhi, the business people I used to meet within the circle of CEOs and Senior Managers were also commonly 10 to 15 years older to me and with family: once again we would not have many shared interests or life styles. However after the turning of the century a larger number of expatriates started coming to Delhi, not only in the corporate word but also in NGOs and among diplomats. The capital evolved and offered more entertainment opportunities out of five-star hotels, with new lounges and restaurants opening and more "party places" spread across the city. It became easier than to go out with friends for a drink in more accessible places other than the few ones reserved for the elites and often too crowded to venture there.

The Delhi Gymkhana club, in the heart of the city, was one of the traditional old clubs in Delhi I happened to visit several times. This used to be an exclusive place for the Brits during the so-called Raj and has maintained its colonial charm in spite of time. Today it is still an exclusive club with several years' waiting lists for membership. However it is possible to be invited there by a member and through the same channel it is also possible to organize private dining in one of their halls. The central ballroom, though renovated several times, has maintained the look of the colonial age, with massive parquet wooden flooring, huge fans hanging from the high ceiling, and some old time pictures on the walls. A curious characteristic of the club is their showing the list of the members who have defaulted the payments in a pin board just at the entrance, where members and guests are supposed to register. I remember having seen known names who had been implied in some scams a decade earlier and were forced to leave the countries; their missing payments are still there well displayed to all guests. A nice custom of this establishment was a sort of youth evening they used to hold once a week, where the members' children were allowed to take some guests into the club. In those evenings the place seemed a completely changed one and the stark contrast between the old-ish looking building and the colored clothes of the young crowd was remarkable.

Differently from Mumbai, hosting a more diverse kind of environment and historically more open to international influences as a port city with people arriving from all over the world, Delhi is a more conservative city, less business-oriented than Mumbai, also due to the fact that being the capital it hosts the administrative structures of the State bureaucracy. Consequently, the attitude of people in the two cities is also different: the coastal people are freer in their way of dressing and speaking, less formal and more open. I thought in fact that living in Mumbai as a single would have been easier than living in Delhi. For the reasons just mentioned and also for the traditional belief that the creation of the family is an essential step in someone's life, the status of being single was something considered almost abnormal and not a topic to be much discussed in public forums or in any way "celebrated." Only during the last years of my stint in the country did I start finding some articles on the press dealing with the subject and activities specifically conceived for singles. In fact I was quite surprised when in 2001 I received a letter from Taj Hotels where a new initiative called Singleton was being launched. It consisted of programs organized during weekends in some of their properties, usually resorts, where being single was a prerequisite to participate. They consisted of different activities—sports, games, and others—structured so that guests had the opportunity of socializing while having fun and relaxing. I did take part in one of these weekends and I still hold good memories of the same. I have even maintained friendship with some of the participants. The program included special attention for the guests, such as an evening candle-lit bath in a scented petal-filled tub or special food treats that made one feel pampered and relaxed.

The years between 2001 and 2003 were indeed the most pleasant period of my life as a single in India. I used to have my consolidated networks of friendships as well as professionals with whom I would regularly meet, party and at times travel. While I had not bonded with many expatriates during my first years, the new wave of arrivals in the relatively younger age segment had seen many more interesting people landing in the capital, and my network of international friends then grew substantially. Together with these friends we organized several activities in sports, culture, and touring. One of the popular ones was a tennis tournament within the Italian community that took place in the Italian Embassy. It had been well organized and, thanks to the fact that the then Italian Ambassador was a passionate player, the Embassy sponsored the day by offering not only the sport structure but also a tasty Italian buffet for all those present. The initiative was so successful that it was repeated for a few years. I enjoyed it very much since tennis was a sport I had been practicing since childhood, and even more thanks to the fact that in one of the editions I managed to win both the single and the double tournaments. I have very good memories of the summers spent in Delhi during those years.

Here the monsoon season starts usually in July and by that time international schools are closed. It is then holiday time for part of the expatriate community and many families decide to go back to their own countries, whereas working husbands stay in town to rejoin the family after a few weeks. A small cosmopolitan group of friends had come together to try and enjoy that month: some of us were singles, some married but temporarily bachelors and wanted to make the best out of our freedom from family engagements. We used to meet very frequently during the week and spend whole weekends together. These were the funniest and most active of the days: we would start with a small group playing cards from the afternoon till early evening. The group would later become larger and continue the evening with a cultural event, such as a movie in the original language or a delicacy tasting session. We would then go for dinner either at a restaurant or to somebody's place. After that we would move for some sport activities (swimming, tennis, volleyball) cum drinks: the favorite spots for such activities were the Embassies, which would normally have sport facilities and were accessible to us since we had diplomats in the group. The early morning hours would be spent together and the group would later split into the polo passionate ones, who would directly go to get the horses ready for a morning chucker, and those more relaxed who would look for a place to have an early breakfast and then go home and rest. All in all there were ways and manners to enjoy the single life in Delhi, in spite of the place not being among the most popular fun or party destinations in Asia. Having said this, living in an environment where most of your friends have families does make you think more about creating your own family, even if this may mean to do so without some degrees of freedom that people living on their own for many years may have got accustomed to.

I had had close friendships during my years in India with local ladies as well as expatriate ones, but none of these had translated into the relationship that would have convinced me to renounce my single status and cross over to the *grihasta* stage. The older one becomes the tougher it is to find a "soul mate." In fact our past experiences create a sort of hard shield around us and our expectations from the possible mate rises to a level difficult to match. I remember that several of my friends had offered to find my lifetime partner and had tried introducing me to eligible prospects. One or two good friends had even requested from me a detailed list of the "must haves" for my future wife, but had sort of given up on the purpose when going through my long lists of characteristics rarely found altogether in a person. Also thanks to this silly game of the "must haves" list I was to eventually meet the person who would become my wife after some time.

On a hot Sunday afternoon of May, almost at the apex of the Delhi dry heat season, I was invited by a friend to join a party in the hotel Oberoi in the vicinity of Connaught Place. My first reaction had been to decline, since I felt too lazy to change and prepare for a party; besides, the idea of driving till downtown was not appealing to me. Very often such parties were rather "hollow": the usual faces sporting the latest designer clothes, maybe also some Bollywood starlets here and there; rarely would one have the chance to meet interesting people and go beyond the routine of small talks. Upon the insistence of my friend, who did not want to go alone and needed a lift to the party, I eventually agreed to go. Once there the scene was not very different from what I had imagined, but I was pleasantly surprised to find a few good friends I did not expect to meet. While talking to one of them, he pointed out to me a girl who not only looked pretty but also wore elegant clothes and seemed to know how to carry them. I looked at the person and had to agree about his statement. Later on during the evening I happened to notice the same girl chatting with a few other friends of mine and took the opportunity to get closer to the group and join the conversation. One of the friends immediately introduced me to the girl and we started a short conversation, interrupted by some other guest wanting to take her somewhere else. The evening continued with the celebration of the host's birthday. This one called on stage the same girl I had been talking to and mentioned that the party was also in her honor, since her birthday had just been a few days earlier. I thought I would not have minded meeting the girl again and before leaving I found a way to start again a conversation and invite her to a party at my place during the weekend. At that moment she was living in Mumbai and was visiting Delhi only for a few days, but she promised that she would do her best to join.

Sure enough she came to the party and we could spend time together chatting and getting to know each other. She went back to Mumbai the subsequent day but I had taken her number and promised to go and see her soon. So I did after a few weeks and since then our relationship started. Only after we had started dating did she reveal to me that the person who had introduced us was the common friend to whom I had given my "must haves" list. Before we had met she had told her more than once that she should meet one of her friends seeking a girl whose characteristics were roughly corresponding to hers. Our long-distance relationship went on for several months and kept on intensifying over time. After more than a year of dating we came to the decision that monthly meetings were no more enough. From my side I could not even consider the idea of moving from Delhi where my company's Head Office was. The only other possibility was that she move back to Delhi, where she had lived for sometime before moving to Mumbai. After her moving we could have a more normal relationship and understand if the same could have worked also on a more serious and permanent basis. It took some time to come to the marriage decision, but after another year or so we did decide to move further and started discussing how to make this happen. Our situation was not the simplest possible, being two people of different nationalities, cultures, and religions who had decided to be together against all odds. Both our families would have something to say about the marriage. In my case I would only have to win the resistance of my mother, who was not particularly happy about the idea of having a daughter-in-law of a different religion. She would have never tried to stop me from doing what I wanted to, but my desire was that she be convinced of this choice and not only resigned to it. In my future wife's family the matter was more complicated. Her sister had already married a person of another religion and the family thought that the second daughter once again marrying a person outside their community would have created problems in finding a wife for the younger brother. Things became easier after our meeting the respective families and gaining the consensus of at least some of them. Eventually even my wife's family came to terms with the idea of our marriage and we started planning for it.

My Big Fat Indo-Italian Wedding

It was spring when we eventually decided to fix a date and start working towards that. The first issue to sort out was what kind of marriage to have and where. The option of a religious one seemed quite difficult, since both of us had no intention of embracing the other's faith and Islam and Christianity are not very compatible as far as the marriage function is concerned. The Muslim marriage is very peculiar and does require that the husband be part of the religion. I did attend one such marriage and I found very strange the fact that the bride is not even present during the ceremony, since this happens between the future husband and the bride's father. I had heard that in some Christian churches in India they did marry couples of different religions, but I would not have liked to force my wife into something completely alien to her. Furthermore, there could have been possible issues on the legal validity of the marriage. Hence the civil route seemed to be the least complex. The place

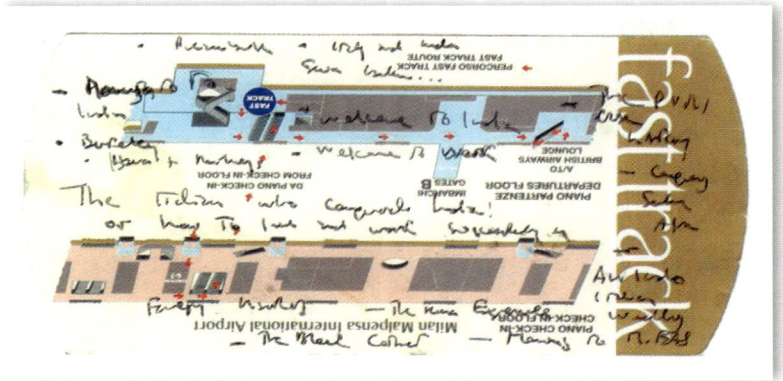

The first words of the book on the airline fast track pass, December 2011

The House in Rajokri, 1999–2007

The Hungarian Cultural Centre
and
Situ Singh Buehler

present

The Joy of Music at Christmas

with solo voices and Ensemble led by Stefano Pelle

The programme includes arias from Bach cantatas, excerpts from Händel's Messiah, trios from Mozart's Nocturnes and Hungarian, German and English Christmas carols

Accompanied by: flute, violin, piano and guitar
Justin McCarthy, Christine Marques, Akemi Ishikawa, Junko Kawashima, Akemi Yotsu, Mariann Kundert, Arun Pathak

on Friday, the 15th December 2000 at 6.30 p.m.
at the Hungarian Cultural Centre, 1-A, Janpath, New Delhi,
(near Hotel Claridges)

The International Opera Ensemble, conducted by Stefano Pelle, performing in New Delhi, December 2000

RAJASTHAN - THE ENDURING PULL & ACROBATIC DANCES
Three destinations: ALWAR, JODHPUR, AND RANAKPUR.

ALWAR : What to SEE? Bala Fort, City Palace - (Musuem, Water Tank, Cenotaph of Maharaja Bhaktiar Singh's Sati)

Sati: A woman who would burn herself alive over the pyre of her dead person. She would become holy enough to be worshipped, usually a cenotaph was built where she burnt herself

Vinay Vilas Palace, **Siliserh Lake** Palace

Sariska - Hunting Lodge - Palace Hotel, and Wild Life Sanctuary

Ancient Sites at - Kali Ghati (to see Mahavir's statue - founder of the Jain Religion, Neel Kanth Mahadeva -temple of Shiva, and Tantric sites)

Kankwari Fort - where Aurangzeb the Mughal Emperor starved two brothers to death

Bargadh - Caves for Buddhist Monks

JODHPUR: Mehrangadh Fort (to see Loha Pol a majestic gate, Moti Mahal pearl palace or the throne room) **Fort Museum** a) Ajit Vilas: Houses Costumes jewellery, watch for bejewelled slippers

b) Phool Mahal: Rajput audience chamber, to see the Lal Der- or Aurangzeb's magnificient red tent

c) Maan Vilas: Houses armoury notice the sword collections

d) Maharaja's Cenotaph - also the shrine of the family goddess -Chamunda Devi

Umed Bhavan Palace Hotel

Mandore Gardens, **Ossian Temple**, Village of Bashoi **community.**

Jodhpur the Blue city.

RANAKPUR the journey from Jodhpur to Ranakpur - the stretch from Pali and Falna craftsmen

Jain Temple: **Chowmukh - Adinath Temple**

Temples of **Parasvnath**, and **Neminanth**, know for mithunas or the erotic sculpture

Notes on Rajasthan from the course 'Window to the Indian Art,' 2001

With his mother (second from left) in a trip to Bhopal, Madhya Pradesh, organized by Navina Jafa (fourth from left in the picture), 2002

Sunday afternoon volleyball in the Rajokri house, 2002

The Royal Enfield modified and personalized for Stefano Pelle, 2003

**NEEMRANA HOTELS
PRESENT**

A CHRISTMAS CELEBRATION

with

The International Opera Ensemble Delhi

on **Saturday, December 20, 2003**

7:00 pm

at

NEEMRANA FORT-PALACE

Conducted by
Stefano Pelle

Situ Singh Buehler	Soprano
Isabelle Stibbe	Soprano
Hur Chul Young	Tenor
Chae Myong Ja	Alto

Piano Accompaniment by
Pearl Drego & Pramod Kingston

Tapan Mullick	Cello
Arun Pathak	Guitar

Chorus

Payal John
Sibylle Von Welck
Diana Rosenow
Subramani Chidambar
John Woodall
Suman Dubey
Madhu John

The International Opera Ensemble performing in Rajasthan, December 2003

With the Management team of PVMI in a two-day out-of-station meeting, 2004

With PVMI Sales and Marketing team during an incentive trip, January 2005

Stefano receives the prize as the winner of the Italian Community Tournament, New Delhi, February 2005

Celebration at Asha Niwas with Gaetano, Anna, Sister Beena, and the children, Christmas 2005.

One of the National Awards for Energy Conservation received by Stefano Pelle on behalf of PVM from the hands of the then President of India, Dr A. P. J. Kalam, December 2005

With some of his staff, February 2006

In Africa with a Nestlé distributor, Lagos, April 2006

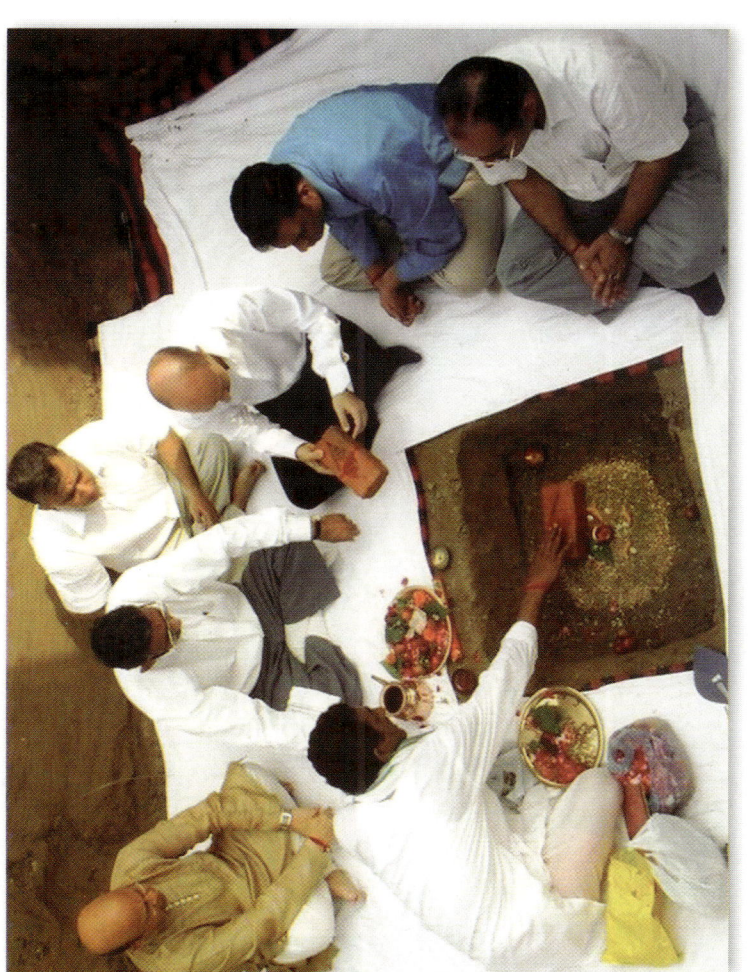

Bhoomi Puja, Rudrapur (Uttarakhand), June 2006

Being conferred with the title of Knight Commander by Italian dignitaries,
New Delhi, July 2006

Stefano's wedding: With his wife Shama at the Rajasthani reception, November 2006

The main reception with the bride and bridegroom's families, November 2006

Visit of R. Prodi, former Italian Prime Minister, New Delhi, 2006

Stefano Pelle with the Italian Ambassador in India, H. E. Giovanni Armellini, at the launch of his first book *Understanding Emerging Markets* in the Italian Embassy in New Delhi, January 2007

Rudrapur Factory inauguration with the India Management Team, June 2007

Traditional Indian greeting, Rudrapur, June 2007

A team-building race with the Asia Pacific Colleagues, July 2007

Stefano and a colleague at a CSR initiative in Chennai, November 2007

In Moscow with family, September 2008

In Africa, visiting the Algerian market with colleagues, January 2009, Algiers

A Friday morning bike ride in the desert close to Dubai, January 2009

Inaugurating the new factory in Bangladesh, June 2009

The School Contact Program in rural India, 2010

Center Shock: Barber

Chlor-mint: Paan Wala

Happydent White: Palace

Some memorable advertisements from Perfetti Van Melle India

was then the next decision to take. The option of Italy would have meant more traveling for her family and possibly some legal issues in the registration of the marriage in India. I had requested the Italian Embassy for the registration of our marriage taking place in India and obtained quite an encouraging reply stating that necessary legal formalities could be done in the Embassy in an hour's time. That facilitated our decision and we eventually concluded that we would have a civil marriage in Delhi and later register it in the Italian Embassy.

Logistically having it there did make sense also in view of the subsequent celebrations: most of our common friends were in Delhi; her family could easily fly there from Kerala, the state in the southern part of India where they hail from; my family and friends had plenty of flights to reach Delhi from various parts of the world. Having the celebrations in Delhi allowed us to use the Rajokri House for the main receptions and helped us accommodate our visiting guests more easily. We eventually came to this decision around July 2006 and we realized then that we needed to start moving fast in the organization since the summer holidays were in between and we would have not had much time left, considering also that people coming from various parts of the world were to plan their travel schedules accordingly. So we started the most urgent task of drawing a list of the people we wanted to invite. People who are familiar with Indian culture, or even those who have watched Hindi movies, know that marriage celebrations in India are quite elaborate. This is very different from marriages in Italy, where one would have the wedding either in a church or in the town hall, followed by a reception which would end up being a (very long) lunch or a dinner; in India people look forward to celebrating the wedding event in several ways and for several days. Usually the various events take place during the span of one week, and the actual wedding ceremony is somewhere in between the various other pre and post marriage rituals and celebrations.

Wedding traditions and customs vary across religions, castes, ethnicities, and regions in the country, but there are some common elements found in many of them. Leaving aside the various formalities happening among the families of the couple to be married, such as the visit of the father of the bridegroom to the bride's house, some events common to many traditions are the *Sangeet*, or the day when ladies sing traditional songs or dance;[10] the *Mehendi*, a gathering often reserved to the ladies where henna is applied on their hands and feet; the procession of the groom to the bride's home, often on a white

---

[10] At times there are separate sangeets for ladies only; other times common ones.

horse or even on an elephant, accompanied by friends and music; the various receptions, hosted by the different sides of the families. The various pre-wedding events are occasions for the families and guests to get to know each other better so that during the subsequent receptions the families and guests have already become familiar with each other. Normally Indian marriages are supposed to be grand. Sources say that one of the richest Indian industrialists spent 60 million dollars for the wedding of his daughter in 2004.[11] I have personally attended the wedding of the daughter of the owner of an international hotel in Delhi and I must say that I was quite impressed. The hotel was closed for a few days in order to prepare it for the celebrations and to host the guests. One of the receptions was held in the pool garden: this had been completely modified and, surprisingly, the swimming pool had disappeared, having been covered to allow a larger space for the banquet. The buffet had over 10 different kinds of cuisines, with ingredients purposely imported from all over the world. In that occasion I ate the largest quantity of Italian Truffle I had ever eaten or I would likely ever eat in my life. A few kilograms of this had been brought from Italy, and the Italian chef, flown in for the event, had cooked it with a special wine costing 100 US dollars per bottle and garnished the dishes with golden leaves.

    I know about north Indian families who have gone bankrupt because of their daughters' marriage expenses. Even without reaching such excesses, I have seen even lower middle class families investing in receptions for hundreds of people and accommodations for dozens of them. I have attended receptions where the number of invitees crossed the thousand. It was certainly not our intention to have a huge event for our marriage, and the fact that it would be held in a "neutral" place like Delhi, home to none of the two families, helped in limiting the number of participants to a number already high for Italian standards but rather modest for Indian ones On the other hand, given the local culture and the perception of our status in the local society and particularly due to the presence of a few high level invitees, we could not afford having a low-profile marriage and receptions. We thought then that we should try and concentrate the various events typical of Indian marriages in two main receptions. Each of these would have a completely different style, one completely Indian, the other more Western. Similarly the locations of the receptions would be two different parts of the large garden of our house, the

---

[11] The wedding of Vanisha Mittal, daughter of Lakshmi Mittal, main shareholders of the Arcelor Mittal steel company, is reported to have cost that much, see Expressindia.com of March 8, 2012, http://www.expressindia.com/latest-news/Daughters-follow-Mukesh-Ambani-Lakshmi-Mittal-to-Forbes-list/355984/.

Chapter 7: An Indo-Italian Wedding | 115

decorations would have very different themes and colors, and even the dress code of the guest was supposed to vary according to this.

In the meantime we had to print our wedding invitations. This matter too was an adventure of its own, since in order to have some invitation cards that were at the same time very traditionally Indian but also elegant and to our taste we had to go looking for the right place in Old Delhi. We visited various shops there till we finally found the one who could give us something up to our expectations. We selected a specific paper, the graphic and the layout, and created a specific logo with our initials. As often it happens in India they had to give us several proofs before getting the final product, and so we kept going through the small streets of Old Delhi where the shop was located. Those who know this part of the city are aware that it is almost impossible to go there by car: so we needed to leave our car parked somewhere close by and take the cycle rickshaw to reach the place. Once we even ventured to go there riding my bike, but we did not dare repeating the experience again. While the tradition in India is to hand-deliver the invitations, in our case most of them had to be sent either by post or scanned and sent by email, considering that a good part of the guests would come from different parts of India or from abroad.

The other interesting adventure was to ensure that we would not have trouble with the administration and bureaucratic machine that would have sanctioned our marriage. Aware of how slow and complex the Indian administrative and legal apparatus can be we went to visit well in advance the Sub-Divisional Magistrate Court. We procured all needed papers and submitted them as per the due deadlines. We also donated a hamper of our candies to the persons involved in the process so as to have them from our side, though their expectations were much higher, particularly after seeing that I, a foreigner, was involved in the process. The magistrate was quite helpful in the process, to the extent of closing an eye about a wrong date written on a certain document. Given the fact that he seemed to be a reasonable person and since we would have not liked to have our union sanctioned in a crowded, noisy, and old place like a sub-divisional Indian Court, we tried our luck and requested him to celebrate the marriage in our place. He eventually agreed to this, provided that it happened on a Saturday, a day when he would not have had a problem in leaving the office. We were very pleased about this, also because for those who wanted to attend the ceremony it would have meant avoiding coming to the Court and waiting there; above all, it reduced the uncertainty of the procedures. Though till the last minute we could not be sure that the Magistrate and his staff would eventually show up, if they did come the signing would have certainly been hassle-free. The other important task was the organization of the accommodation for the guests.

We had approximately 40 people coming from out of Delhi, some from different places in India, others from Singapore, Italy, and other European countries. We tried to have our immediate families staying with us in our place and in the nearby house kindly made available by our landlord, but the other thirty or so people had to be accommodated somewhere. Luckily there was a resort just next to our house and we were able to book a few rooms there: this also facilitated the logistics, since guests staying there would have not needed transportation to reach our place. For the rest of the guests we managed to find a few hotels not too far and cars which could take them around. Luckily we had booked the rooms well in advance since November is the peak of the tourism season in north India and also the moment of the year when the maximum number of weddings happen. For this hotel rates are extremely high, up to double the low season ones and even for those rates it is difficult to find available rooms. Last but not the least: we had to organize the reception. Surprisingly, this would not have been a very difficult thing, had the two of us—future husband and wife—not been as perfectionists as we are. We did try to find help in wedding planning firms, but those we had consulted did not meet our requirements.

Eventually we took the precious help of a person in my company who became the point of reference for the different vendors involved. I requested her boss to give her leaves a few days before the marriage and she did take quite a bit of pressure off our shoulders. Also, my secretary and another colleague did help us and, despite the stress, we managed to organize almost everything as per our expectations. Apart from the two receptions organized by us, a third one was offered to us from our friend Ravi, who also happened to be one of my best men. This took place three days before the wedding and was limited to some of our resident friends and those few others who had already reached from abroad. It was held on a roof garden in Gurgaon and unfortunately coincided with an evening of strong wind, causing some of the guests to catch a seasonal flu typical of that season in Delhi. For the first reception, the ethnic Indian one, we decided to have the Sangeet and Mehendi together. Just a few weeks earlier my future wife and I had visited a slum in Delhi inhabited by Rajasthani communities: some of them were performing artistes, while some others had small businesses such as selling of bangles and other Indian handicrafts. We decided that we should try and use their services for our first reception instead of hiring professional performers. By doing this we would have ensured that they could earn some money as well as enjoy a nice evening and a good meal. We were also happy since we could not have had anything more authentic for our Indian reception.

It turned out to be a brilliant idea and all the guests did enjoy their dances, music, henna[12] works, the astrologist, the bangles stall, and the Parrot reading.[13] The set up of this reception was the part of the lawn just in front of the main house entrance. We had recreated a sort of square of a typical village with tents and stalls where the Rajasthani boys and girls displayed their various activities; there was a gazebo where the food was kept and a main tent at the end of the lawn where a few dozen people could sit. Since we had chosen the Rajasthan ethnic theme, the dominant colors were orange and maroon: the whole décor of the tents, dining tables, stalls, and couches had such colors and the flowers used in the décor were mainly marigolds. A few of the boys and girls kept performing typical music and dances, involving also the guests in the same. For the latter part of the evening a dance floor had been installed in a corner and a DJ with a vast repertoire of music—from Indian classical, to Punjabi and various western kinds of music, with emphasis on the pop music of the 1980s and 1990s—made available.

The second reception happened two days after the ethnic one and had a completely different set-up. It was hosted in the back part of the house garden, a larger area than the one where the previous reception had taken place, part of which was landscaped with slopes going up and down: right in the middle of this there was a small hillock with a stage on it, the ideal place where the marriage could have been celebrated. Here the theme was more Western, the dominant colors silver, white and black and the decorations more formal; so also was the setting of the dining tables. White flowers and dozens of small lights decorated the trees all around and the tables, and Western classical music was played in the background. In this reception we wanted to include the tradition of the bridegroom going to the bride's place, the bride leaving her place as well as the ritual of the marriage itself. While the actual legal marriage had happened in the afternoon of the same day in presence of the families, witnesses, and only a few close friends, during the reception we would simulate a short ritual that was to remind of a wedding ceremony. Both of us were to reach the central stage, bridegroom first and bride later, accompanied by four girls holding a golden veil on her head. Here we were to remain sitting on some sort of "Divan" for some time[14] and eventually exchange garlands to symbolize the exchange of promises for our future together. Soon after this,

---

[12] A sort of natural ink used for different purposes, among which also dying the hair.
[13] A parrot picking up the tarot cards, which are then read by its master.
[14] The ritual of the newly-wedded couple sitting on a sofa and the guests coming to them to talk, bringing gifts or taking pictures with them is very common in Indian marriages.

fireworks would start and the reception would continue with the dinner and the married couple joining the guests. All the described events were supposed to happen in the initial part of the evening in the sequence just mentioned, the first phase of which was my entering the venue of the reception. So as to include the traditional ritual of the bridegroom riding to the bride's home, I had planned to reach the venue riding an elephant. Guests had begun coming in from 8 p.m. onwards and my entry was scheduled around 9 p.m., so as to leave to the guests the necessary time to arrive, settle down, and be able to watch the whole ritual from their place. The elephant was supposed to come by 6 p.m. or so and wait somewhere close by, in order to have some rehearsal. Since by 9 p.m. there was no trace of the animal I started becoming seriously worried because the whole plan was being delayed. By that time I had already sent a few of my staff out to try and find alternatives for the entrance, such as a white horse, another very common "vehicle" used in marriages. Almost every evening during the marriage season in Delhi one would see such horses going from place to place to be part of such rituals, but that night there was no such animal around, and the only hope was that the elephant would eventually show up. Luckily, by 9:30 p.m., one of my people roaming around to find some solution spotted the pachyderm and his rider slowly moving towards our direction, almost one kilometer away. They eventually arrived around 10 p.m. and I could finally sigh with relief, unaware that the troubles linked to the beast were not yet over.

    I climbed on to the elephant which slowly walked the path from my main gate to the reception venue: the entrance was a surprise for most of the guests and was welcomed by long rounds of applauses, as well as by a few gun shots of one of my security guards who had possibly had a drink too much. I was then supposed to get off the animal and walk to the central stage, but to do so the elephant would have had to kneel down and let me get off, whereas he seemed to have no intention of doing so. His master tried several times to force him down, but he just refused to budge and, after each attempt of his pal convincing him to bend down, became more and more irritated to the point of walking around in a sort of ballet and risking to crash the guests who had gathered around us. We were subsequently told that the animal had got irritated by the gun shots, the lights and the sounds, and this caused his refusal to follow his boss' orders. After almost 10 minutes of unsuccessful attempts I decided to jump down, though from that height and in my wedding dress was not the most comfortable choice. Luckily my staff was fast to catch me and I could finally touch the ground amidst the euphoric encouragements of the laughing guests.

The rest of the planned events happened as scheduled, but it was past 10:30 p.m. when the simulated wedding ceremony was over and the actual reception could start. Luckily there was no other surprise in the evening and all guests enjoyed the event; they kept congratulating us for the organization and successful outcome of such an unusual and articulated reception. Many years have passed but when I socially meet some of the participants they still tell other friends about my wedding, claiming that that was the most beautiful and spectacular wedding they had ever attended; next they start telling about the elephant ballet and my jump, an episode that had clearly been the climax of the celebrations.

8

THE RUSSIAN ROULETTE

The New Faces of Russia

The results obtained in India and in the surrounding countries did not go unnoticed and it was decided that I be promoted to Vice President of the Group and Chief Operating Officer of a region. Our Group is structured into five geographical areas, each of which is handled by a Vice President and COO. There are also five other VPs with functional competences such as HR, Finance, Marketing, R&D and Development & Innovation. I was to keep handling south Asia, which included the sub-continent with the addition of Myanmar and Afghanistan. This sub-region, previously merged with Asia Pacific, had in the meantime turned into an area worth considering a region on its own. In addition to this I was given the task to also handle Russia and the CIS countries. Clubbing Russia with south Asia was a rather unusual choice, but since that country had been a problematic one it was decided to provide me with the opportunity of trying to turn around the results of the local operating company.

My elevation to the new role had happened in September 2005 and in the last quarter of that year I went for the first time to Moscow, where our factory and local offices were located. The plant was actually 30 kilometers west of Moscow, off the highway going to Riga. The first time I visited the place I was enchanted by the forest I had to cross on the way to the plant. Inside and all around the borders of the forest there were many residential sites, several of which were under construction. Some were Dacias, the well-known countryside residences where Muscovites spend their weekends and holidays. They represent an institution for the Russian people and every person dreams of owning one and spending the happy moments of their family life there. They are used as bases to go fishing in summer or ice skating on the frozen rivers and lakes during the long and cold winters. Most of them also have vegetable gardens where families grow their own produce. Interestingly, even those families who cannot afford the luxury of a second residence do practice their own farming by renting small plots of land, at times as small as 10 square meters, to grow their vegetables.

I came to know later on that the houses in the area surrounding the plant were progressively becoming the first residence of many Muscovites, particularly upper class families with young children that had started preferring a healthier life to that of the city, due to the sky-rocketing prices of the residential units in Moscow. The same V. Putin, then the President of Russia, was told to be spending most of his time in a residence just outside the city. This represented a major hassle for those living in the areas linking the President's house to the Kremlin, since at some given times in the morning and evening the traffic was stopped to allow his motorcade to drive undisturbed from one place to the other. It was done mainly for security reasons but also to avoid the traffic in Moscow, one of the worst I have ever experienced. Many areas of the city, as well as the ring road around it and the roads leading to the two main airports, are continuously jammed; the traffic does not follow a regular pattern one could predict in order to avoid it. The President is not the only one to enjoy traffic-free rides: most of the VIPs, not necessarily politicians, drive beside jams with their blinking lights and sirens to avoid the long queues. Some roads have a lane conceived mainly for this purpose.

One can easily perceive the large divide between the rich ones and the rest of the people. Large black cars followed by security; the ostentation of the most expensive jewelry and luxury brands; large houses with very tall walls in the most exclusive areas, and above all the often arrogant attitude in public places; all this differentiates the elites of former oligarchs now evolved into rich and powerful businessmen from the rest of the people. Though international brands of clothes and accessories are also rather common among the upper middle class members, who do not hesitate to spend the equivalent of two months of their salaries for a Louis Vuitton bag, the large majority of the middle class do not own a car and live in the outskirts or in suburbs of the main cities. I have often noticed a marked difference between the way men and women of such stratum of the society dress and take care of themselves. Men seem not to be particularly interested in fashion and brands[1] whereas

---

[1] This is however less true for the younger generations where, possibly due to the effect of globalization, boys are also more brand conscious and follow more fashion trends in clothes.

women are very sensitive to the latest trends and spend large amounts of time and money for their personal care and look. It is indeed surprising to see the number of luxury cars being driven in Moscow: I remember walking by a recently opened hotel close to the Red Square and seeing three Rolls Royce parked in front of it. It might have been one of the rare times in my life I had seen three of those cars together. On the other hand the fortunate lot of common people owning cars very often have Lada vehicles, the most popular locally-made car that used to be one of the few makes available during the USSR era.

While the richest live in huge mansions with Italian-designed interiors and imported furniture and expatriates rent central apartments for US$ 15,000 per month, middle class families live in large and often old complexes, often in the outskirts of Moscow; the lower class families still share the same roof with other families, a heritage of the communist system. Outside the main cities one still sees many old wooden houses dating back to decades ago in very precarious conditions. Stark contrasts coexist in such a huge nation with a territory so large as to extend across 12 different time zones. At that time President Putin was still extremely popular[2] since he had given back to the country part of the pride lost subsequently to the fall of the Soviet regime. After several years of GDP fall, currency depreciation, and people getting poorer and desperate, the President had contributed to bringing back growth to the economy, keeping inflation under control and creating new jobs also by attracting foreign investors who had come to the country seeking to exploit the potential of a large population eager to increase their standards of life. In 2006 *The Economist* had come out with a cover with Putin dressed with a mafia sort of hat caved in and a petrol pump in his hands held like a gun, under the headline "Do not mess with Russia." The page appropriately depicted the new attitude of the nation full of the advantages deriving from the dependency of many countries on its natural gas and oil resources.

This new Russia had a different face when compared with the stereotypes one would have associated with the old regime. It was a country with a new breed of millionaires such as Roman Abramovich, the owner of a renowned European football team;[3] with a new generation of sports heroes, such as Maria Sharapova, not only an athlete but also a businesswoman who created

---

[2] Today, after Putin's pursuit of his third presidential mandate, the alleged rigged elections and many unrealized promises, his popularity seems to have drastically reduced.
[3] The team is the English Premier league Chelsea Football Club. Abramovich is one of the richest persons in Russia; he is also the Governor of the Far East State of Chukotka.

her own lines of fashion apparels and accessories; with younger politicians such as Dmitry Medvedev, Deputy Prime Minister at the age of 40 and later President before turning 45. However, despite the apparent wave of changes, many aspects of the old regime remained unvaried. For instance the almighty secret service that, though under a different label,[4] kept on pulling the strings of many sectors of the country; the limitations in the freedom of speech and the suspect disappearance of many journalists and writers; the misadventures of those who had dared challenge the regime in some way; among these the unlucky CEO of the largest local oil company[5] who has been spending the last few years in prison after unclear accusations never definitely proven. The country's large bureaucratic machine has not changed much and I had to witness this during the years I handled the local company and interacted with the Russian institutions. In one of my visits to the country I had reached Moscow Sheremetyevo airport very early on a Sunday morning. The immigration process was always a painful moment of the trip, with endless queues and arrogant officers who would ask questions in Russian and deal with passengers as if they were doing them a huge favor. That day something seemed to be going wrong with my passport, and they asked me to sit and wait, initially without giving me any explanation. After almost one hour I was told that the problem was in the fact that my valid visa was on my old passport (attached to the new one), whereas the new valid passport I had shown did not have a visa. Despite my attempts to explain that the passport where I had the visa had run out of pages and I had been obliged to get a new one, they did not seem or want to understand my words, and I had to wait in the immigration hall from six to nine in the morning without anyone telling me what would happen next.

After several hours of unproductive wait, being now a more decent time to call somebody (on a Sunday morning), I contacted a local friend who could speak to them in Russian. The immigration people initially refused to take my phone and, when I finally managed to convince one of them to do so, he hardly listened to my friend's explanation. I then called my local company but the day being a Sunday, I was not able to talk to anybody. Eventually I phoned the Group HR VP in Italy and requested him to contact

---

[4] In 1991 the KGB was renamed FSB and was formally re-oriented towards commercial purposes. However, with the growing power of Putin, a former KGB member, it soon reverted to its traditional tasks.
[5] The company is Yukos Oil and its former Chairman and CEO, M. Khodorkovsky, arrested in October 2003, charged with fraud and tax evasion.

somebody through the diplomatic circuit; unfortunately he also could not trace anybody on a Sunday morning. After five frustrating hours of waiting I was led to the office of a relatively young and educated English-speaking officer. Finally I could communicate with somebody who was willing to listen and talk to me. I could explain the situation to her and she highlighted to me that the visa was directly linked with the passport number, hence when I had obtained a new passport my visa would have automatically lost validity. As per their law I was trying to enter the country without a valid visa, hence I was subject to being imprisoned and subsequently deported. I had to wait in her office one more hour and finally I could talk to the CEO of my local company, who could contact somebody who talked to this officer. I had to write a declaration where I admitted to be violating the Russian immigration law and undertook not to do this again in the future; having done this I paid for a new visa and around midday I was finally able to enter the country.

This was not the only occasion when I personally experienced the Red Tape and harassment of the Russian administration. During my first visits in the country I was walking with an Italian friend resident in Moscow on Tverskaya, one of the large roads leading to the Red Square. We had finished our dinner and were heading to a bar to meet other friends when a policeman stopped us and asked for our documents. My friend had his papers proving his local residence but I was not carrying my passport and was only able to show some other personal identity document, apparently not good enough for him. The policeman insisted then that we had to follow him to the police station so that he could verify my identity and visa and highlighted to us that the process might take a few hours, or even the whole night. Only when my friend took him in confidence and decided to pay the "fine" for my omission were we allowed to go and continue our evening walk. Despite the vast changes brought to the country by the opening of the market to capitalism and foreign investments, heritages of the old regime keep coexisting at various levels of the local institutions with the new faces of the nation.

PVM's Industrial Adventure

Perfetti had had a presence in Russia since the 1990s. It was distributed through Van Melle already before the takeover of the same. Once the integration was completed, thanks to the strength of the former Van Melle brands in this country also the sales of the Perfetti brand gained salience. The business had been developing well with sales growing and good margins and thanks to such good results the former Van Melle had initiated the project to set up a local manufacturing plant. The idea behind this was to save custom duties on the imports (approximately 25 percent) while improving time to market in Russia and also in the CIS countries. Before the Perfetti take over, a large plot of land had been bought but had not yet been registered in the name of the company. The design of the plant had been agreed upon by the management and the initial bureaucratic process to obtain the necessary permit had started. The company had engaged a few consultants to get help in dealing with local authorities. Through them they had initiated the various steps to obtain the land registration, a prerequisite to be able to obtain the approval for an industrial project.

However, several months had passed by and, for reasons initially not very clear, the registration of the land was still pending. In the meanwhile, the project had progressed: the company which was to build the plant had been selected and an agreement with them had been signed. Given the delays it was suggested that, while waiting for the administrative process to happen, the first steps in cleaning the land and preparing it for the construction be taken. Works had then begun and the execution of the contract had started; the first payments were made and the project clock started ticking. By the time the land had been cleared and leveled and was ready for the first stage of construction, there had not been any further progress on the registration. With the contractor having mobilized his equipment and initiated the preliminary works, any decline in the pace of work would have implied expenses to be reimbursed to him. Misguided by the consultants who communicated false expectations about the quick resolution of the pending administrative issues and caught in the tricky mechanisms of the running expenses payable to the contractor for the delay, the company decided to continue the construction of the plant. Months passed and the building came up gradually, but the promises of obtaining the registration were not kept and the reason why this had not happened finally surfaced. The land was in an area linked to the army, hence considered of national interest; it could not have been sold to private foreign investors without some special permissions. Actions were then initiated to sort out the issue, but the Russian bureaucracy is known to be heavy and slow.

Months kept passing by and heaps of documentations were produced but the solution to the matter seemed nowhere close. In the meantime the plant building was almost completed, the first machineries had started arriving and the first workers had been hired. In fact several years had passed since the beginning of the project. After Van Melle had become part of the Perfetti Group some of the people involved in the first stage of the project had left causing further difficulties. When I was given the responsibility of the country the situation had come to a paradox: the factory had been built, some of the production lines had been commissioned but formally the land did not yet belong to PVM and the plant did not even exist. Its project had not yet been presented for approval and consequently the building permission permit was still to be requested. Considering that every day of inactivity was causing losses for several thousands of Euros, we had to find the way to start production at the earliest. Therefore we requested and obtained from the local authorities the permit to start some trials. A plant that did not formally exist could not logically be granted the permit to start some trials, but often in that country things happened without logical explanations.

Under the trials permit we were able to produce and sell at least for a few months, since the permit had to be renewed every semester. Only in 2006, also thanks to the help of the Italian Embassy and other influential players, were we able to obtain the registration of the land in the name of the local subsidiary and we could start the actual process of presenting an industrial plan to the local authorities. The first step of this was the presentation of the plant lay out, including the main factory and utilities, to the health authority of the region. Various approvals had to be obtained at regional and central level and often this implied two different stages of applications. While we obtained an in-principle approval for the design relatively quickly—compared to the years spent for getting the land registration—the consent had several conditions attached to be verified at a subsequent stage. The application for the building plan could eventually be submitted, though in reality the plant was not only already existing but also already in production. In some weeks the permission to build was granted but once again subject to strict conditions: one of these was the fact of having a water Effluent Treatment Plant (ETP) much more effective than the one already built, so as to deliver "fish quality" outlet water. PVM operates factories all over the world and is known to be a good corporate citizen and abide all local laws and regulations; however never before had one of the existing plants been requested to have such a high quality of effluent water. In order to reach such a level, the existing ETP needed to be upgraded with a substantial investment, the depreciation of which would have further affected the bottom line of the operating company. The upgrading was carried out during the following months, so as to be ready at the time of the commissioning inspection. In parallel to this the gas connection had to be obtained, another important stage towards the completion of the plant. During the first "trial" period factory and offices—located in this—were run through diesel generators. However the final configuration foresaw that the power plant would have used gas, much cheaper than the diesel and for which the generators had been procured. Obtaining the gas connection was not an easy task and implied the presentation of many documents and applications. The process was complicated by the fact that part of the pipeline that was to serve our factory fell in a sort of "no man's land" between us and the neighbors. With hard efforts we ensured that the connection could be granted and the gas power plant started.

The final step of approvals was then the commissioning of the plant. Curiously we requested the commissioning inspection only a few weeks after obtaining the building approval: the various authorities could have wondered how such a huge plant could be completed in such a record time! The first inspection happened a few weeks later and the regional authority provided first a pre-approval and subsequently also the balance approvals. It had taken seven years since the beginning of the project to have a full-fledged factory with all due permits and licenses to legally run local production. This had been the longest time to complete an industrial project in the PVM Group and possibly the most expensive process ever accomplished. The initial cost budgeted for the project had more than doubled and the company had accumulated large pre-operative losses. However the learning of such complex delivery would have been precious for the future operations in Russia as well as in other emerging countries.

Competing in Eurasia

The Russian Federation is the largest country in the world, with a territory extending from Norway to Alaska, covering about one eighth of the earth's inhabited land area. It would be a mistake to consider this nation as one market. When also the CIS countries are clubbed to the Federation they form together a conglomerate of different nations, cultures and markets so vast that several strategies need to be employed in order to be able to effectively compete. When I took the responsibility of the extended Russia in 2005 the local Operating Company was going through the industrial problems just described. Such situations take a large part of the management's attention and may become a cause of distraction from the core business. Also, due to this the local company had not been performing very well during the previous years, both in terms of top and bottom line results. This was one of those cases where a company that is expanding its operations internationally loses out while moving from a trading operation to a green field with direct investments. In fact sales were doing relatively well during the 1990s but the sudden change of business model destabilized the existing organization with serious prejudice to growth and profitability. Urgent corrective actions needed to be taken, both at product mix level and in the organizational structure. Among several brands and products sold in Russia and the neighboring countries, in this market, PVM had two successful brands in its portfolio—Mentos and Fruit-tella. We decided to build on these in order to expand the business and revive the growth. The products sold under such brands were the traditional chewy candies in stick packs, pillars of the former Van Melle Company. The candy segment was large in size, constituting almost 87 percent of the volumes of the combined candy and gum market, but the value of this segment was only 44 percent of the total, with the gums rapidly gaining share. Even in terms of growth candies were growing slowly, whereas gums recorded growth rates well above the double digit threshold.[6] Within the candies, the segment with the highest growth was that of the jellies. In gums two main international competitors shared the market,[7] with hardly any presence of other relevant national brands. In such a situation they were able to enjoy the dominant positions and had created high entry barriers both in terms of shelf space in the outlets and for the high promotional investments in the point of purchase and advertising. PVM Russia saw the opportunity of utilizing the strength and awareness of the Mentos brand in order to make an entry in a large and growing segment dominated by only two players.

The fact that PVM has a strong presence in gums in many countries worldwide and a consolidated knowhow in the development of gum products ensured that the new launches would have qualitatively been at least at par compared to the existing competitors. However the spending capacity of the competitors was certainly higher than that of PVM Russia, which was still in the red and used to compete only in the less profitable segment of candies. Having considered all the possible opportunities and threats, including the fact that one of the mentioned competitors had just entered the candy segment, we finally took the decision to launch a gum under the Mentos brand name in the Russian market. The product was to have a shape similar to the Mentos candy, but a lower weight. It was to be initially imported packed in a flip top box with a side opening. Due to the duties and the cost of freight the packs were sold at a premium of approximately 20 percent[8] compared to the main format of the existing market leader. An international advertising

---

[6] As per Nielsen data the growth of the gums in 2007 vs. previous year had been 13 percent.
[7] Historically, the Wrigley's company had been the market leader with the brand Orbit holding approximately 70 percent of the market. The competitor was the brand Dirol from Cadbury, with the balance of the market share.
[8] Mentos was sold at 12 Roubles vs. the price of 10 Roubles of Wrigley's Orbit.

commercial was aired and sampling plans through magazines and in store complemented the launch. Due to the strength of the competitors and their reaction to the launch, it was not easy to gain significant presence in supermarkets. The delayed distribution and the hard-to-justify premium price translated into a lukewarm acceptance of consumers for the new product, though in qualitative researches the product itself was considered either superior or at par against the competitors. Several corrective actions were then taken. The price could be changed thanks to a new blister format of nine pieces that replaced the 12 pieces box. We started importing the product in bulk and packing it locally to save custom duty and the differential in labor costs.

Additional new formats were launched, aiming particularly at a distribution channel more accessible to PVM. A range of attractive bottles containing a higher number of pieces (30 and 60) were launched at premium prices for sales mainly in the petrol stations. A new local campaign that emphasized the possible usage also on the go, in this case in the car, was also aired in parallel to the international one. Bottles were a novelty in the market and gave Mentos gum momentum positions in the petrol stations and more popularity among consumers: the increased demand made easier the entry into other distribution channels. New product formats and variants[9] were progressively introduced and the brand sales as well as its market share started increasing. After little over two years from the launch in supermarkets, where the entry had initially been difficult, the brand managed to gain a market share of approximately six percent, a satisfactory result given the market situation and the fact that the competitors had been in the market for several decades. Its share in the petrol stations was much higher and even after the launch of bottles from the competitors Mentos remained the most popular gum in such formats. The results obtained encouraged us to procure a production line so as to avoid the extra costs of importing the bulk products: the improved margins provided a better promotional investing capacity that led to improved sales results.

In the meantime an important international acquisition had happened in the PVM Group: the Spanish company Chupa Chups had been bought in the year 2006. The Brand Chupa Chups had international presence and recognition, but the company had not been doing well for a few years. Also in this case Perfetti had cooperated with Chupa at a distribution level in several countries and the main shareholders of the companies had developed a good relationship. Such international acquisition had to become particularly

---

[9] The variants were Mentos Pure Fresh, Mentos Blast, and Mentos Cube.

important for PVM Russia, since the Chupa Chups Company had a manufacturing plant in Saint Petersburg. We took over the local company with the task of leading the integration process locally. Parts of the years 2006 and 2007 were dedicated to integrate the management teams, the distribution networks and the Finance and IT Departments. Logistically the location of the Chupa factory and offices in the other main Russian Metropolis complemented PVM's plant and offices located close to the capital. The brand portfolios were also complementary, being Chupa mostly in lollipops, segments where PVM had a strong presence in some Asian markets but not in Russia. It was certainly a good opportunity for PVM to strengthen its muscles in the candy segment, but also its distribution strength vis-à-vis the trade and media. Furthermore the high awareness of the brand Chupa Chups among the Russian consumers provided a great opportunity to launch new products under the same name.

Such an opportunity was exploited in the occasion of the launch of a proprietary product produced and marketed by PVM in several countries under a different brand but launched under the brand name Chupa Chups in Russia. The uniqueness of the product, candy floss with bubble gum inside, the strength of the brand Chupa and an appropriate price point yielded good success and turned into one of the first brand synergies achieved in the local integration process. Another important strategic move for PVM Russia was the entry into the jelly segment, a promising and growing one where international players did not have a strong presence. The products were bought from a third party and launched in several formats at different prices under the Fruit-tella brand. Also in this case the encouraging results achieved as well as the potential of the segment prompted us to localize the production: a high output jelly line was purchased and installed in the local factory, thus improving the possibility of providing a wider range of products and better flexibility in the formats offered. The new launches in the mentioned segments and the synergy obtained thanks to the integration revived the growth in the Russian company's sales.

After several years of stagnation 2006 saw a growth of over 23 percent in the value of the sales of PVM Russia. The subsequent year was when the combined entity merged their sales; hence the overall value saw a jump of over 80 percent. On a comparable basis 2008 recorded again double-digit growth, with several brands including Chupa seeing increases both in volumes and in value. Thanks to these results and to the fact that both factories were now producing at higher utilization, the overall losses of the integrated company were reduced, thus paving the way towards an operating break even.

9

SETTLING DOWN IN THE MIDDLE EAST

UAE at a Glance

One of my first tasks as Vice-President of the PVM Group was to find my successor in India. I thought that the time had come for the local operating company to have its first Indian Managing Director. With the help of a Head Hunting company we started the search and a few months later we found the candidate who was to take over from me. Since the new person came from outside the Group and from a different industry I thought that the handover should take all the necessary time. Once I was convinced that he had learned enough to be able to handle the operations on his own I started considering moving my office outside the country so as to enhance his autonomy and also in order to have a more detached perspective of all the four operating companies part of my geographical area. Also in view of the fact that there were plans to start studying opportunities in Africa, I thought that a location connected to that continent as well as to south Asia and Russia would have been convenient. Ideally the new regional headquarters had to have direct flights to all my frequent destinations and also ensure good connections with the corporate headquarters in Europe.

Dubai had all such requisites, being in the middle of the areas I was to handle and having a national airline ensuring seamless connections not only to the countries I had to travel to at that moment but also towards many other destinations where I might have needed to travel in future. The city was located between south Asia and Italy; had good business IT and communications infrastructures; was in the same time zone as Russia, and was recognized as a place with a business-friendly environment. On top of this it also allowed a comfortable life and an interesting mix of cultures. We studied then how to open an office in Dubai and found out that the process appeared relatively simple. It implied the creation of a local company and obtaining a trade license, even if no trade was to be done. Once we got all necessary information from various sources, including local authorities we met during exploratory trips, we presented the plan and got the approval from the Corporate Headquarters. In April 2007 we created Perfetti Van Melle Middle East and opened the regional office within a free zone. The localization in such a zone allowed us to have full ownership of the company, whereas as per the law of the land entities created outside those zones need to have a local partner with at least 51 percent share.

When we actually started living and working in the UAE we realized that things were not as simple as they had been presented to us and that there was a well-studied marketing strategy behind the way the Emirate used to project its image to the world. This strategy, together with an admirable long-term vision from the fathers of the United Emirates, were what have made this nation a true oasis of tolerance and progress in an arid land surrounded by the desert. Many of the neighboring countries trying to imitate Dubai have not been able to achieve similar development, at least from the human point of view, and have yet to remove some of the anachronistic laws and rules that restrict the freedom of their societies as well as of visiting tourists. One such example is Saudi Arabia, among the richest nations in the area. Here women are still forbidden to drive on their own or to meet any other man apart from their husband or a member of the family. During the last few years women have been fighting for their rights, but so far they have only obtained some concessions. Interestingly, only a few days before the starting of the London Olympics, obviously too late for any possible preparation, the women athletes of the Saudi teams have been authorized to take part in the event. Iran is another case: here a very strict police ensure that all women, including those visiting the countries, have their body and hair fully covered to the point of threatening them or even cutting their hair or beating them if they do not comply with their orders. The impression one has when entering this country is that the police and the institutions have the supreme and indisputable power over the inhabitants and visitors. A known person, who, invited by the government and treated as a VIP, had recently visited Iran for humanitarian purposes, told me that upon his arrival an officer had asked him to wait in a lounge for his passport to be stamped. After he had been waiting some time he had asked another officer how long the passport stamping procedure would take: the reply given was "ten minutes or ten hours, depending on the will of the immigration officer."

Chapter 9: Settling Down in the Middle East | 133

To better understand how the UAE have become what they are today it is beneficial to go back in time to a few decades ago when some of these states were still a British protectorate called the Trucial States. The origin of such a name came from a treaty signed in 1853 with the UK, under which the Sheikdoms agreed to a perpetual maritime truce with the British. This truce was necessary in order to protect the British expeditions for the Indian trade from pirates' attacks off the coast of Ras al Khaimah.[1] Later on the relationship between the British and the said states became closer, till the signing of another treaty in 1893 where, in view of the colonialist aims of other European countries, the sheikhs agreed not to dispose of any territory except to the UK and not to enter into relationships with any foreign government other than the UK without its consent. The British committed in return to protect the Trucial coast from all aggressions by sea and to help in case of land attacks. Towards the end of the 1960s, the British Government declared its intentions to put an end to the protectorate by the beginning of the subsequent decade. The various states, too small to be independent nations, decided to create a federation in order to ensure synergies in fields such as security and external policies, while also maintaining certain autonomies in internal affairs and socio-cultural matters.

Therefore, on December 2, 1971, the United Arab Emirates Federation came into existence.[2] The Sheikh ruling the richest and most powerful Emirate, namely Abu Dhabi, selected as capital city, became the President of the Federation. The Vice Presidency went to the Dubai ruler, also designated Prime Minister. All other Sheikhs were part of a body called the Supreme Council of Rulers, which holds the Executive power; a Federal National Council was formed to decide about federal laws and regulations.[3] A common currency, the Arab Emirates Dirham (AED), was created and pegged to the US dollar.[4] The autonomy in policies within the individual emirates allows the coexistence of very liberal and tolerant emirates like Dubai—highly urbanized, where spirits are allowed,[5] most of the women dress the western way, and restaurants and night clubs flourish all over the territory—with

---

[1] This was also called the "pirates coast."
[2] The original Federation comprised six states, whereas Ras al Khaimah joined later, on February 11, 1972.
[3] This 40-people partly elective body has in reality more consultative than actual legislative powers.
[4] One US$ is equal to 3.67 AED.
[5] Spirits have some restrictions though: they can be bought in specialized outlets against presentation of an annually purchased liquor license, issued only to non-Muslim applicants. Limited quantities can be purchased while entering the country at the airports' Duty-Free shops. On a few days declared "dry," alcohol cannot be served.

the bordering Sharjah, a "dry" emirate where spirits are not allowed, or Um al Qwain, more rural and traditional. Even between Dubai and Abu Dhabi there are substantial differences, the latter being more conservative and less tolerant; the former freer and with a wider availability of shopping malls with international outlets, restaurants and entertainment activities. Many people working in Abu Dhabi decide to live in Dubai and commute. This has become easier since 2011, after the opening of a new bridge and road crossing, via the recently developed islands,[6] linking the capital to Dubai and bringing down the travel time between the two cities to about 70 minutes. In the past there was a certain rivalry between the two main emirates in trying to attract foreign investments and redesigning and modernizing their own infrastructures.

Abu Dhabi has largely developed its business infrastructure during the last five years and today is the place where the big businesses happen. This is due to the wealth of the UAE coming from its oil resources, allowing it to have one of the world's richest sovereign funds. Dubai is still where the highest number of expatriates chooses to live, buy houses, and party. The history of this young nation has seen it acquiring during the last decade larger international visibility and recognition and progressively climbing the ladder of several ranks, including the Human Development Index.[7] It currently ranks 42nd in the world for ease of starting a business according to the World Bank and IFC Doing Business 2012 report, three positions higher than the previous year. Incredible progresses have been made in a territory that, up to the late 1960s, used to be a bunch of arid lands with few fishing villages, and a few trading centers. The vision of the personality recognized as the Father of the Nation, Sheik Zayed bin Sultan Al Nahayan and of a few other far-sighted members of his immediate and enlarged family have transformed the landscapes of some small towns in the desert into world famous cosmopolitan cities. Now they host millions of foreigners from dozens of different countries and they have become an example of peaceful coexistence among various races, religions, and nationalities. The total population of the UAE is approximately 7.5 million people[8] but the percentage of expatriates is above

---

[6] Saadiyat and Yas Islands; the bridge is a 10-lane, 1.4 km-long one named Shaikh Khalifa Bridge.
[7] The United Arab Emirates ranked 30th in the index of the just-released UN Human Development Report; they were the top Arab country in the list of 187 countries. The index was part of the "Human Development Report 2011, Sustainability and Equity: A Better Future for All." The six Arab Gulf States were the top Arab countries. Qatar ranked 37, Bahrain 42, Saudi Arabia 56, Kuwait 63, and Oman 89. Available at http://gulfnews.com/news/gulf/uae/general /uae-ranked-30th-un-development-index-and-as-top-arab-country-1.922764.
[8] World Bank, see http://data.worldbank.org/country/united-arab-emirates.

80 percent of the total[9] and it is estimated that over 200 nationalities live together in the country.[10] The per capita GDP hovers around US$ 40,000 and the GDP growth used to be between three and four percent in the pre-crisis years;[11] it seems to be on its way to achieve similar rates again in the current year. Oil and gas resources represented the key driver of growth for the country during the last 40 years. The first exploration of oil fields happened in the late 1950s and export of oil started a few years later. In the span of 10 years, thanks to the steep rise of crude prices in 1973, funds flowing into the country increased exponentially. However, if emirates like Abu Dhabi still depend heavily on oil,[12] the revenues coming from the oil sector for Dubai now make only six percent of the total GDP. It was thanks to the depletion of the natural reserves that initially Dubai and later also Abu Dhabi and the other emirates decided to diversify more and more in other sectors such as trade, tourism, and other services.

In a document titled "The Abu Dhabi Economic Vision 2030" issued by the Government of Abu Dhabi in November 2008, the rulers project that in little over 20 years from then the non-oil revenues of the emirate would represent 64 percent of the GDP: consequently, those of the UAE would become around three-quarters of the GDP or more. In order to enhance such diversification the Khalifa fund was launched in 2007 to provide financial and professional assistance to local enterprises. Since then it funded 367 projects in several industries, among which 30 percent were in the industrial sector.[13] Still in the perspective of diversification and more specifically in the energy industry the country bid and eventually obtained to become the host venue for the International Renewable Energy Agency (IRENA). Part of the merit of this achievement goes to the Masdar project, a city being constructed in the vicinity of Abu Dhabi planned to entirely rely on renewable energy with a sustainable zero waste and zero carbon ecology. And the achievement of the nations have been many more. Two world class airlines operate from

---

[9] World Bank and CIA estimate 19 percent of local population, whereas as per the UAE National Bureau of Statistics the total population is 8.2 million, out of which only about 12 percent are nationals.
[10] Abu Dhabi eGovernment Gateway, see http://www.abudhabi.ae/egovPoolPortal_WAR/appmanager/ADeGP/Citizen?_nfpb=true&_pageLabel=p20192&lang=en.
[11] In 2009 the GDP de-grew by 1.6 percent but it started growing again around 1.4 percent in 2010, see http://data.worldbank.org/indicator/NY.GDP.MKTP.KD.ZG.
[12] The non-oil GDP in Abu Dhabi was projected to reach about 48 percent in 2011, see *Emirates 24/7 Business*, October 11, 2011. Available at http://www.emirates247.com/business/abu-dhabi-gdp-to-top-dh1-5trn-2011-10-11-1.422819.
[13] See Hassan, F. 2012. "Rewarding Innovation," *Gulf News*, March 28, 2012.

the capital and from Dubai: they have won numerous awards and their airports—particularly the Dubai one—have become hubs connecting Asia with Europe and the rest of the world.

The Dubai international Airport has recently added a new terminal dedicated to its own airline.[14] This is supposedly the world's largest passenger terminal and one of the world largest buildings in terms of floor space; it has increased the airport passenger capacity to over 60 million passengers per year, against last year's traffic of 51 million: once the Concourse 3 is inaugurated, sometime during 2012, the total capacity will reach 80 million. Another even larger international airport, Dubai World Central, is being built[15] and is projected to have a capacity of over 120 million passengers.[16] Dubai built in less than four years the Dubai Metro, a mass transportation system running for almost 75 kilometers and connecting several areas of the city with Jebel Ali, one of the world's largest free zones and port. The two Metro lines (Green and Red) have also created the new record of being the longest driverless metro network in the world.[17] Abu Dhabi has just started a similar project consisting of a Metro and light-rail transit system that will extend for about 130 kilometers and is expected to be completed by 2016.[18] Off the Dubai coast there are the world's largest man-made islands, three palm-shaped ones and a large archipelago called "The World" for its shape. Unfortunately some of these projects have not been completed because of the financial crisis of 2008 that has also stalled many other real estate developments.

Despite this, the Burj Khalifa, the world's tallest building with its 829 meters, hosting a hotel, offices, and residential luxury apartments, was inaugurated in 2010. This has become one of the icons of the UAE, together with Burj Al Arab, the sail-shaped seven-star luxury hotel built on a man-made island, which had been for years the pride of the nation and symbol of the progress and modernization of the same. Since 2009 Abu Dhabi has been hosting a Formula 1 grand prix on Yas Island, a reclaimed land island with several hotels, a thematic amusement park called Ferrari World—the first ever Ferrari theme park—and several other tourist attractions to come in the future. The island was named the world's leading tourism project and Middle East

---

[14] Terminal Three, entirely dedicated to Emirates airline, was opened in October 2008.
[15] The cargo sections had already opened in 2010.
[16] See http://www.airport.ae/al-maktoum-international-airport-dubai-world-central-uae.html
[17] Source: gulfnews.com, February 15th, 2012, "Dubai Metro Creates New World Record," http://gulfnews.com/news/gulf/uae/traffic-transport/dubai-metro-creates-new-world-record-1.984105.
[18] Source: *Gulf News*, March 8, 2012, Dubai Edition, "Abu Dhabi Begins Work on Metro and Light-rail Design."

leading tourism development project by the World Travel Awards in 2009 and 2011, respectively.[19]

Living and Working in Dubai

I moved to Dubai in April 2007. A colleague of mine had already moved a few weeks earlier and he helped in facilitating the visa process and suggesting some of the useful tips one needs to know when moving to a new country. I had planned to come alone for the first weeks, leaving my wife back in India so that I could settle some of the administrative issues before her arrival. To be a resident of Dubai one needs to have a job, which entitles one to get a visa from the employer; in case of spouse and family they can be on the visa of the working husband/wife. I needed then to get my own residence visa before being able to sponsor my wife. The first few days were devoted to the various procedures for creating the local company, finding the office space, procuring the visas, and starting to look for accommodations. The company we created in April 2007 was already our second company, since during a previous exploratory trip we had applied for a company in the Jebel Ali free zone, which had been incorporated a few months later. Any company with a trade license in a free zone needs to have office space in the same, and the Jebel Ali zone was not able at that moment to give us adequate office space. Hence we had to create another company in a different free zone where we were able to find the space we needed. Therefore for the first year we ended up having a one-room office—which we used only a few times as a meeting room—in the Jebel Ali free zone and the operating office in the DMCC (Dubai Multi Commodities Centre) Jumeira Lake Tower (JLT) free zone, where we had found the needed office space. Looking back it seems almost incredible that we had to struggle to find an office in a moment when Dubai was booming and the demand both for residential and commercial space was far superior to the offer. In those days one had to decide on the spot about renting or buying a property, since the day after it could have already been rented or sold, or the price might have increased.

The building where we took our office was one of the first towers to be completed in the free zone: today the JLT free zone has many commercial

---

[19] Gangal, N. 2009. "Yas Island Named World's Leading Tourism Project," *Arabian Business*, November 11, 2009. Available at http://www.worldtravelawards.com/award-middle-easts-leading-tourism-development-project-2011.

towers, some fully or partly occupied and operating; others completed but not yet commissioned for lack of possible tenants; others being constructed. The area had been planned in the pre-crisis years, whereas after the financial meltdown in 2008, the effects of which hit the economy of the UAE in 2009, the consequences on the real estate market were devastating. In 2010, when we renewed the lease for our office, we agreed on a price that was 40 percent of the one originally fixed in 2007. We also had a similar experience in searching for residential accommodations. Our budget for the Dubai operations had been presented and approved based on the prices of December 2006: a few months later, prices had increased by almost 30 percent and we were not able to find anything acceptable within the budget limits. However after the crisis we could renegotiate the rents by over 20 percent. Furnishing the office, hired only as a shell, was a rather lengthy process. One had to obtain several permits from the free zone, the Environmental Health and Safety Authority, the Central Engineering Department, the building management as well as from the owner of the property. Work authorizations have become even more difficult today when the building is in operation and close to full occupancy; apart from the said permits and authorizations for the vendors to enter the building and bring or remove materials from the same, further approvals from various authorities are to be obtained.

Moving from New Delhi to Dubai was very difficult but also very easy. The Indian capital, and in general the Indian nation, is so rich in arts, culture, history, and natural beauties that the comparison with any other "young" country would almost be unfair. India is the world's largest democracy and its people are hospitable, helpful and tolerant. The low labor cost allows comforts such as abundant domestic help which are unthinkable in the West. The fact of having spent almost nine years of my life in such a country, having married an Indian woman and conceived our first child there made my transfer even more difficult. The first comment from my wife on a look-and-see trip in 2006 after landing in Dubai was literally: *questo posto non mi piace* (I do not like this place); it was spoken in a well-articulated Italian accent—rather unusual since we normally communicate in English—with the clear purpose of highlighting her disappointment. We took some time to find the place that would have become our home. We were looking for a house in New Dubai, the part of the city on the southern coast beyond Bur Dubai. Most of the nice residential houses are in the areas called Jumeira and Uum Suqueim, but for the kind of house we had in mind the prices of these areas were unaffordable at that point in time.

After visiting well over 50 places, among which were some horribly decorated ones with sinks in the drawing room or heavy-colored stain glasses at

Chapter 9: Settling Down in the Middle East | 139

all windows, we had short-listed two houses, one in Uum Suqueim and the other in a new area called Al Barsha. Eventually we selected this last, which was larger and even cheaper, though the surroundings were not as developed as in the other area. The first night spent in the house was quite a shock: we were woken up by some loud voices in the heart of the night and got rather scared. It took us a few seconds to realize that the "shouting" was nothing but the call to prayer coming from the nearby mosques. We could not sleep anymore, worried for our future nights but glad to have signed only a one year lease. However, after a few weeks we would no more hear the early morning prayers and were able to peacefully sleep throughout the night. Another episode, on the occasion of an invitation to the wedding of our landlord's son, which occurred a few months later, reminded us that we were now living in a Muslim country. Though the card mentioned only my name I thought that the invite was extended to my spouse too: that would have been the norm in India. Not being familiar with the local customs but unwilling to arrive empty handed, my wife and I reached the reception with a large flower bouquet.[20] The first surprise was that the reception was only for men. Luckily the venue was a hotel, so I could drop my wife in the lobby and join the party. The second one came at the moment of joining the reception. I was carrying the flowers with both my hands and trying to find the right person to hand them over, but none of the hosts seemed to be willing to receive them. It took a few minutes before one of the participants, possibly a friend of the hosts, saw my embarrassment and came to my rescue by picking up the bouquet and allowing me to shake hands with the hosts. The third surprise was the humongous amount of food served; I realized later on that this happens quite often when Arab people host parties. The invitees were between 100 and 150, but the food would have sufficed for at least 400.

Life in Dubai turned out to be much less vibrant and interesting than in New Delhi. On the other hand driving on six lanes well-asphalted roads, having no power cut whatsoever, seamless telephone and internet connections, and a smooth and relaxed drive to the office was making quite a difference in the daily routine; particularly when coming from a city depending on generators, with congested roads that made driving difficult and jerky, and beggars that continuously knocked on your window. Despite the state-of-the-art road system, driving in Dubai is not the easiest of experiences one can have in the emirate. Only some privileged citizens from a restricted list of countries

---

[20] Due to the scarcity of water, flowers are very expensive in the UAE. The starting price for a small bouquet is US$ 50.

can avail of the benefit of obtaining a driving license by exchange: in this case one has to undergo only a sight test and present his valid driving license to get, in less than half an hour, the UAE one. Those who are not amongst the privileged have to attend a minimum of ten costly driving lessons before adventuring in a theory and practice exam, very unlikely to be passed at the first attempt, hence requiring more driving classes. The whole process usually takes no less than two months and not negligible expenses, which are to some extent part of the hidden costs of living in a (formally) tax-free nation. Once the deserved license is obtained the adventure of driving in an ever changing city starts.

I have yet to find a reliable GPS device that can safely take me to a destination in the new Dubai, where almost every month roads are closed, diverted, enlarged, re-opened, and again closed due to the continuous evolution of the urban landscape. One needs to rely on one's own knowledge and on the road signs, not the clearest and well displayed part of the city infrastructure. The fact that distances are substantial in a city that is spread in length for over 50 kilometers has led to the creation of wide and long roads where the average speed is rather high compared to the typical urban centre.[21] In order to help maintain smooth traffic flows, u-turns are usually forbidden on large roads: hence a distraction may cost you 10 additional miles to get back to the missed crossroad, or take you to a remote and unknown place from where it becomes very hard to find the right direction again. Apart from the mentioned difficulties there are hazards caused by the speeding craze, often by spoiled children of rich and influential locals. They are not concerned about safety or speed limits and cruise at outrageous speeds with their brand new Ferrari while zig-zagging on the main commuting roads. They do not care about the speed cameras, very frequent in Dubai, nor about the police, who may be taken into confidence by their networked fathers. At times one gets to hear about road accidents being met by youth while driving around 250 kilometers per hour on ordinary roads. Such behavior pushes the emirate's police to be very strict about speed limits (for common people) and even stricter on drinking and driving. Dubai is not "dry" like some other emirates, and is in general a tolerant place. Drinking is allowed with some restrictions but there is zero tolerance for drinking and driving. The enforcement of such rules is becoming stricter and stricter, to the point that people caught driving even the morning after a drinking night, when traces of alcohol may still be detectable, have to pay for the consequences to the extent of being jailed and deported.

---

[21] I recorded an average of 43 km/hr while driving in Dubai, well above the average speed of 20–25 km/hr usually recorded in a city like Rome or New Delhi.

Chapter 9: Settling Down in the Middle East | 141

This has justified the creation of a service called "safe driver," which sends drivers to bring people home in their own car at any time of the day and night for the cost of approximately US$ 40. The alternative is using taxis, usually cheap and reliable, apart from Thursday nights, when they become absolutely untraceable. Twice I had to go to the airport on a Thursday and had a confirmed taxi booking at a certain time in the evening, but no taxi showed up. I complained to the local Road Authority[22] but they simply told me in an apologetic way that no taxis were available to take my call. There is certainly scope for improvement in such booking service, which has already taken place since the summer of 2012. In general the quality of life in Dubai is good. Those who love the sun are happy to see it shining almost every day of the year, apart from the rare showers during at best 10 days in the winter months or the few days of dust storms, when the skyline becomes almost surreal and it is difficult to walk without adequate protection. Sea lovers can swim throughout the year in relatively clean and blue waters with long, white, and well-organized beaches. Power is reliable and relatively cheap: on the other hand water is scarce and expensive. In a usual bill of the DEWA, the electricity and water authority, the cost of water for a house is almost equivalent to that of the electricity. In such bills there is another bit of hidden cost of living, since a tax of 5 percent of the rent paid is levied, normally on the highest paid rent. After we managed to renegotiate the annual rent as a consequence of the crisis, we applied to the DEWA for the proportional reduction of the tax but we never succeeded in obtaining it. The residence visa cost is another of such hidden ones. Once it was renewable every three years but recently it has been made renewable annually. In order to obtain it one has to undergo medical tests in designated government hospitals. The overall costs of the process can be between US$ 2,000 and 3,000 per renewal. When visas are changed identity cards need to be changed also, with consequent investments of time and money.

Cars and vehicles in general are very affordable in the UAE compared to other countries. I bought my motorbike here for an amount that is 40 percent of its cost in India and 70 percent of the price I would have paid in Italy. However, every year one has to submit the vehicle for revision to authorized centers where it is inspected and released with an annual registration renewal. Also in this case there is a certain investment in time (one to two hours) and money (approximately US$ 100), which can vary according to the modality of procedure selected (for the VIP one it takes usually 20 minutes and

---

[22] The RTA—Road and Traffic Authority—which is the main taxi supplier in Dubai.

hundred and fifty dollars). Despite the hidden costs just mentioned, the fact that there is no income tax plays a major role in attracting companies and individuals to the country. Emirates like Sharjah and Ras Al Khaimah have started free zones with cheaper annual fees and are actively trying to attract foreign investors; Dubai was the fore-runner in the free zones, considering its strive, driven by the lack of long-term oil reserves, to diversify its economy. The idea of creating specific areas of the emirates dedicated to specialized industries (egs, Media City, Knowledge Village, Healthcare City, etc.) and the effort to attract the largest world companies with special incentives such as subsidized office rents shows the long-term vision of the rulers of the country. They had clear in their minds that such world-renowned brands were the key to creating an international image and working environment. The building of a state-of-the-art infrastructure was fundamental for this goal and translated into massive investments that have completely changed the landscape of some cities.

A major difference I have noticed between working in the UAE compared to working in India is the substantially lower level of corruption. Usually red tape and corruption go hand in hand in emerging countries, since it is often within the rusty mechanisms of a heavy bureaucracy that corrupt individuals take advantage of delays and difficulties to obtain bribes. Not so in the UAE, where, despite the façade of hassle-free administrative institutions, red tape does exist at several levels. This is possibly a by-product of the large intervention of the State in the economy, typical of most of the Arab world. However this does not coexist with corruption, perhaps due to the fact that public employees are well-paid and often have more benefits than those working in the private sector. This is evident when comparing the Indian Police with that of the UAE, the former being generally poorly educated, inefficient, and corrupt while the latter is more educated, helpful, and usually kind.

Not all that glitters is gold in the UAE. There are also less known aspects of this nation, clearly not publicly displayed or highlighted by the local media. The fact that such sides do not have visibility already says something about the freedom of speech in the country, which, not being a democracy, does impose some freedom restrictions. The press is censored and biased in favor of the governing elite. The protection of labor for some categories hardly exists: the few rare times that distressed workers have tried public protest for more than justified reasons have seen the authorities repressing the same and their employers taking actions against the initiatives. Laws and regulations may be changed overnight and there is hardly any possibility of appealing. In disputes with public institutions courts tend to favor these rather than individuals; in disputes among individuals there is a bias towards locals against foreigners. Many of these issues are highlighted in an article appearing in a British newspaper in 2009.[23] Last but not the least, Dubai, like the largest part of the Arab nations, is a sort of autocratic regime, though an enlightened one. If we look at what the city was 40 years ago, the progress made also at social level is huge. Local residents, who did not have water or electricity and had to go for higher education to Kuwait or India, have today many facilities such as free or subsidized housing and utility costs; many local and international universities are now present in the country and for locals education is paid till the highest levels.

Emiratis can also avail of free healthcare to the extent of being sent abroad in case of necessity. Despite the fact that they do not have much of a saying in the ruling of the country, they do support their own government and their rulers. Moves towards a greater involvement of the citizens have also been made in the recent past, with the introduction of representative elections for 50 percent of the Federal National Council. "Democracy is no panacea for all ills," as a specialist writer on Middle East affairs wrote in a local paper in a very well written and actual article,[24] considering the context of the Arab Spring. "Any system that can provide people with a decent standard of living, homes, jobs, healthcare, education, and essential freedoms can be an option," the writer stated. One could argue about the extent of the freedoms in the UAE, but having lived here for over five years I must say that I do not feel particularly constrained. One needs to keep in mind that, despite its secular and liberal stand, the UAE are still an Islamic nation: hence, expatriates need to respect the local religion and the mores of the place. Not rarely does one read in the papers about foreigners sent to jails for acts that in their country would be considered normal, but here are regarded as very offensive. Among these are kissing in public places; indulging in close contact with the partner; even showing the middle finger to someone. Recently a lady has been jailed for 30 days having made this gesture to a policeman. The British Consulate has been quite active trying to educate its own resident community about such issues, since a few Britons caught in such circumstances have been jailed and subsequently deported. Also in this case, it is just a matter of being culturally sensitive and respectful. A recent survey on world happiness and satisfaction

---

[23] "The Dark Side of Dubai," *The Independent*, April 7, 2009. Available at http://www.independent.co.uk/opinion/commentators/johann-hari/the-dark-side-of-dubai-1664368.html?mid=556.
[24] Linda S. Heard, "Democracy Is No Panacea for All Ills," *Gulf News*, April 10, 2012, Dubai Edition.

quoted in a local newspaper[25] ranked the UAE at the 17th place, and first among the Arab Nations. Dubai's ruler, Sheik Mohammed Al Maktum, was quoted to have said that "the government saw as its duty to provide decent living standards and assure the prosperity of all citizens."[26] Considering the overall picture of life in Dubai I am convinced that the positive sides outnumber the negative ones and the city state can offer comfortable life standards and a convenient working environment, together with a cosmopolitan flavor rarely found in other parts of the world.

Arab Spring and the Middle East

The end of 2010 witnessed the start of an unprecedented wave of unrest that would dramatically change the face of the Arab World. The sparkle happened in December 2010 in a small town in Tunisia with the desperate gesture of a young street vendor[27] who set fire to himself to protest against the harassment of the police which had confiscated his goods and humiliated him. He died after a few days and, soon after the incident, people started flooding the streets to give voice to feelings that had been repressed for decades. After one month from the incident Tunisia's President Ben Ali, who had ruled for over 20 years, was forced to flee the country and seek refuge first in France, which refused him, and eventually in Saudi Arabia. What would have remained an isolated incident only 20 years ago, thanks to the power of the World Wide Web, social networks, and the mobile communication technology, became an unstoppable tide of riots, first in the north African countries and later in the Middle East. Algeria, Egypt, and Libya followed: the masses, driven by the youth, expressed their anger against governments who had oppressed them for years, deprived them of fundamental rights, repressed their freedoms and dignity, and failed to redistribute the wealth of the nation concentrated in the hands of the ruling elites. For a long time it had been argued that the spread of the third wave of democracy around the world had stopped at the

---

[25] Mohammed, "Citizens' Happiness at Centre of Our Policies," *Gulf News*, Dubai Edition, April 8, 2012. The article quotes a UN survey, whereas we have found a similar survey done by the Columbia University, the Earth Institute, on March 2012. Available at http://www.earth.columbia.edu/sitefiles/file/Sachs%20Writing/2012/World%20Happiness%20Report.pdf.
[26] See note 25.
[27] Mohamed Bouazizi was his name, and the incident had happened in the town of Sidi Bouzid.

borders of the Arab World and that the Arab political system had stagnated due to the lack of any major political reform.[28] What were the causes of such tumultuous events called the Arab Spring that brought about the toppling of four autocratic regimes in one year? To better understand them we need some background information about the region. The last 40 years have seen a major change in the demographics of the Middle East and North Africa (MENA) region: a high birth rate has created a large base of young people who have progressively entered the work force. During the years 1996–2006 this has grown annually three times as much as in the rest of the developing world, thus creating the "largest rates of youth unemployment in the world. In Jordan for instance more than 70 percent of unemployed are under the age of 29 years."[29]

Together with its getting younger, this part of the world has become more and more educated: during the last 20 years of the twentieth century the

Table 9.1 Unemployment around the World

Region	Total unemployment (thousands), 2011	Youth unemployment rate (percent), 2011
CIS/Central & East Europe	15,513	17.7
Dev. Economies & the EU	43,547	17.9
East Asia	35,538	8.8
Latin America & the Caribbean	20,527	13.3
Middle East	7,119	26.2
North Africa	7,786	27.1
South Asia	25,024	9.9
S.E. Asia and the Pacific	14,577	13.4
Sub-Saharan Africa	27,599	12.8

Source: ILO, Global Employment Trends 2012.

---

[28] Abdullah Al Shayji, "Arab Spring Impacts Gulf Politics More Than Its People," *Gulf News*, March 5, 2012, Dubai Edition.
[29] A. Malik and B. Awadallah, "The Economics of Arab Spring," CSAE paper, December 2011.

Middle East, starting from a very low base, recorded the fastest education rise among any other region in the world.[30] While similar demographic trends were recorded also in other emerging countries like the Asian ones, where structural reforms generated huge economic opportunities and the growth of a vast middle class, in the MENA region the economic structure of the nation state did not change to adapt to the demographic evolution. The lack of economic reforms did not create adequate opportunities for young people, resulting in a mismatch between the jobs' demand and offer and reducing the hopes for social mobility. In 2009 the global youth unemployment recorded its largest annual increase; in 2010 it was at 12.8 percent, against the global adult unemployment rate of 4.8 percent.[31] Compared to these figures the unemployment rates of Middle East and North Africa in 2010 were 25.5 and 23.8, respectively; one year later in 2011, as a consequence of the effects of the Arab Spring on the economies of these areas, the rates had reached 26.2 and 27.1.[32] Even more striking in these regions is the female youth unemployment, reaching 39.4 percent in the Middle East and 34.1 percent in North Africa.

The above data provide the explanation of the discontent among a better educated youth across the regions: they were connected through the social networks and became the driving force behind the Arab Spring, causing radical political changes. Protest happened not only in North Africa but also in the Middle East, namely in Bahrain, Oman, Yemen, and eventually in Syria. While the local government with the help of forces from the GCC managed to suppress the protests in Bahrain, Yemen's President A. Saleh was eventually forced to step down in February 2012, one year since the first riots. While this book is being written Syria's rebellion is still going on. The death toll of this was estimated by a human rights organization[33] to have crossed 40,000 people by November 2012. It is interesting to notice that the nations where the protests have eventually ended up toppling the governments[34] are those where one of two pillars of the Arab model of preserving social order, that is,

---

[30] See note 29.
[31] See UN Report, *Gulf News*, February 7, 2012, page 26, Dubai Edition.
[32] See ILO, Global Employment trend as reported in Gulf News, February 7, 2012, page 26. Dubai Edition.
[33] The Syrian Observatory for Human Rights on November 23, 2012. Available at http://www.globalpost.com/dispatch/news/regions/middle-east/syria/121123/syrian-death-toll-over-40000-says-rights-group.
[34] With the exception of Algeria, and we explain why a few lines later.

repression and redistribution,[35] has not been implemented or maintained. Tunisia and Egypt are countries relatively devoid of natural resources but with abundant labor resources, at that time rather disappointed by the high unemployment rates and decades of repression. Libya has abundant natural resources but the wealth coming from them has not been redistributed among the people. While its leaders for 40 years had secured billions of dollars in foreign countries for themselves, the common man could not afford to pay the increasing prices of basic food for his family.

In June 2012 the people of Egypt elected their new democratically elected President: M. Mursi, a US-trained engineer won a close presidential run off[36] to become the first Islamist to be elected in this position. His victory and the consequent defeat of the candidate that had had a major role in the previous regime, highlights the will of the majority of Egyptians to turn the page to the past. In Yemen, where over 40 percent of the population lived below the poverty line, people protested for their economic conditions, unemployment as well as the government proposal to perpetuate a regime[37] which had lasted too long. In many years of ruling President Saleh had also concentrated among members of his family military, civil and economic power, and wealth. This had alienated almost "all relevant political and social groups within his own ruling party, the opposition parties, the military and security institutions and society at large."[38] Like in Tunisia, Egypt, and Libya, where the rulers had put their own interests ahead of those of the people, exasperating the increasingly poor masses, in Yemen such a mistake was probably the most critical factor in the collapse of Saleh's regime.

Interestingly other countries in North Africa and the Middle East, though initially shaken by protests, did not experience the drastic changes taking place in the mentioned countries. That is the case of Algeria, where riots did happen in December 2010 for a few months. This country is rich in natural resources, particularly gas and oil, but its people do not benefit from the same and from the rising price of hydrocarbons. "It continues to lack just

---

[35] See note 29.

[36] He obtained 51.7 percent votes against his rival A. Shafiq, former Prime Minister during Mubarak's rule.

[37] An additional reason for the protest was Saleh's attempt to unilaterally change the electoral law and amend the constitution.

[38] See A. Al-Faqhi, "The Yemen Uprising: Imperatives for Change and Potential Risks (ARI)," Real Istituto Elcano, March 21, 2011, http://www.realinstitutoelcano.org/wps/portal/rielcano_eng/Content?WCM_GLOBAL_CONTEXT=/elcano/elcano_in/zonas_in/ari58-2011.

about everything, be it housing, health, or jobs, and what it does possess is deficient and requires rebuilding."[39] Also in this case repression marked the history of the country, but not wealth redistribution. However, differently from the other countries, Algeria had been torn by a civil war for over 10 years till a relatively recent past, a conflict that had left well over 100,000 dead and missing. Such facts were a deterrent for the population that did not certainly have a strong appetite for rebellions anymore. Apart from this there was neither a cohesive and strong political opposition in the country that could join the youth riots, nor a strong link between the capital, where the initial demonstrations had happened, and the provinces. Furthermore, the regime managed to bribe the military by increasing their salary by 50 percent retrospectively for three years so as to ensure their loyalty in the occasion of the riots.[40] Therefore the riots did not continue after April 2011.

In the Middle East—apart from Syria—only Bahrain and Saudi Arabia, and marginally Oman, were hit by the Arab Spring. Oman saw riots in the port city of Sohar in February 2011, where hundreds of demonstrators demanded jobs and an end to corruption. Oman's Sultan Qaboos swiftly responded by raising government salaries, increasing the minimum wages by 40 percent and unemployment benefits to almost US$ 400 a month (150 reals). He also sacked 12 cabinet ministers a few weeks after the unrest subsided.[41] The sultanate has, however, good record in terms of health, education and income. Its Sultan even granted women the right to vote and stand for elections as early as 1994 and today Oman has three female cabinet ministers.[42] The country has been leading a smart foreign policy, trying to balance his links with Iran while being an active member of the Gulf Cooperation Council (GCC).[43] In an extraordinary GCC ministerial meeting held in the Saudi capital of Riyadh in March 2010, the UAE Foreign Minister pledged on behalf of the Gulf Alliance US$ 20 billion in special assistance to Oman and Bahrain as part of an effort to help stabilize social unrest.[44] No intervention was necessary in Oman. The Bahrain situation was different, where 2,000

---

[39] Rabah Gheezali, "Why Has the Arab Spring Not Spread to Algeria?" *Huff Post World*, April 3, 2011, http://www.huffingtonpost.com/rabah-ghezali/why-has-the-arab-spring-n_b_844182.html

[40] Source: Why Has the Arab Spring Not Spread to Algeria, quoted above.

[41] Sigurd Neubauer, "How the Arab Spring Skirted Oman," *Huff Post World*, December 13, 2011.

[42] Source: How the Arab Spring Skirted Oman, quoted above.

[43] GCC comprises Bahrain, Oman, Kuwait, Qatar, Saudi Arabia, and the UAE.

[44] Source: How the Arab Spring Skirted Oman, quoted above.

troops, the majority of which was sent by Saudi Arabia, entered the neighbor nation as part of a force operating under the aegis of the GCC. Here we start seeing among the Arabian Gulf countries the largest and richest, Saudi Arabia, trying to ensure the role of supervisory power vis-à-vis its neighbours. In 2011 Saudi had been watching with unease as Bahrain's Shiite[45] majority staged weeks of protests against a Sunni monarchy, fearing that if the protesters prevailed, Iran, its bitter regional rival, could expand its influence and inspire unrest elsewhere. What could be seen as a tail of the Arab Spring happened in Jordan in October 2012, when anti-government demonstrators took to the road in Amman, led by the largest opposition party, the Islamic Action Front, to demand political reforms. Once again the influence of the Muslim Brotherhood which has emerged as the winner in other Arab Springs hit-states is driving the change in a country where the movement had been so far rather subdued. A day before the demonstration King Abdullah dissolved the parliament and called for early elections. A transitional government was to be created to oversee the elections due by the year-end.[46] Looking at the wider region, in the post-World War II era its geopolitics has been dominated by a balance of power among the three most important nations, namely Iran, Iraq, and Saudi Arabia. During the Iran–Iraq war of the 1980s most of the Gulf States sided with Iraq, some remained neutral,[47] but Saudi Arabia clearly supported Iraq, accentuating even more the rivalry with Iran.

After the USA led the war with Saddam Hussein, Iraq lost its regional influence in the delicate equilibrium of the area; the stand-off between Saudi Arabia and Iran appeared more and more evident. Also, other Sunni states started sensing a growing influence in the area of the Shiite dominated Iran, particularly since Iran seemed to be able to mould the post-USA era of Iraq. When elections in this country were decided to be held, Saudi Arabia's Sunni monarchy worked in the background to protect the Sunni minority while

---

[45] The distinction between Sunnis and Shiites is the major diversification present within the members of the worldwide Islamic community. The original schism happened soon after the death of Prophet Muhammad and was caused by different opinions about his legitimate successors. Over time the main difference has become the importance of the role of Imams among the two groups. Sunnis are the majority (80/90 percent of the total) and Shiites are mainly concentrated in Iran, Bahrain, Pakistan, and few other countries.

[46] See Osama Al Sharif, "Jordan's Politics in Cross-hairs," *Gulf News*, October 8, 2012, Dubai Edition.

[47] Interestingly Dubai kept supporting Iran, due to its trade relation with the neighbor nation. Even today in Dubai live a considerable number of Iranians, many of whom keep on doing business from here with their native country.

Iran dialoged with the Shiite groups and the two major Kurdish parties. "Iraq's March 2010 elections seemed to indicate that Iran's efforts had paid off. Immediately after the disputed elections, three of the top four candidates turned up in Tehran for 'consultations' with Iranian officials."[48] Though it is not clear how Iraq will eventually re-emerge as a key player in the region, the cold treatment by most Sunni Arab states of the Shiite-dominated government of Prime Minister Nouri al Maliki seems to have had the effect of pushing this nation even closer towards Iran.[49] In March 2012 an Arab League summit was held in Baghdad and marked a tangible sign of the potential re-emergence of the country in the geopolitical scenario of the area. Though the summit had low attendance, partly for security reasons and partly to reflect the disapproval of Iraq's marginalization of the minority Sunni community, the event set the tone for a more important fact to happen in 2013, the taking of the Arab League chairmanship by Iraq. Perhaps during that period the relationship between Arab countries and Iraq may improve. Saudi Arabia has so far consistently refused to deal with the Iraqi Prime Minister, even more after the refusal of this last to condemn Syrian President Al Assad for the violent suppression of the riots.[50] An interesting article by a British author and journalist[51] states that Saudi Arabia, after quelling some riots in its eastern province allegedly fomented by a "foreign country,"[52] acted behind the scene in the Arab Spring. They started with offering refuge and refusing to extradite the deposed Tunisian leader; had a strong role in guiding the Muslim Brotherhood to power in Egypt; hosted the injured Yemen President; had a leading role in the repression in Bahrain.

By the end of 2011 Saudi had out-maneuvered its rival Iran. In the ongoing Syria crisis, Riyadh was quick to withdraw its ambassador to Damascus and condemn the crackdown on Syrian people, though forgetting that they also had crushed their own people's riots just a few months earlier. A strong variable in the future of the region will be the outcome of the Syria crisis. Here

---

[48] Afshin Molavi, "Iran and the Gulf States," *The Iran Primer*, The USA Institute of Peace. Available at http://iranprimer.usip.org/resource/iran-and-gulf-states.
[49] See Meghan L. O'Sullivan, "Iraq Can Re-emerge as Key Player," *Gulf News*, March 31, 2012, Dubai Edition.
[50] See Roula Khalaf, "A Setback for the Resurgent Country," *Financial Times*, reprinted by *Gulf News*, April 8, 2012, Dubai Edition.
[51] John R. Bradley, "Saudi Arabia's Invisible Hand in the Arab Spring," *Foreign Affairs*, October 13, 2011, http://www.foreignaffairs.com/articles/136473/john-r-bradley/saudi-arabias-invisible-hand-in-the-arab-spring.
[52] Likely referring to Iran.

not only is the influence of Saudi and Iran felt in the evolving scenario, since the strategic location of the country with part of its coast along the Mediterranean Sea and bordering with Iraq, Turkey, Lebanon, Israel, and Jordan makes it an important hub between the Levant and the Middle East. What had started in 2011 as one of the Arab Spring's pro-democracy protest and has eventually ended up being a violent civil war between the ruling government and the opposition rebels, now seems to have the potential to expand beyond the Syrian borders and destabilize the region. A worrying step towards such a scenario happened in October 2012 when some mortar shells from Syria hit Turkey. The episode was said to have been accidental and killed five Turkish civilians. However when a second shell hit land near a plant belonging to the Turkish Grain Board (TMO), not far from Akcakala, where the first incident had happened, Turkey started retaliating and fired some shells against Syrian military targets across the border. The Turkish Prime Minister also warned Syria that its country would not shy away if provoked.[53]

The other important player in such a crisis is Russia, which has been offering its continued support to the ruling regime, possibly in order to reassert its role and influence in the region. Russia, together with China, vetoed a draft UN Security Council draft resolution calling on President Bashar to step down[54]; there are rumors about Russia keeping on supplying arms to the regime and having reinforced their presence in the naval base of Tartus established under a Russia-Syria Treaty of 1971. In fact the Arab Spring has secluded Russia from the region, since Lybia, an old time ally of Russia, seems now closer to the West and Egypt. Even Iraq, a former ally, may establish different alliances in future. Throughout the Iran nuclear issue[55] Russia has supported the country by helping build nuclear power plants, trying to mitigate the international sanctions against it while also having a very active role in the negotiations with the UN representative Nations. Here Moscow, apart from the geopolitical influence, has also economic interests, since it had been selling to Teheran fuel for the nuclear plant. In the summer of 2010 the heads of the nuclear authorities of the two countries held a joint conference on

---

[53] See Nick Craben, "Crisis Deepens as Turkey Fires More Retaliatory Strikes at Syria," *Daily Mail*, October 8, 2012, http://www.dailymail.co.uk/news/article-2213980/Syria-Turkey-clash-Crisis-deepens-Turkey-fires-retaliatory-strikes-fourth-consecutive-day.html.

[54] See O. Al Sharif, "Syria is Battleground for Russia and US," *Gulf News*, April 9, 2012, Dubai Edition.

[55] The alleged enriching of uranium for a nuclear bomb, though Iran keeps on stating that they are for energy purposes, and the threat from Israel to bomb the facilities in the country.

occasion of the initiation of the enriched fuel supply to the plant of Bushehr, in Southern Iran.

In April 2012 talks between Iranian officials and the so-called 5 plus group[56] were held in Istanbul and, also thanks to ground work done by Russia, were said to have been successful. With V. Putin back to the Presidential seat, it is likely that a stronger stand against the growing influence of the USA in the region will be taken. And all this may further complicate the Saudi-Iran stand-off and the overall Middle East geopolitical scenario. The UAE have been rather neutral in such a confrontation, since on the one hand they share with Saudi Arabia the membership of the GCC, the union of the Arab States in the Arabia Peninsula; on the other hand, due to the geographic proximity, they have had for many years strong economic ties with Iran. A dispute over three islands off the coast of the Ras al Khaimah emirate[57] occupied by Iran in 1971 and claimed by the UAE has recently been reignited by a visit of the Iranian President to the islands in the spring of 2012. In case a solution is not found, the UAE may distance itself from Iran and rather take sides with Saudi Arabia.

---

[56] USA, Russia, China, England, France plus Germany. The positive outcome of the talks was reported in an article by A. Safty entitled "Nethanyau War Aims Take a Hit," appearing in *Gulf News* (Dubai Edition) on April 23, 2012.
[57] Abu Mousa, Greater and Lesser Tunbs.

10

REAL ESTATE AND EMERGING MARKETS

An Expatriate's Perspective

One of the first priorities of an expatriate arriving in a new country is usually that of finding appropriate housing for him and his family. If he also has the task of setting up a new office, he would need to survey the commercial properties market. In case he is in charge of starting a green or brown field project he would then investigate the availability of industrial land or perhaps of already-existing factories for rent or sales. Therefore, be it for personal or professional reasons, expatriates need to get at least some idea about the real estate markets of their host country. What may happen is that at times, having been exposed to such a sector, expatriates start considering investing in it, particularly when the expatriation happens in countries where real estate may offer very good returns. This is often the case of emerging countries, in many of which the property market has been booming during the first decade of the new century. Such a surge has happened thanks to the fast economic growth leading to high demand for commercial and residential estates so as to accommodate the growth of the industrialized work-force. The consequent expansion of the middle classes of the same countries has also caused a higher demand for higher value assets. The progressive opening to foreign investments in several sectors, the fast growth of the population and the rapid urbanization happening in many such countries during the recent years have multiplied the value of real estate properties there.

An example of this is Russia, where, during the years 2000 to 2007, an incredible growth of the property market was recorded, "with secondary market prices skyrocketing by 436 percent while primary market prices rose 362 percent."[1] Rents of prime properties in central Moscow were and still remain, despite the recent slowdown, among the highest in the world. Another example is Brazil, where the estate market had been relatively stable during the last decade but has started growing soon after the global crisis in 2008. Two major events, the FIFA World Cup in 2014 and the Olympics in 2016, are providing a large stimulus to this market and have already attracted the attention of real estate investors. In 2009 Rio was one of the few cities to record an increase beyond 20 percent of prime rentals; in 2010 office vacancy rates were at 5 to 10 percent, rather low by current international standards, and rental values were rising.[2] The recent housing boom is challenging the government which needs to address a shortage of 6.3 million homes.[3] Real estate markets are booming not only among the BRICs but also in many other countries in Asia and Africa. It is extremely difficult to rent a decent three-bedroom apartment in one of the areas where usually expatriates live in Lagos,[4] the business capital of Nigeria, for less than US$ 5,000 per month, a price to which one needs to add the cost of utilities and maintenance. Prices of offices in the city of Luanda, Angola, were reported to be among the highest in the Middle East and Africa (MEA) region, well higher than cities such as Doha or Muscat.[5]

Therefore expatriates who are posted in emerging countries develop—not rarely—interest in the real estate sector and decide to invest in this. Many companies foresee that expatriates' accommodation cost be taken care of by the employer: in similar circumstances a good investment possibility for the employee would be that of buying the house in the host country where he

---

[1] See "Russia Housing Market Still Depressed," in *Global Property Guide*, September 30, 2011. Available at http://www.globalpropertyguide.com/Europe/Russia.

[2] Jones Lang Lasalle, "Global Market Perspective March 2010: A BRIC Built Recovery?" on http://www.joneslanglasalle.com/MediaResources/EU/Marketing/Global-Market-Perspective-March-2010_final.pdf.

[3] See G. Coppola and N. Brandt, "Brazil Housing Boom Forcing Switch to Private Market: Mortgages," *Bloomberg Businessweek*, April 10, 2012. Available at http://www.businessweek.com/news/2012-04-09/brazil-housing-boom-forcing-switch-to-private-market-mortgages.

[4] Such areas are Victoria Island and Ikhoy.

[5] See Cushman and Wakefield, "Emerging Markets: Africa and The Middle East Research," 2006, available on http://www.cushwake.com/cwglobal/jsp/kcReportDetail.jsp?Country=c14200228p&Language=EN&catId=100004&pId=c5100064p. Doha is the capital of Qatar, Muscat of Oman.

resides and renting it out to his company. Not all companies' policies accept such a possibility, but if the deal is agreed so that the rent paid is slightly below the market price it may end up being a win-win situation for both parties. Some companies, particularly the subsidiaries operating in emerging countries, grant house loans to their senior resources so as to enable them to eventually own the place where they live. Usually such provisions are meant as retention tools for local resources that would not otherwise be able to own a property; if they are also applicable to expatriates the investment opportunities in the host country may become even more interesting. Let us try to illustrate this with a simplified example. If the price of a house is 100 a buyer may be able to purchase this through a down payment of 20, while borrowing the balance of 80 through a bank loan. In this case the property will be mortgaged to the bank and the buyer may need to pay a yearly payment to the bank of 5 for 20 years (principal of 80 plus interest of 20). In case the expatriate buyer agrees with its company that he will rent out the property to the same for his own use for an annual rent of 5[6] or slightly less than that, he could use the rent money to repay the loan installment and exploit the benefit offered by the company to eventually own his residence in the host country. If he is posted somewhere else after a few years he may still find a tenant who could pay to him a rent equivalent to the loan installment. In case he can get a loan from his own company at a preferential interest rate, hence lowering the amount of the monthly installment, he may even be able to save some money out of the rent.

The example is oversimplified and in reality there could be additional expenses[7] and situations when the rent paid is lower than the installments. However what was described could be an opportunity worth considering by the expatriate. When evaluating possible investments one would need to carefully study the legal environment of the country as well as to ensure that the projected return on the investments justifies the risks linked to the same. Often the decision to invest in real estate in the host country is made after having lived there for some time, once risks and opportunities implied in the deal have been considered: a thorough check about the local property laws (e.g., on the possibility of full ownership for a foreign resident) is, however advisable. The choice of the right property to invest in would reduce the risks and

---

[6] Usually property would give a return on the investment of 5 percent or so, hence the mentioned rental price.

[7] For instance, the loan insurances or the common fees for the house if it is in a residential complex.

maximize the return on the investment. A safe option is to buy only premium properties built by the best developers in premium locations. Though the initial investment may be higher, the risk of major structural problems and consequent high maintenance costs may result in being significantly lower, while the chances of finding better tenants higher. When for budget constraints or lack of availability it is not possible to find premium properties in good locations, one should look at a property with distinguishing uniqueness, so as to be differentiated from the many others available in the market. The last but not the least element to consider is the time horizon of the deal: in case this is longer than the possible expatriate's stint in the country one would need to keep in mind the practicalities of managing the property from a remote location and plan about the best possible way to do so. It would be wise to diversify the typology of investments in real estates: one may consider not only residential but also commercial ones or even just lands, though in many countries there are restrictions upon foreign citizens' owning bare land. In a larger perspective it would also be preferable to invest in more than one country in order to balance the risks among the same. In terms of an overall investment portfolio one may look at keeping the real estate investments within a reasonable percentage of one's own total wealth, since such forms of investment may not be quickly liquidated in case of an unforeseen sudden need.

Investing in India

In the initial chapters of this book we talked about the fantastic economic growth of India during the new century. One of the governments ruling India during the years 2000s had created the motto "India Shining" to emphasize how the economic development of this nation was giving it a new shine in the new world economic and political order. The sustained GDP growth of over 7 percent during those years and the implications of such growth were the reasons behind the exponential surge of the real estate sector, which is expected to reach the size of US$ 180 billion by the end of the current decade.[8] Together with the GDP development, driven by the service sector and specifically the IT and Financial services, India experienced a rapidly growing urbanization that led to a strong demand for commercial estates—mainly office spaces—and an exponential demand for affordable houses. In view of the expected rapid evolution of the sector the Indian Government had well drafted the rules for the industry and this helped the rapid development of

---

[8] See "India Brand Equity Foundation", April 2010, www.ibef.org.

the same. Foreign Direct Investments up to 100 percent were allowed under the automatic route for most of the assets classes. Thanks to this, besides the large local players such as DLF,[9] Unitech, and Raheja, foreign developers have also invested in India from the Middle East (Emaar and Nakheel) and other countries, and large financial groups as Citigroup, Deutsche Bank, and Morgan Stanley have played a role in the development of the sector.

From a highly fragmented sector the industry has evolved into a semi-organized one: the national developers have a large presence across the country, but regional ones are aggressively expanding.[10] While in the past the developments had happened mainly in the large metropolitan areas of Delhi and NCR, Mumbai, and Bangalore, later on, with the shift of the services to the second tier cities such as Hyderabad and Pune, also these cities experienced a real estate boom. Even the most recent reports[11] suggest that in these cities the IT occupiers continue to expand and create demand both for commercial and residential spaces.

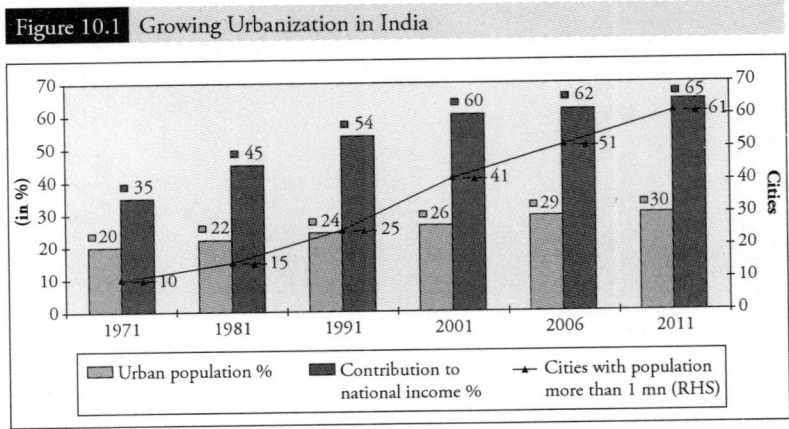

Figure 10.1 Growing Urbanization in India

Source: National Institute of Urban Affairs, UNDP, Ernst & Young analysis, as reported by IBEF.

---

[9] This is the same developer who built the new Gurgaon, the area described in the third chapter where the corporate office of Perfetti Van Melle India was located.
[10] See India Brand Equity Foundation mentioned earlier.
[11] Jones Lang Lasalle, "Global Market Perspective," fourth quarter 2012, February 2, 2012, http://www.joneslanglasalle.com/GMP/en-gb/Pages/Global-Market-Perspective-Global-Property.aspx.

When I learned that I would be moving from India I thought that leaving the country after so many years without taking advantage of the incredible growth of its real estate market would have been a pity. Therefore I started looking for a possible investment. Initially my idea was to find an apartment in one of the premium expatriate locations in South Delhi. With this objective in mind I started surveying the areas I liked in search of a suitable residential property. My idea when investing in a residence is that I should like it and possibly not mind living there in case at some point in time circumstances led me to do so. I visited a few locations such as Vasant Vihar, Shanti Niketan, and Malcha Marg. Located close to the Diplomatic Enclave these are usually considered among the most premium localities in South Delhi. After Amrita Shergil Marg and Golf Links, very central and elegant areas with hardly any available place and prices in the range of Hong Kong and Tokyo, those I was exploring were the best residential areas of the city, hence rather easy to rent out. However already at that time property prices had considerably increased—almost doubled—compared to the previous year, when I had started looking at the market, and a three bedroom apartment would have been available for over US$ 1 million. At that moment the price seemed to me far too high (though today a similar apartment would be sold for a price double that), since with the same amount one would have been able to find maybe a slightly smaller sized three bedroom apartment in a central area of Paris.

Since I had kept aside a certain budget for such investment I decided to change my searching scope and looked at an upcoming area of Delhi, the new business district of Gurgaon. Here prices were still in the range of what I intended investing, but many high-rise residential towers were being built in the heart of the business hub and the area was becoming a cement jungle. While dozens of offices and residences were under construction, the basic infrastructures were not being sized for such a wide development. Anybody with a pinch of forward vision would have perceived the danger of huge bottlenecks both in the traffic and in the power and water situation. I thought that I should try and find a place out of the central business district, in the vicinity of the same and along the expansion axis of the city. Since very many residential towers were coming up, I needed to find a differentiating element: eventually I found that in a complex of small town houses about fifteen minutes away from the main downtown New Gurgaon. It was a self-contained community of villas in a gated community immersed in the greenery with full power back-up, security, sport facilities, and a club house. As soon as I was shown the complex I felt that it was the right investment. The villas were just being handed over in that period, so the sales deed could happen in the span of a few days. Within one week I had paid the money, signed the deed, got it registered, and got the house key. It took some time to decorate the place and add a personal touch to it with some woodwork, lights, and bathroom fixtures. A few weeks after finishing the works I found a good opportunity to rent it out.

Recently I checked the resale value of the property and was pleased to know that, despite the slow-down due to the 2008–2009 crisis, I could easily sell it for three times its original value. A more "scientific" proof of the good investment choice was a report of the fourth quarter of 2011 from a renowned international real estate agency[12] stating that the average achievable selling price in Gurgaon for high segment residences had increased by 22 percent against the same period of the previous year. However not all investments in India are so successful and hassle free. In 2007, advised by some colleagues I had subscribed to an offer of a reputed company[13] who was to develop some land in Faridabad, a suburb of Delhi. I paid an initial token to book the plot while the rest of the payments should have followed at several stages of the project. I waited three years but no development happened. When even the same company hinted that the project would have not progressed due to the aftermath of the global financial meltdown I requested the reimbursement of the booking amount. For over one year I could not get any response from the developer, not even after writing to the Managing Director or calling him, since he refused to take my calls. Eventually I had to threaten them with a legal notice in order to recover the amount with the accrued interests.

A person known to me had another not very successful investment in a plot of land in the state of Uttarakhand, where he and a few partners had bought some plots of lands when it seemed that their value was bound to keep growing indefinitely. After a few years due to financial needs he got out of the investment and with difficulties he managed to recover the amount originally invested. Beside the market volatility when investing in a residential property in India one needs to be wary also of the reliability of the seller. It is not rare to find people who try to sell without being entitled to do so, at times even showing an apparently valid title deed. If one decides to buy directly from a well-reputed builder there should not be surprises in terms of title validity,

---

[12] Cushman & Wakefield, Marketbeat Residential Snapshot NCR, available at http://www.cushwake.com/cwmbs4q11/PDF/ncr_res_4q11.pdf.
[13] The company was Vipul, an Indian Group in Real Estate and facility management.

but delays in the deliveries and sub-optimal finishing may still happen. I had another interesting personal experience when I decided to build our holiday home in Goa. I had been searching for an old Portuguese house for a long time but had not been able to find one up to my expectations, when I met a broker who proposed to build one for me from scratch in cooperation with a local builder. I was hesitant since I would not want to have a modern-looking house but was eventually convinced to go ahead in the deal when I saw some of the houses in Portuguese style they had built. We agreed on the terms and conditions and signed the deal. Here I made the mistake of entering into a turn-key contract where I would buy the land and the house to be built on it and they were to deliver to me by a certain deadline a finished house with a few agreed specifications. Before signing I had done my due diligence both on the land and on the party, but despite this the building of the house would have taken time, effort, and frustration for me, my wife, and a friend who, living in Goa, had offered to help in the matter.

The first problems started with delays on the agreed timetable due to disputes between the builder and the village Panchayat.[14] The phases of payment for the project were structured so that at the casting of the first floor I would have already paid a large part of the due amount. This stage was achieved quite rapidly, but it was just soon after that casting that the alleged dispute had happened and the work had halted. The second surprise came when I visited the construction site for the first time and I realized that the plot I had bought had become much smaller, since a non marginal part of the same, well over 100 square meters, had been used to make a road on the back. While the builder had mentioned to me that part of the side plot would have been used for a road, nothing had been told to me about the back. When I requested explanations I was told that they had to do that in order to pacify the Panchayat and allow the work to go on. Due to this change, the layout of the plot had become more congested and needed some adjustments. Therefore we agreed to shift the swimming pool in an area that was to be left as a garden only. Prior to doing this they had to apply again to the Panchayat for the change of land use (from garden to building) for that area and this caused delay. It took several months after the works could start again to complete the shell of the house and begin work in the interior.

At that point the first problems of sub-standard finishing and material started. Possibly this was due to the fact that the delays had also impacted the

---

[14] The word literally means assembly of five. Such bodies represent units of administration at three levels: village, block, and district; they are formally called Gram Panchayat and are present as system of local governance in India and other countries in South Asia.

overall costs of the developer and the fixed amount indicated in the contract led them to try and maintain their margins by saving as much as possible on the materials. Eventually we agreed that I would have paid any "better" finishing I would have wanted: it would have meant extra costs for me but at least I could get the desired quality. Building a house in remote, even if I had an Italian friend on site supervising the works, turned out to be very difficult. Particularly in places like India, where it is hard to get good quality of finishing, the walls end up having bumps, the tiling work not being proper, the woodwork very tentative, and so on for other details. The last surprise came at the time of getting the final approval for the project completion, which would allow us to get possession of it and start living in the house. The process was taking a long time and again the developer blamed it on the Panchayat. As a déjà-vu experience they came up with the request of enlarging the side road from the current width of up to three or four meters, as it was supposedly indicated in the original project. Once more this implied a loss of additional land from my side, which I was eventually forced to accept in order to sort the issue out. Despite all this, from an investor's perspective also this opportunity did make sense: for the cost of a 50-square meter flat in the outskirts of Rome I was able to buy a villa with a built surface 10 times bigger on a large plot of land in one of the most sought-after tourist destinations in India.

Middle and Far East Opportunities

A recent report on cost of living from the Economist Intelligence Unit[15] states that out of the 10 most expensive cities in the world five are located in East Asia and two in Australia. Tokyo, Osaka Kobe, and Singapore rank at the 2nd, 3rd, and 9th place, respectively; Sidney and Melbourne at the 7th and 8th. The cost of the living index includes a number of indicators among which figures the housing cost. More specifically on the real estate residential properties, a ranking by the Global Property Guide[16] places Hong Kong, Singapore, and Tokyo at the 3rd, 5th, and 8th places respectively in terms of price per square meter for an apartment in a central area. Historically, such cities have hosted

---

[15] "Worldwide Cost of Living 2012," by EIU, available at http://www.eiu.com/public/thankyou_download.aspx?activity=download&campaignid=wcol2012.

[16] "World's Most Expensive Cities," on http://www.globalpropertyguide.com/most-expensive-cities, consulted on 25/4/2012.

among the world's most expensive homes, even though prices have had ups and downs during the years. Tokyo, for instance, experienced a severe asset bubble during the late 1980s, after two decades of continuous increases in prices of land.[17] Japan was affected by the global financial crisis and house prices in the main eight cities fell by 8 percent in 2009.[18] After a recovery in 2010, in the aftermath of the March 2011 earthquake, the average price of new Tokyo condominiums fell by 7.2 percent.[19] However, with a projected population of over 35 million people in 2020[20] and due to the strong space restrictions, the Tokyo real estate market—representing 70 percent of the Japanese one, the third world largest[21]—is bound to remain among the most expensive in the world. Even the Singapore market suffered after the financial crisis: its economy contracted 9.5 percent during the first quarter of 2009, and there was a 24.9 percent house price fall during the first half of the year.[22] However, in the subsequent half of the year, residential property prices surged almost 16 percent and the growth continued the next year to slow down only in 2011, also due to the economy being affected by the western economies' crises. Despite this, industry analysts still think that home owners can expect a 10–15 percent capital appreciation on their properties over the next five years.[23] Tokyo and Singapore are not located/cannot be considered in emerging countries, but I have mentioned them as benchmarks with other cities in such countries, such as Shanghai and Bangkok.

China experienced its first real estate boom in the early 1990s, as the consequence of housing reforms carried out in some cities.[24] Further reforms by the

---

[17] "From 1970 to 1980, land prices in Japan rose 200 percent (23.5 percent in real terms), and 238.5 percent in the six major cities (39.3 percent in real terms). Then during the 1980s, there was a 103 percent increase nationally (61.6 percent in real terms) and a 272.2 percent rise in the six major cities (196.4 percent in real terms)," see "Japanese House Prices Continue to Fall," http://www.globalpropertyguide.com/Asia/Japan/Price-History.

[18] Source: Japanese House Prices Continue to Fall, quoted above.

[19] Source: The Land Institute of Japan as reported by Global Property Guide on 25/1/2012.

[20] Source: East Asia Real Estate Investment Market 2011, by Nomura Research Institute, November 2011.

[21] Source: East Asia Real Estate Investment by NRI quoted above.

[22] Source: Global Property Guide, "Singapore Real Estate Price Surging," Nuwire Investor, December 4, 2009. http://www.nuwireinvestor.com/articles/singapore-real-estate-prices-surging-54181.aspx.

[23] "Real Estate Prices Stall in Singapore," Nuwire Investor, September 12, 2011, http://www.nuwireinvestor.com/articles/real-estate-prices-stall-in-singapore-57767.aspx.

[24] The cities were Shenzhen and Shanghai. Source: "China Real Estate Market in China Knowledge," http://www.chinaknowledge.com/Business/CBGdetails.aspx?subchap=4&content=21.

Chinese government in 1994 and 1998 "established the market mechanism in both housing production and housing consumption."[25] By the end of the twentieth century and the first years of the current one, the annual investment in housing in China increased by six times and almost every major city here saw house prices sky rocketing. In 2004, the government started issuing policies to regulate the housing industry in order to control soaring housing prices and discourage speculation.[26] A post-financial crisis stimulus package introduced in November 2008 by the government further fueled the growth of property prices.[27] Buyers took advantage of looser lending conditions and lower interest rates, and developers were able to easily get loans with the lowered capital requirements. In 2010, the government had to intervene again with market cooling measures by regulating more strictly mortgages and introducing new property taxes. Such measures, combined with increased interest rates and other inflation fighting ones, eventually caused a slowdown in the market. In spite of the continuous increase in prices per square meter in Shanghai—for comparable residential units—they are still half those of Tokyo, 40 percent of Singapore and 35 percent of those in Hong Kong. Considering that rental yields for similar properties in Shanghai are around 2.7 percent compared to the 2.9 of Singapore and 3.2 of Hong Kong, the Chinese city represents a more affordable investment opportunity among the mentioned ones. An even better investment opportunity in the Far East is Bangkok, where the price per square meter is less than half that of Shanghai and rental yields, around 6.5 percent, are almost two and a half time those of the Chinese metropolis.[28] Bangkok has remarkably improved its infrastructures during the last decades and today offers a quality of life not very different from the other large Asian metropolises, with a much lower overall cost of living.[29]

Investment opportunities are also there in the Middle East region. While some of these countries have been affected by the financial crisis and more

---

[25] Source: "Housing Policy and Finance in China: A Literature Review," prepared for U.S. Department of Housing and Urban Development by Lan Deng, Qingyun Shen, Lin Wang, November 2009, http://www.chinaplanning.org/Publications/Lan%20Deng%20-%20Housing%20Policy%20and%20Finance%20In%20China.pdf.

[26] Source: "Housing Policy and Finance in China: A Literature Review," quoted above.

[27] The package included reducing the property deed tax rate for first-time home buyers, certain stamp duty, and business tax exemptions.

[28] World most expensive cities quoted above on Global Property Guide mentioned above.

[29] A 2010 survey from Mercer ranked Hong Kong the 8th highest world city for cost of living for expatriates, Singapore the 11th, Shanghai the 25th, and Bangkok at the 121st slot; see "Global World Cost of Living" ranking on http://www.finfacts.ie/costofliving.htm.

Figure 10.2 Residential Properties: World's Most Expensive Cities

Rank	City/Country	Buying Price US$ Per Sq. M.	Price/Rent Ratio (x)	Rent per Month ($)	Gross Rental Yield
1	Monaco	53,226	58x	9,212	1.73 percent
2	London, UK	20,505	23x	8,830	4.31 percent
3	Hong Kong	19,323	31x	6,235	3.23 percent
5	Singapore	16,727	34x	4,905	2.94 percent
8	Tokyo	13,855	23x	5,993	4,33 percent
20	Shanghai, China	6,932	38x	1,841	2.66 percent
49	Bangkok, Thailand	3,300	15x	2,143	6.49 percent

Source: Global Property Guide.
Note: Based on the average for a 120 square meter apartment typically in a prime inner city area.

recently by the Arab Spring,[30] some markets seem to be recovering well and attracting the interest of investors. As mentioned earlier in these pages, the MENA region is experiencing a very high population growth and has a very young overall age profile. These factors drive the rate of household formation, and, consequently, the housing demand. Industry sources estimates that in Saudi Arabia one million new households will be created by 2015.[31] Among the very interesting residential property markets of the region emerges that of Jordan, with rental yields crossing 9 percent;[32] Lebanon with yields close to 4.7 percent; UAE with yields just below 7 percent, in between the mentioned two countries. In UAE there are two very distinct residential markets, one for nationals and one for expatriates. The first one deals also with subsidized housing and does not fully follow market movements. The second one for expatriates consists of two main segments, a very low level one mainly for construction workers, a business-to-business segment negotiated between developers and local employers, and a second one catering to the middle and upper-income expatriates. This is the segment attracting foreign investors.

---

[30] Oman and Bahrain are among these.
[31] Jones Lang Lasalle, "Why Affordable Housing Matters," available at http://www.joneslangla-salle-mena.com/ResearchLevel1/JLLMENA_Affordable percent 20Housing_2011.pdf.
[32] Source: Global Property Guide, http://www.globalpropertyguide.com/Middle-East/rent-yields.

While some of the smaller emirates like Ajman had tried following the development of Dubai and Abu Dhabi by launching large residential projects, only some of these have survived the 2008 financial crisis. I recently drove along the road passing through what was supposed to be a residential project for hundreds of thousands of people, costing billions of dollars. A large and modern-looking sales office and a few model houses are what actually ended up being built of that project. These structures are still there today and can be seen from the road: they look like cathedrals in the desert since all around them there is no sign of the huge complex that was to be constructed. It is useful to recall what had happened in the years past to have a better idea of what was behind projects like the one mentioned in Ajman.

During the year 2006–2007, the UAE and particularly Dubai, were literally going crazy with growth and developments. Europe seemed to have finally realized the existence of an ultra-modern place built in the desert hosting a number of architectural wonders and breaking new world records every year. In such a place making money was easy, life was good, and there were no taxes. The number of residents of Dubai was increasing by hundreds of thousands every year. With such a hunger for houses the market was clearly a landlord-driven one: rents were paid in advance for one full year and could increase by 10 or 20 percent every semester.[33] Sources reported that at the peak of such craze in Dubai there were between 15 and 25 percent of the world's tower cranes.[34] While this was an estimate and the actual percentage might have been lower, I do remember that at that moment in any part of Dubai where I was I could turn my head and see at least 15–20 cranes around me. The Dubai economy had been based on trade in the past and on oil later on. As already mentioned earlier, when this started depleting the emirate decided to replace it with tourism and other activities. Dubai aspired to become the financial hub of the Middle East through the creation of DIFC, a financial free zone with a separate jurisdiction, and the Dubai bourse.

The real estate sector became a very important part of the economy, around which a huge business revolved and thousands of jobs were created. The financial crisis in 2008–2009 drastically reduced the funds available in the market, caused the stalling of the whole financial system and the consequent collapse of the real estate market. People were used to buying properties with

---

[33] There was the theoretical possibility to appeal to a local authority if the landlord decided to be unreasonable and steeply increase the rent demanded, but the benchmark on which the decision would take place were market prices, and these were continuously escalating.

[34] See "Dubai's Forest of Cranes Grows Thin," *The National*, September 24, 2009, http://www.thenational.ae/news/uae-news/dubais-forest-of-cranes-grows-thin.

a minimum down payment, since banks used to finance up to 90 percent of their cost and sell them, either at the project stage or already built, a few weeks or months later at a higher price. With the credit crunch buyers disappeared; those who had purchased on credit to resell had to start re-paying the loans but could not find buyers ready to purchase the properties or tenants to rent them out. Thousand of defaulters left the country in financial disarray. Many of the developers went bankrupt and even Nakheel, the state-owned builder of the Palms and other gigantic projects, risked the bankrupt with the risk of dragging the Dubai Government into a solvency crisis. Their debts had to be re-negotiated and the emirate of Abu Dhabi is said to have intervened to bail out the highly indebted Dubai emirate.[35] After reaching the bottom in the first part of 2011, the Dubai residential property market started picking up again in 2012. With the economy again showing a moderate growth driven by trade, tourism, and the hospitality sector, the confidence of investors shows signs of having returned and the demand for high quality well located assets is showing signs of revival. Prime residential buildings are witnessing increases in price and rentals and are expected to further increase during 2012, whereas secondary locations are still suffering. With prices per square meter having declined up to 50 percent against the peak in 2008 but now showing a positive outlook, investments in residential prime locations are becoming more and more interesting, given the level of rental yields. Despite being in the heart of the region troubled by the Arab Spring, Dubai has to some extent benefited from the repercussions of the movement, since capitals (and also people) moving away from countries like Egypt and Syria have flown to the most stable nation in the region, helping revive its economy and the property market.

---

[35] This is said to have been the reason why the Burj skyscraper mentioned above, which was to be called Burj Dubai, was instead at the moment of its inauguration in 2010 renamed Burj Khalifa, in honor of the Sheik Khalifa Al Nayan, President of the UAE and Ruler of Abu Dhabi, who had helped during such difficult times.

11

STARTING UP IN THE DARK CONTINENT

Africa Shining

Surrounded by the sea, just a few hundred miles south of Europe and bordering with the Arabian Peninsula on its north-west, lies Africa. This continent represents the last frontier for business growth, a part of the word where so far many multinational companies have not yet had the opportunity—or at times the courage—to invest. With almost one billion people, more than half of them below 24 years of age,[1] the demographics of Africa are certainly one of its strengths. It is estimated that by 2050 over two billion people will have been living there. Having then overtaken China and India, the continent will host the largest and possibly the youngest world population. Little over 10 years ago one of the renowned international economic magazines[2] had defined Africa "a hopeless continent." Such hastened judgment had to prove wrong in the subsequent years; today the general sentiment is that Africa is for business potential what Asia was 20 years ago, and it is bound to become one of the emerging drivers of growth for the world's economy.

The mainland is commonly divided into north Africa and the sub-Saharan Africa (SSA), with the eastern and western regions being part of this last. Business wise north Africa is often assimilated to the Middle East Region, also due to the common ethnic origin, religion and language (Arabic) of the

---

[1] See "Africa Open for Business," report by The Economist Intelligence Unit, 2012.
[2] It was *The Economist* as reported in the "Africa Open for Business," mentioned in note 1.

majority of their populations. The northern states are closer to Europe, not only geographically but also in the aspirations of their people; more so in the Maghreb, comprising Morocco, Algeria, and Tunisia, where the influence of France is largely felt. Such a link, heritage of the colonial period, is also still robust in some of the west African states and obviously in the Island of Reunion, a French overseas department. South Africa and some of the southern states are the most modern and developed parts of the continent, though not the fastest growing in terms of GDP. Nigeria, Ethiopia, Egypt, and the Democratic Republic of Congo (DRC) have the largest populations: among these Ethiopia shows the highest potential for growth in the coming years (above 8 percent per year), followed by the DRC and Nigeria.[3] All these three countries have a large population base, hence high potential for future economic and human development. In 2012 countries like Libya and Sierra Leone will see much higher growth rates due to "one off" events.[4] Other relatively large economies expected to grow at rate above seven percent are Angola, Ghana, and Mozambique.

In the eastern region, Tanzania and Kenya are also foreseen to reach growth rates in the region of 7 percent, the latter having also a rather large population base. Considering the size of the GDP and its potential, as well as the demographic dividend, the five power houses of the continent are said to be South Africa, Nigeria, Angola, Ethiopia, and Kenya; as close followers come Sudan, Tanzania, and the DRC.[5] Along with the population and the growing middle classes, highly interesting for market seeking companies, Africa's natural wealth of commodities has been so far the main reason behind the Foreign Direct Investments of resource seeking international companies. According to a multinational consulting firm[6] mining and metals, oil, gas, and other exploitable resources are the sectors holding the best potential to attract investors, followed soon after by consumer products. For many years Africa's economy was almost insulated from the rest of the world and developed nations had an aid-centered approach towards the continent against the development policies they effected in emerging nations such as the BRIC ones. This is the main reason why Africa's share of the world trade hovers around

---

[3] See "Where to Invest in Africa," RMB FICC Research, August 8, 2011.
[4] See "Into Africa," report from The Economist Intelligence Unit, 2012. Euromonitor (A New Era for African Developments) estimates that Libya GDP will grow in excess of 70 percent, coming from a dip of 61 percent in 2011; Sierra Leone will grow in excess of 35 percent. Available at http://blog.euromonitor.com/2012/06/a-new-era-for-african-development.html.
[5] See note 3.
[6] Ernst and Young; as quoted in the paper referred to in note 3.

Chapter 11: Starting Up in the Dark Continent | 169

2 percent and it also explains why Sub Saharan Africa received in 2010 only about 3 percent of the global Foreign Direct Investment.[7]

While such figures definitely do not reflect the potential of the continent, its relative insulation vis-à-vis the world economy has proven beneficial during the recent global downturn, when the SSA recovered fast from any previous external shock to become the world's second fastest growing region after Emerging Asia.[8] However the weight of Africa in the world's economy is bound to change. Since the turning of the century emerging nations such as China have started nurturing stronger links with many African countries. Beijing uses a model similar to that used in other Asian countries: they help build infrastructures and offer financial assistance against the right of exploiting the local natural resources. In 2011 12.4 percent of all exports from Africa went to China,[9] a country hungry for commodities in which Africa is rich. According to a report from an international banking group[10] "South Africa's mineral deposits, worth an estimated $2.5 trillions (excluding energy minerals) are the richest in the world."[11] Precious metals are also abundant in the continent: a recent geological survey[12] stated that 89 percent of the world's reserves of platinum, 66 percent of diamonds and 16 percent of gold are hosted here and most of these are still untapped. From an export perspective petroleum and gas top the list followed by iron ore and precious metals.[13]

Other countries are following China in the race to Africa: Malaysia, Brazil, and India are more and more present in the continent. The shares of Africa's export to these countries, particularly the last two, are growing and, in 2010, had reached three and six percent, respectively.[14] Trade with India grew four-fold between 2004 and 2009 and is expected to grow beyond US$ 75 billion by 2015.[15] Indian FDI stock in Africa is estimated at US$ 30–35 billion, whereas China at approximately the double.[16] Improving the shaky

---

[7] See D. Moyo, "Africa Can Remind the World of the Capitalist Way," *Financial Times*, February 2, 2012, Dubai.
[8] See M. Siddiqui, "World Growth Now Depends on Africa," *African Business*, 382 (January 2012).
[9] See note 1.
[10] Citigroup, as reported by *The Economist*, December 3–9 2011, in the article "Nationalization in South Africa," a debate that will persist.
[11] *The Economist*, December 3–9 2011 quoted in note 10.
[12] US Geological Survey 2010.
[13] "Where to Invest in Africa," RMB FICC Research, August 15, 2011.
[14] See note 8.
[15] V. Noury, "Trade Level Grow by 400% in Five Years," *African Business* 382 (January 2012).
[16] See note 8.

infrastructure in most of the African countries is a colossal task. Chad, Angola, and Nigeria are the countries with the weakest infrastructures whereas South Africa, Mauritius, Botswana, and Namibia are among the best of the lot.[17] While the investment to GDP ratio for these is still low compared to Asian nations,[18] progress is being made in some fields: one of these is communication. Africa has today more than 600 million mobile phone users and a tenth of its land mass is covered by mobile-internet services.[19] Considering the generally bad conditions of roads and the difficulties and time required to move around, such communication links have helped immensely in financial transactions—this is the case for mobile banking—and telephonic agro information. Therefore trade is gaining pace, particularly among the various Regional Economic Communities created in the different regions of the continent, some of which have evolved or are evolving into monetary unions.[20] Trade barriers are progressively being dismantled and tariffs being lowered. A factor helping in this is the reduced political rivalry among nations. The general political situation of the continent is improving, when compared to the initial post-independence years, during which not a single president or government—except for Mauritius—had been peacefully ousted.[21]

Since the first example in Benin in 1991 democratic systems have become more and more frequent and the number of dictators and regimes across the nations are gradually decreasing. So are the armed conflicts: in the period 2001–2010 Africa has seen 14 conflicts coming to an end, though three new ones have emerged.[22] Such improved conditions have favored the continent's overall economic growth that touched almost six percent in 2011, despite the generalized world economy slow down; a similar pace is expected for 2012. Though starting from a relatively low base during the past decade six of the world's 10 fastest growing countries were African.[23] Despite the huge opportunities that all the above represent there is still a large number of people of the continent living in poverty: in many places higher growth has not

---

[17] World Economic Forum. See note 13.
[18] 22 percent in SSA compared to 42 percent in emerging Asia; see note 13.
[19] "Africa Rising," *The Economist*, December 3–9, 2011. Also available online at http://www.economist.com/node/21541015.
[20] There are seven main Regional Economic Communities, the members of which are at times overlapping. UEMOA, a community of eight French speaking countries, has already established a common currency and WAMZ plans to introduce a single currency in 2015.
[21] See note 19.
[22] See http://www.ploughshares.ca/content/2011-armed-conflicts-report.
[23] *The Economist*, see note 19.

yet fully translated into job creations, though many Africans are benefiting from the same. There are still several repressive and non-democratic governments. There is wide-spread over-regulation of business and corruption and in general the ease of doing business in most of the nations remains rather low. Social protection and higher quality of lives are still to reach many of the African countries.

On the other hand, an African business magazine[24] states that 78 percent of SSA governments undertook at least one positive reform in 2010. A few countries have drastically improved their frame of law and order: among these Nigeria, where a few years ago one could not walk in the streets; Rwanda, which is becoming more and more a safe and stable nation; Kenya, which introduced a new constitution in 2010 and overhauled the existing judicial structure also by including a Supreme Court. Several nations have been strengthening ties and international companies are making inroads into the continent. Investors used to be initially resource seekers but, thanks to the demographic dividend and the emerging middle classes, they are gradually becoming market seekers and are looking at the continent with increased interest. As Asia was for the twentieth century, Africa is bound to become the engine of the world's growth for the decades to come.

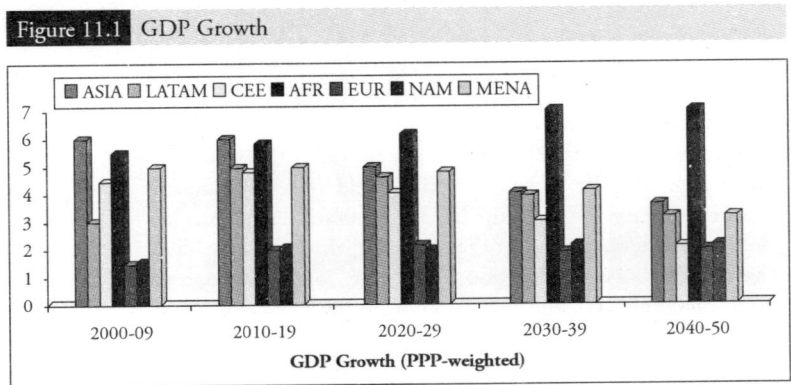

Figure 11.1 GDP Growth

Source: IMF, Goldman Sachs Global ECS Research.

---

[24] V. Noury, "Rwanda Most Business Friendly in E. Africa," *African Business*, 382 (January 2012). While the year quoted in the article when the reforms have happened is 2012 we reckon that is a typographical error, since other data in the same refer to 2012 and the magazine was published in January 2012.

Making Inroads into Africa

Almost half of Perfetti Van Melle's revenues are still coming from Europe, where the Group has its origins. In the last 20 years PVM has gained a strong share in the Asian sugar confectionery market. Also, thanks to the introduction of Mentos Gum, PVM today has also a significant presence in the American sugar confectionery market. On the other hand the Group's presence in Africa is still marginal. This was the reason why, a few years ago, I was given the assignment to study some of the African countries so as to select the most potential ones for us and start building our business there. With this objective I explored several countries in north and west Africa in view of a possible investment there. In 2007 I visited Egypt, the third most populous African nation, and had been positively impressed by the warmth of its people and its cultural heritage. A large population and its sweet tooth were certainly favorable factors to consider in view of an entry in the country. However, one of the international sugar confectionery players had understood the potential of this market much before us. Having been operating in the country for decades and having also acquired local players, they had built a stronghold very difficult to attack. While the quality of the products present in the market at that moment was rather average and Perfetti Van Melle with its know how would have certainly been able to introduce higher quality offers, market prices were rather low, thus creating a barrier for new entrants.

We did, however, start some business there, though with higher price formats that limited our presence to an upper niche of the market. As it often happens in emerging countries with heavy red tape, we took some time to receive the import licenses for our products. Sales are gradually showing encouraging results and the positive trend continued even in 2011 despite the Arab Spring. In 2012, the uncertain political situation has taken a toll on the general development of the economy, thus also impacting the growth of the fast moving consumer goods industry. To some extent we did experience a minimal impact at the beginning of the year, since, as a consequence of the mentioned uncertainty, our distributor was reluctant to buy a large quantity of goods. Luckily, this situation did not last long enough to impact our pipeline of products in the market: once the nation went towards a more defined democratic orientation and elections were announced and later effected, even our local partner became reassured, replenished his stock and re-started his drive of our sales. We took advantage of such renovated push in a moment where other companies were still hesitating and we see our sales on a good growth path that should lead to double our turnover by the end of the year 2012.

Chapter 11: Starting Up in the Dark Continent | 173

In 2009 I had traveled to Algeria to gain an insight of the market opportunities there. Differently from Egypt, I had found the sugar confectionery market here less developed and with no local direct investments from international confectionery players. The trade was very fragmented with hardly any modern trade except for one outlet with the name of a large international retailing chain but actually owned and managed by local shareholders. The site for a second of such outlets had been selected but its construction had never happened. Here we had a first-hand experience of how sudden changes in the legal framework could be a high deterrent for foreign investments. During the first years of the new century the government had decided to attract foreign investments and had allowed foreign ownership up to 100 percent in specific sectors. Subsequently, multinationals such as Danone had entered the country, progressively bought over their partner and, after a difficult start, were recording good business growth. In the telecom sector an international player[25] had set up a profitable business and found the way to minimize their fiscal liability through a smart corporate architecture. This fact was possibly one of the factors that triggered the sudden change of orientation of the local government in 2009. When we were just about to close a deal with a possible local partner, the law on ownership of foreign investments changed and international investors were forced to have a local majority partner in order to set up a company. In that occasion we received unexpected good support from the Italian Trade Commission:[26] through this we could meet local authorities in order to better interpret the circular of the President to his ministries that was eventually converted into law of the new regime for foreign investments. As a consequence of that change our local venture never happened eventually.

Only recently have we again started exploring a possible entry into the country but for many months we have been struggling to obtain the various permissions to import our products. When we finally could start some business we had further delays linked to problems experienced by our distributor that pushed us to find an alternate one. Algiers is not among the most

---

[25] Orascom, a telecom company owned by an Egyptian Tycoon with presence in several countries in the MENA region.
[26] A few years ago the Italian economic institutions that were to help Italian companies expand abroad were divided into three bodies: the Economic Sections of the Embassies, the local Chambers of Commerce and the Italian Trade Commissions (ICE). Such divisions did not really help Italian investors abroad and the organizations were eventually unified a few years ago into what was called the *sportello unico,* literally the "single window." In rare cases—like the one I mention here—thanks to the proactive interventions of their responsible, some of the local ICE offices were effectively providing support to Italian investors.

beautiful cities I have visited, but I still have nice memories of it. Together with some colleagues we had managed to slot a short tour of the local Kasbah during a market visit and a local guide had taken us through some improbably narrow stairs and hidden doors to the terrace of an old building with a stunning view of the city. Later on the same guide took us to a small "patisserie" hidden in a corner of the old town where we ate delicious local sweets, too good not to bring some back home. I recently traveled to Tunisia, where we run our business in partnership with a local group. They are a diversified company into retailing, manufacturing, and distribution. We have been associated with them for some time and our sales are being built slowly but steadily. Recent changes in laws have hindered the imports of some of our products, due to unexpected prohibitions of ingredients normally allowed in food in many other countries.

In April 2012 I met the owner of the local partner company in Tunis for a very pleasant dinner in a restaurant set up by a retired doctor in the ground floor of his house. Our partner, Mr Tahar, is a charming and cultured person and he surprised me when he mentioned that he had decided to be associated with our company not so much for the possible profit deriving from the partnership, as because he wanted to better understand the business model of multinational companies in fast-moving consumer goods. There is always enough to learn from smart entrepreneurs and one of the reasons why I enjoy my demanding job and the extensive traveling linked to it is the opportunity to meet interesting people, discover new cultures and habits and keep enriching my own knowledge.

In the north African region Libya is a country with very good business opportunities today. The war that put an end to 40 years of regime has left the country severely damaged but its people finally free to act and express their own opinions on how to rebuild the nation and create a democracy. The elections held in the summer of 2012 have been greeted by the people with an overwhelming enthusiasm. Our business was stalled in 2011, but we have seen a strong restart in 2012, driven by a renovated impetus from our distribution partner, who expects a much brighter future in a freer and fairer political and business environment. Now that the country is more open some of the unusual restrictions on some ingredients, which had been imposed during the previous regimes, seem to be bound to disappear, hence offering us good opportunities to enlarge our range of products. Considering that the population in Libya is relatively small[27] we are now re-building here the sizable business we used to have in past years, making the country one of the strongholds of the region for

---

[27] The estimated population is 6.7 million, as per the CIA Fact Book, 2012. Available at https://www.cia.gov/library/publications/the-world-factbook/geos/ly.html.

Chapter 11: Starting Up in the Dark Continent | 175

Perfetti Van Melle. We also have some presence in a few countries of eastern and central Africa, where we have selected some priority markets and have started investing in the same. Kenya and Ethiopia seem to offer interesting potential but the Democratic Republic of Congo and Angola are also part of our priority list. PVM has had a presence in South Africa for a few years already. In the early years of the last decade we had set up a small sales and marketing subsidiary there. We had started importing some of our bubble gum products under a regional brand but had found a very strong competition from local players selling products at very low prices. The freight and custom duties did not allow us to effectively compete in this segment and we decided to focus our attention on some other more profitable ones. Apart from various imported products coming from several countries including Argentina and Colombia, there are two main international players particularly strong in the gums market, one of which also produces locally.

While our business is now growing we are still a relatively small player in this market, but our set-up here has allowed us to study other countries in the southern part of Africa. We have already managed to develop a healthy business in the islands of Mauritius and Reunion and other countries are now being approached. In west Africa I traveled a few times to Ghana and Nigeria. Ivory Coast was a country in this region which in the past had attracted foreign investors for its relatively stable political situation and comfortable life style. It was said to be the best-run country in the area before the coup of 1999; military and political unrest during the subsequent years drastically changed the scene. Multinationals such as Nestlé, who used to have their regional headquarters there, decided to move their offices to Ghana, even today one of the better countries of the area both in terms of ease of doing business and quality of life. For our business Ghana represents a good example of a healthy and growing operation. Here we have been able to succeed in the gum segment also, a difficult one for us to tackle in the SSA region. We have been using a talented local advertising agency to develop good quality locally produced advertisements at very reasonable costs.

In this area, the country with the highest potential is certainly Nigeria, with its 150 million people and a sustained GDP growth of six to seven percent for the last few years. The first time I visited the country in 2006, I was rather frightened by the news in the papers and the reputation of a very dangerous place it had gained. My trip had been kindly organized by the local Nestlé subsidiary, thanks to the request of a friend who used to work in the Swiss Group. Upon landing in Lagos I was greeted by the General Manager of the local Nestlé company. We traveled in his armored car with a local policeman seated in the front seat and an armed security team escorting us in another car. I received a card that the company used to distribute to their guests with some "dos and don'ts," among which were the strong suggestions not to get out of the hotel alone, not to open the door of the room to unknown people, and other scary advice that certainly did not contribute to improve my perception of the country. I keep going to Nigeria off and on and I find that the security situation has certainly improved over the years.

In Lagos, the business capital, one feels how vibrant the environment is, in the country considered Africa's powerhouse. Thousands of traders crowd the streets of the city, selling snacks and water to shoe racks and kitchen accessories throughout the days and nights. They are particularly concentrated in proximity of the traffic jams, so as to have more time to display their merchandise and conclude the sales deal: such vendors are called "go slow" and through them a volume as high as the 20 percent of the overall sales in the country are said to be sold. Many roads in Lagos or other roads starting from here in different directions cross large open markets with hundreds of outlets, kiosks, tabletops, or even just individuals sitting with their goods displayed on a piece of plastic on the floor in front of them. I happened to socially meet a few local business men who have created their successful practice in the country. Most of them had studied in the UK or in the USA and, after a few years in those countries where they often still had interests or properties, they had come back to Nigeria to start their own companies. They showed off branded clothes and accessories as a statement of their success and earned thousands of dollars per day, often dealing with multinationals doing business in the country. Despite the messy appearance of the local infrastructures (e.g., bad roads and pathetic power situation) and visible poverty spread in pockets, the Nigerian market has attracted not only resource seekers such as the major international oil companies, but also some of the FMCG large brands. It is a fact that Heineken, the Dutch beer multinational present for many years in the country in a joint venture with a local partner, has earned astonishing profits from the local operations here, in some years—in excess of two hundred million Euros.

Fifty Countries, Thousand Cultures

Africa is said to have been the birthplace of the human race a few million years ago. People across the over fifty countries[28] in the continent are extremely

---

[28] 54 or 55 are the numbers usually mentioned when counting the African countries, though other numbers are also quoted (e.g., 46) according to other criteria. In fact some of the countries—for example the Canary Islands and Cueta—are not independent and some are parts of other countries (e.g., St Helena is part of the UK and Reunion part of France).

diverse, speak different languages, practice hundreds of religions, live in a variety of places, and are engaged in a wide range of economic activities.[29] While today its inhabitants are mostly of indigenous origins, over the centuries people from many parts of the word have immigrated to Africa and eventually settled there. Since the seventh century Arabs have crossed over from the Middle East and have settled in the northern part, bringing with them the Islamic religion. Europeans started settling in the seventeenth century in the south, continued to immigrate during the colonial period, and many of them took root in various parts of the continent such as South Africa, Zimbabwe, and other nations of the north. Asians came during the colonial period and created settlements in several parts, particularly in east and south Africa. There are hundreds of tribes throughout the continent, each of them with different languages, cultures, and habits. From the famous Maasai herders and warriors who dominated the plains of east Africa to the nomadic Tuareg, who used to live predominantly in the northern desert. The Zulu are still the largest ethnic group of the south, whereas the Yoruba are among the largest cultural groups in the continent and live numerous in the west, particularly in Nigeria and Benin;[30] the Berbers have lived in the northern states of Morocco, Algeria, Egypt, and other states for a long time, since references to them are found as early as 3000 BC.[31] One can notice the tribal origins of some individuals by looking at the scars or marks on their face, purposely made as decorations—with function similar to tattoos—carried by many individuals with pride and by some others with a slight embarrassment.

There are hundreds of sub-cultures of the various ethnic groups and the languages are as many. Just in Zambia, a country of 10 million people, there are 70 languages, of which six are recognized as official. South Africa has 11 official languages.[32] Interestingly in South Africa there is an Indo-European language, Afrikaans, developed 300 years ago by the Dutch colonizers, which is no more spoken either in Europe or in Asia. Since it was brought by the Europeans but had influences from slaves who had come from Malaysia it is similar to Dutch but with Malay influences. It is estimated that the languages spoken in Africa are between 1,500 and 2,000,[33] divided into four main

---

[29] See "African People and Culture," *Africa Guide*. Available at http://www.africaguide.com/culture/.

[30] Many Yoruba were forcibly brought to America and have influenced many Afro-American traditions in North America as well as in the Caribbean region.

[31] See "African People and Culture," *Africa Guide*. Available at http://www.africaguide.com/culture/tribes/index.htm.

[32] See "Language Diversity in Southern Africa," *Exploring Africa Teachers*. Availbale at http://exploringafrica.matrix.msu.edu/teachers/curriculum/m20/activity3.php.

[33] See http://www.nationsonline.org/oneworld/african_languages.htm.

groups: Afro-Asiatic in the north, Nilo-Saharian in the central and eastern regions, Niger-Saharian (Niger Congo)—the largest group with over 1,000 languages—in central, eastern, and southern Africa and Khoisian, in some part of the western and southern region. With such a huge diversity of people, traditions and languages it would not be possible to talk about one unified African culture. However, dividing the continent into the four regions to some extent corresponding with the above-mentioned four language groupings, we may try to draw similarities and differences among some of the main cultures spread among the same, also by utilizing the tool of the cultural dimensions developed by Geert Hofstede (GH) already mentioned in chapter four.

Starting from north Africa, let us take Morocco as a nation representing the region, or at least the Maghreb area. According to the GH analysis this country records very high values for the Power Distance–PD (70) and Uncertainty Avoidance–UA (68) dimensions, coupled with low score for Individualism–ID (25) and a just above average value of Masculinity–MA (53). The picture painted by such a grid would reveal a collectivist and strongly hierarchical society. Such high values of powered distance and uncertainty avoidance highlight a need of strong rules and codes of belief and behavior: it is likely that people in such societies may welcome a strong government, even an autocratic one, which is able to "reassure" its citizens and look after the welfare of the nation. Egypt shows scores very similar to Morocco, though with a lower value of the MA dimension (45). Interestingly, the value of the cultural dimensions in north Africa are very similar to those found in many Arab Societies (e.g., Saudi Arabia, where PD and UA are extremely high—95 and 80; MA is rather high—60 and ID is low—25), where rulers have almost absolute power and people accept this with rare instances of rebellion. To some extent this explains the fact that the regions of Middle East and north Africa are often considered as one cluster, where the Islamic roots and the common language create trans-national societies with similar fundamental values and cultures. The actual political situations of these regions with strong governments and in some cases dictators who have dominated the political scene for decades up to the Arab Spring, well reflects the finding of the above cultural dimension analysis. Though on the GH website the data for Tunisia are not available, from my personal experience I would reckon that this country may be slightly different compared to the cluster just examined, with a likely lower value of the MA dimension as well as of PD and UA. I would assume this by looking at the relatively high presence of women in the workplace as well as at the less prominent hierarchy attitude compared to the other two nations just examined. France is a clear model for this society, which must have taken from there a more developed feminine cultural dimension and perhaps also a lower acceptance of authority. If that was proven true we would also have a justification of the origin of the Arab Spring movement in this country.

Islam is spread also in other parts of Africa, but does not seem to have had the same capacity to mold the society's culture one could find in the north African region, possibly because in west Africa Islam has also been blended with the local cultures. The religion began penetrating the western region around the ninth century through missionary efforts and trade network. Since then it kept growing and producing important centers of learning; today it is embraced by approximately 50 percent of the population of west Africa, with peaks of 99 percent in Mauritania and 92 percent in Senegal.[34] When analyzing this region[35] through the cultural dimensions model, we also find here a high score for PD (78) and low score for ID highlighting collectivistic societies, similarly to the north. But the scores of UA and MA are much lower (54 and 46 respectively), hence showing a lower acceptance of strong rules and beliefs and a more feminine society. The additional interesting finding to be underlined here is the very low value of the fifth cultural dimension, Long term Orientation–LO (16), linked to the teaching of Confucianism and to the search for virtue and a future-oriented perspective. Such a low value implies a small propensity to save and impatience for achieving quick results.

While a similar attitude is commonly found in most African countries, in my personal experience I found that in this region, and more particularly in Nigeria, it is even more accentuated. People here seem to be living just for the day, without even considering that there could be a tomorrow. They tend to spend most of their salary in the first days after receiving them[36] and would not hesitate to invest an amount equivalent to two or three salaries in a branded fashion accessory; in general they seem not to care about what the future may bring, but instead being very focused to get something "here and now" so as to enjoy immediate gratification. A similar attitude seems to provide an explanation for some facts of life that I noticed while working in Africa. The first one is the endemic corruption rooted in the way of living in many of these nations. People long to make a quick "hit" and enjoy it as soon as they can, without thinking about the possible consequences of acts that may have legal implications. Such an attitude is so widely spread that requests

---

[34] See *Exploring Africa Teachers*. Available at http://exploringafrica.matrix.msu.edu/teachers/curriculum/m17/activity3.php.
[35] The Index clubs together three countries: Nigeria, Ghana, and Sierra Leone.
[36] I have noticed a similar attitude towards spending also in some south east Asian societies like those of the Philippines and to some extent Indonesia, where salaries are paid twice monthly (on the 1st and the 16th) to avoid that they are fully spent during the first half of the month.

for bribes are made openly, without even trying to disguise them, as it may happen in other parts of the emerging world. Another stunning fact that one notices, particularly if coming from a western European country or from the USA, is that the value of a human life is extremely low in Africa, even lower than in Asia. People are ready to kill for as little as a few dollars. Death at all ages is a fact of everyday life, be it due to accidental causes—a road accident, an electric shock provoked by a broken power wire—or to very preventable diseases. With such premises it is then better to live by the day, as the strong "short-termism" highlighted in the GH analysis shows. I remember having seen a motorbike sporting a black board instead of the number plate with a red writing on it reading "tomorrow who knows." Apart from finding this hilarious I thought it summarized very well what was just mentioned about the attitude of the Nigerian common man.

This craving for immediate gratification may help explain the very high consumption of beer in a country the population of which is half Muslim. Against the average of the west Africa cluster Nigeria shows a higher score in the ID dimension. This is reflected in the high number of small entrepreneurs populating the roads of the cities. In my direct experience I realized that many Nigerians look at subordinate employment as a way to make money and set up their own business. When we examine the cultural dimensions of the east Africa cluster,[37] we notice immediately two main differences with the western region: the substantially lower scores for PD (64) and MA (41). The reasons for such diversity could be on one side the wider variety of religious groups, not predominantly Muslim (e.g., approximately 70 percent of Kenyans are Christians); on the other side the more recent colonial history that saw strong Italian influences in one of the cluster states and European and Asian immigration in others. An additional reason could be the balanced social and economic development of one of the cluster countries, namely Tanzania, which may influence the overall cultural score-cards. Interestingly, Tanzanians have the reputation of being the most laid-back people of the region, possibly also due to the country's recent socialist past. People from Uganda are instead said to be street smart and more determined to get what they want, up to the extent of cheating to achieve their objective.

During my trips in the region I could notice that eastern Africans, particularly people from Kenya, are generally friendlier and less aggressive than their western counterparts. They also tend to be more hospitable, fun loving

---

[37] In the G. Hofstede site this is represented by Ethiopia, Kenya, Tanzania, and Zimbabwe, but Uganda is also usually considered to be in the east Africa region.

and genuine. I noticed that it is very easy to talk to anyone in the streets and have a laugh with them. I also noticed that people here mingle in a much easier way than in South Africa for instance, where the race factor is still very important in social relations. The *hakuna matata*[38] attitude summarizes the helpful and relaxed approach of this people. I have also observed that Kenyan women tend to be more reserved and shy in their interaction with *mzungu*, that is a white man, when compared to Nigerian women, who are normally more relaxed and extroverted. Rather different cultural profiles of societies emerge from the analysis of the south African region. Starting from the Republic of South Africa we notice a very high ID dimension (65), possibly the highest so far encountered in all regional clusters examined. This implies a "high preference for a loosely-knit social framework in which individuals are expected to take care of themselves and their immediate families only"[39] very different from the collectivistic societies found in the other regions and more similar to values found in western societies such as the north American. Power Distance and Uncertainty Avoidance dimensions seem to be quite balanced (both at 49) and rather lower than the other regions. Differently, Zambia has higher PD values (60) and lower ID (35), but surprisingly also lower MA (40 against 60 in the RSA) which denotes a rather feminine society.

As already mentioned above, what I have attempted in this brief cultural trip across Africa is only a quick glance at the variety of regional cultures through a useful tool provided by a scholar and my personal observations during my traveling and working here. Such short overview does not pretend to be either a rigorous or a complete analysis of the immense cultural heritage of the African continent. A direct implication of the large differences highlighted among the various African regions is the different approach investors will need to use when planning to do business in these. Not only foreign investors but also local ones have failed due to the wrong assumption that a business model working in a region could have been replicated *"sic et simpliciter"* in another. A South African fast food chain, for instance, had opened a few years ago in a west African country, declaring the intention to change the fast food business in that country. They had trained the best professionals, opened shops in high street locations, at times even with drive-throughs. However, less than one year after the launch, they had shut down.[40]

---

[38] In Swahili, the Kenyan national language; it could be translated as "no problem," "it can be done" or "take it easy."
[39] Geert Hostede site in http://geert-hofstede.com/south-africa.html.
[40] See K. Dumor, "Getting Vocal with Local," *Msafiri: Kenya Airways*, 81 (May–June).

12

THE BRICs OVER THE PAST DECADE

Projections and Actuality

The acronym BRIC appeared for the first time in a paper dated November 2001 from Goldman Sachs:[1] among other findings the report also suggested that Brazil, Russia, India, and China should have been included in the G7 and some of the Euro nations removed from that body. Two years later another paper[2] dealt more specifically with the economic data of the BRIC, projecting the same to the year 2050 in order to show what major change was about to happen with the surge of the BRIC nations. The publication attracted the attention of various media and governments. Since then the word BRIC has become a rather known and used term to indicate the most potential of the emerging countries, whose economies have recorded among the highest growth rates worldwide. The basic conclusions of those papers were that those countries were driving the global growth and would have become among the largest world economies by the year 2050. At the time of publishing the first paper the world's share of the BRIC's GDP was about 14 percent; it would have drastically increased during the first half of the twenty-first century, up to the point of becoming about 25 percent in 2010 and possibly 40 percent in 2050. The projections were based on a model that considered several variables, among which the labor force growth, the capital

---

[1] Goldman Sachs, "Building Better Global Economic BRICS," *Global Economics Paper* No. 66 (2001), available on http://www.goldmansachs.com/our-thinking/brics/brics-reports-pdfs/build-better-brics.pdf.
[2] Goldman Sachs, "Dreaming with the BRICS: The Path to 2050," *Global Economics Paper* No. 99 (2003), available on http://www.goldmansachs.com/our-thinking/brics/brics-dream.html.

Chapter 12: The BRICs Over the Past Decade | 183

accumulation and the exchange rate trends. The appreciation of the currencies of such countries would have played an important role in the rising share of the world's GDP of the mentioned countries, also in view of the fact that the GDP data were considered in US$. The Goldman Sachs (GS) BRIC papers were meant to show the potential of these countries: the second one, as stated in its title, wanted to highlight a possible path of evolution, though not necessarily the only one, of the economies of these countries towards a much stronger role within the world's economy. The implications of the conclusions of the papers were that a great transformation of the global spending power was under way, accompanied by a shift in importance in the role of such emerging nations within the world's economic and political scenario. GS kept updating their initial projections with other papers dealing with the same topics, among which a paper in 2005[3] which added a second cluster called N-11, representing the next eleven high potential emerging countries after the BRICs, and another in 2009,[4] following the 2008 financial crisis, looking at how such countries had withstood the crisis for years. After over ten years from the first appearance of the acronym it is interesting to look back at what the reality has been against the projected numbers, so as to revalidate the importance of the most potential emerging countries and their future role. The first observation one could make is that the attention from the media, the governments and the investors drawn by the BRICs papers highlighting their potential also as investment destinations have certainly contributed to the actual flowing of large capitals in the same, hence have ended up being almost a self-fulfilling prophecy. This could have not happened but for the strong fundamentals of the countries rightly captured in the mentioned papers. In general the growth delivered by the BRIC countries was not very different from the projections made, with a variation of 1–1.5 percentage point. The stars of the decade were certainly China and India, which outperformed the original forecasts with an average growth exceeding ten percent (against the forecasted 7.6) for the former and almost touching seven percent (vs. 5.7) for the latter. On the other hand Brazil averaged 3.3 percent GDP growth and Russia 5.5, hence have underperformed against the original projections of 3.45 and 5.85 respectively, perhaps partly due to the recent world financial crisis. In terms of GDP level, the four countries were in 2010 as an aggregate at US$ 10,972 billion against a projection distinctly too pessimistic of

---

[3] How Solid Are the BRICS, *GEP* 134, 2005.
[4] "The Long Term Outlook for the BRICs and N-11 Post Crisis," *Global Economics Paper* No. 192, December 4, 2009.

5,442,[5] with China having almost doubled the projected GDP level, similarly to the other countries with the exception of Brazil that has tripled the forecasted level. As far as the per capita GDP is concerned in 2012 Brazil and Russia stood at a similar level, slightly above the US$ 10,000 milestone, with Brazil tripling the projections, also thanks to the currency appreciation, and being slightly higher than Russia, which on the other hand had multiplied by four its average per capita GDP against the year 2000 and doubled the figure projected by GS. China had crossed the 4,300 mark (vs. the projected 2,223) whereas India lagged behind at 1,256, being among the four countries the one that achieved the lowest increase in this indicator.[6] Therefore the last decade has seen a truly remarkable achievement by the BRICs, with their share of growth rising sharply and constituting nearly half of the overall global growth. Their contribution to global trade has also drastically increased from a level close to 3 percent at the turning of the century to about 14 percent in the year 2010. Similarly during the same period also the BRICs equity market returns have by far exceeded those of any developed market, leading to the quadrupling of their total market capitalization. Their share of the global GDP has grown to 25 percent compared to 11 percent in 1990. GS had forecasted that the different BRICs Economies would have overtaken the G7 ones for the size of their GDP at some given point in times. For instance China was to surpass Germany in 2009, while it did so two years in advance: it was to surpass Japan around 2016, while it did so in 2010. Similarly Brazil is catching up with France much faster than the foreseen 2030, and may possibly overtake it in the span of three years or so. The faster race of the BRICs, apart from their overall better achievements, is also to be attributed to the consequences of the 2008 financial crisis as well as the most recent European crisis due to the possible exit from the Eurozone of Greece. The European nations are those who suffered the most from the two combined crises, while the BRICs, though initially impacted, showed a much better resilience, also thanks to improvements in macroeconomic policies in their economies. The

---

[5] These data are though not entirely comparable, since in the original paper of 2003 the basis was the US$ of that year, whereas the data in 2010 are based on the 2010 US$. The large difference is also possibly explained by different currency exchanges assumptions vs. their actual trends. Brazil's nominal exchange rate against the US$ for instance has steeply appreciated and is now almost 100 percent stronger than what it was in 2003. This is the reason why the assumptions on appreciation of the currencies were changed in the paper No. 208 published in December 2011.

[6] For India the forecast was exceeded by 56 percent, hence a relatively lower gap vs. the actual doubling and tripling of the 2003 GS forecast for the other BRIC countries.

following two decades will possibly be still dominated by such cluster of countries, particularly till the year 2010. In a paper recently published[7] Goldman Sachs formulated with fine tuned assumptions the forecast for the coming 40 years, not only for the BRICs but also for the N-11 and the G7. They foresee that, having achieved their peak average growth[8] in the first decade of the century, BRICs will still be the cluster with the higher growth in the current decade, but will progressively be outgrown by the N-11, which will become the fastest growing cluster from 2030 to 2050.[9] Since the BRICs would still see substantial growth during the next 15 years and the N-11 will also accelerate their emergence during the same period, despite the not exciting performances of the G7 countries the overall world GDP development should see an acceleration in the coming years, with a global growth crossing 4 percent in the current decade (vs. 3.5 percent of the previous one). This would come as a consequence of the larger weight of such countries within the global economies' GDP. Of the four countries India is foreseen to progressively outgrow China, and remain the only economy among the group to sustain a growth in excess of 7 percent in the current decade and one point lower in the next one.[10] Geographically speaking, while Asia will continue to have an overall high but stable growth (around 6 percent) in the current decade, Latin America should see an acceleration of the same in the same period taking it to an average not too far from Asia (about 5 percent). The champion of the coming 40 years will be Africa, which should reach an average growth similar to Asia during the current decade and further accelerate to cross the 7 percent landmark from 2030 to 2050. According to the GS latest projections a cluster of Sub Saharan African countries will be the main driver of growth during the mentioned years. In terms of absolute GDP level in US$ by 2020 Asia will be 1.5 times bigger than North America and 1.7 times bigger than Europe: by 2050 it will have become 3 and 3.7 times bigger than North America and Europe respectively. It is easily understandable that the economic clout that emerging countries will gain during the coming years will completely reverse the global political situation and the world needs to be ready for this.

---

[7] "The BRICs 10 Years On: Halfway Through the Great Transformation," *Global Economic Paper* No. 208, December 7, 2011.
[8] The average PPP weighted growth was about 8 percent in 2001–2010.
[9] During these years the growth rates of the N11 would be around 5 percent.
[10] The most recent slowdown in India GDP growth (foreseen at 6.5 percent in the FY 2011–2012) would however seem to lead to different conclusions.

The BRICs Get Their Act Together

In June 2009, possibly a period that marked the peak of the financial crisis for the main emerging markets, the leaders of the BRIC Nations met in Yekaterinburg to discuss a number of topics, with special focus but not limited to the financial and economic changes necessary to avoide or at least reduce the damages of another possible future crisis. For the first time a cluster that was not previously existing if not for economic analysis and studies were becoming a real forum where the head of the BRIC nations could discuss, decide and cooperate with common goals. Prior to such meeting there had been instances of cooperation among the leaders of these countries in the occasion of other forums such as the WTO meetings or other assemblies on climate change. But the Yekaterinburg conference marked the first of a series of meetings that would have seen a new drive from such countries to create a body with a growing international influence to reaffirm the interests of the emerging nations vis-à-vis other forums such as the G7, where Western ones had still the lion's share. The meeting's conclusions were summarized in a common declaration that stated the points agreed and set the ground for the subsequent gatherings of the members that would happen yearly and would be hosted every time by one of the four countries. This declaration was mainly centered on financial and monetary actions to face the consequences of the recent crisis: in fact the first six of the sixteen-point statement were dealing with such issues. However three of the subsequent points dealt with environment and energy issues and the rest mentioned various intents to strengthen cooperation in different fields—science, education, assistance—among the four countries. The last two items in the document reaffirmed the need for multilateral diplomacy and the aspirations of India and Brazil within the United Nations; they also stated that the next meeting would be held in Brazil. Less than one year later in April 2010 the countries' leaders met again in Brasilia. By this time the world economic situation, and particularly the economies of the concerned four nations, had improved and it was clear that such countries were playing a wider role in helping the world growth: this was acknowledged more than once in the joint declaration issued also after the meeting. Such document touches upon general themes such as Development, Agriculture, Energy and Climate change. It mentions in its central part about needed reforms of institutions such as the IMF and World Bank. Interestingly it also states that the BRIC leaders have instructed their Finance Ministers to look into "regional monetary arrangements and discuss modalities of cooperation between our countries in this area." In fact in preparation to this second gathering of the country' leaders other meetings had been held: among these one in Moscow for the Ministers of Agriculture and Agrarian development; an exchange program for Magistrates and Judges held in Brazil; various other meetings on security issues and statistical exchanges. Also this declaration, as the previous one, contains paragraphs on energy emphasizing the need to develop cleaner and sustainable power systems: production and use of biofuels and renewable energies are specifically mentioned, though keeping an open door to a "more efficient use of fossil fuel." Climate change is recognized as a serious threat requiring strengthened global action: this represents a remarkable step ahead against the position of denial of any commitment about this issue previously shown by some of these countries. Two additional BRIC nations' meetings were held in April 2011 and March 2012, in Sanya, China and New Delhi, India respectively. Interestingly the acronym gained a last letter when the four nations were joined by a fifth one, South Africa. The joint declarations issued after this meeting are much more concise and general when compared to the previous two. After welcoming the new entry in the initial paragraph it is emphasized that now the BRICS stretch among different continents is the home of nearly three billion people and they aim to significantly contributing to the "development of humanity and establishing a more equitable and fair world." Later in the text it is further emphasized the strengthening of the cooperation on regional issues, not only among the BRICS but also with other countries and particularly emerging ones. The countries state their commitment to multilateral diplomacy and the central role of the United Nations, while on the other hand highlighting the need of a comprehensive reforms of this institution and of its Security Council: here the Big Brothers already part of the council reiterate the importance of the other three nations by supporting their aspirations to play a greater role in the UN. Once again, as already happened during the first BRIC meeting, this point is written with reference to the India long bid for a permanent seat in that Council. Though the language of the statement is intentionally kept vague, in this case, the sentence follows a paragraph mentioning the Security Council, hence making the inference to this more immediate.[11] In reality in a past as recent as two months earlier China had raised objections to quick reforms of the UN and indirectly to the India bid.[12] The Sanya summit marked the appearance of some concrete proposals in the area of Finance,

---

[11] While the previous declaration had a statement on the aspirations of India very similar to the one here quoted, there the Security Council was not mentioned at all.
[12] See "China Opposes India's Call for Quick UNSC reforms," *The Indian Express,* February 17, 2011, available on http://www.indianexpress.com/news/china-opposes-indias-call-for-quick-unsc-reforms/751286/0.

the framework of which had been created in the previous meetings, where the leaders agreed to consider the prospects for trade in local currencies. However the most interesting conclusions are found in the joint declaration issued on the occasion of the fourth BRICS meeting, held in Delhi in the Spring of 2012, in a time when the Western world, and particularly the Euro area, seemed to be aiming for a double dip recession also affecting the economies of the emerging markets. In the initial part of the document the five nations blame the aggressive policy actions taken by the Western Central Banks for causing a spill over of capital into the emerging market economies and excessive volatility of commodity prices. Hence they call for greater international oversight and reform and identify in the international economic cooperation the primary role of the G20. The change of roles and weights of nations that used to hardly have any say in the decision making forums of the developed countries a few years earlier is remarkable and seem now to be "scolding" those countries and directing them to act for the good of the world's economy and prosperity. They state being worried about the slow pace of reform in the IMF and call for the leadership of the World Bank to be given to the emerging nations, so they can gain a stronger representation in the international financial architecture. Point 13 of the document deals with a "BRICS-led South–South development bank" a major topic announced in principle in the earlier meetings and now being mandated to the Finance Ministers of the cluster so as to be examined and re-discussed in South Africa in the 2013 BRICS forum. The central section of the declaration covers the delicate matters of the open conflicts in various areas of the globe. The Syria crisis is mentioned with careful words so as to find common ground where the nations had had different approaches.[13] References are made to the Afghanistan situation, to the possible escalation of the Iran conflict and last but not least to the Israeli-Palestinian conflict, appearing for the first time among the topics discussed since the forum has started meeting. Even in this document, as in the previous two, the same sentence about the aspirations of India, Brazil and South Africa to a role within the UN is reiterated. The repetition of such statement in a vague form highlights the inability of reaching a consensus among the members about the enlargement of the Security Council. References are made to climate change and clean energy, this time also including "a safe nuclear energy for peaceful purposes" as well as to a report coordinated by India with a special focus on synergies and

---

[13] India and South Africa had voted in favor of an Arab League sponsored resolution against the ruling government in the UN Security Council whereas Russia and China had vetoed the same.

complementarities of the countries' economies. If some of the major statements discussed during the mentioned meetings will actually translate into reality the bloc of the BRICS is bound to become more and more integrated and consequently more powerful compared to its developed countries counterpart. The seamless flow of cross country credit that may happen as a consequence of the creation of the common development bank would further enhance the intra BRICS trade and investments and possibly contribute to the improvement of the infrastructures in the various countries. More coordinated efforts in external affairs will carry a larger weight and possibly succeed where the efforts of the individual countries may fail. Even on the humanitarian side, the statements in support of a more equitable and fair world could go a long way to also push the developed countries to a larger effort in this direction. Last but not least the commitment expressed on the climate change and new energy front open a new era in a field that till only a few years ago did not seem to be acknowledged by some of these countries.

BRICS and the Green Revolution

The latest entry in the BRICS hosted in Durban a two-week long Climate Change conference in November/December 2011. This marked two decades since the United Nations Framework Convention on Climate Change was formed[14] to cooperatively consider actions in order to limit the average global temperature increases to two degrees Celsius from pre-industrial levels. The expectations before the conference were rather low, due to the previous semi-failures of the various meetings held in 2009[15] in preparation of the Copenhagen meeting in December 2009 and the modest progress made in Cancun in 2010. Already in the 1990s,[16] it had become clear that there was a net divide between "North" and "South" based on diverging interest vis-à-vis the objective of reducing the carbon emissions and minimizing the climate change issue. The "South" group represented those developing countries that felt that possible limitations in the emissions would have hindered their economic

---

[14] 1992 was the year of the meeting in Rio de Janeiro of the UNCED—Conference on Environment and Development—that opened for signature the Framework Convention. The body was preceded by an International Negotiating Committee for a Framework convention created vide resolution of the United Nations General Assembly no. 45/212 of December 21, 1990. The actual convention entered into force on March 21, 1994.
[15] Three rounds of negotiations were held in Bonn and one in Tianjin, China.
[16] Since the second conference on Climate Change held in Geneva in 1990.

development. Among them, China, the country with the highest global CO_2 emissions, had clashed with the US, the nation with the second highest emissions, during the Cancun conference. The representatives of this nation surprised the world during the Durban meeting by entertaining the possibility of accepting emission limits (though with caveats[17]). Overall the conference, that seemed to be bound for a major failure till the last day of talks, was not an overwhelming success but represented for sure a step forward. One important achievement reached here was the agreement to extend the Kyoto protocol,[18] due to expire in 2012, until 2017. The US, who had refused to sign the Kyoto protocol, accepted to search for an agreement with "legal force." The participants agreed to create a new treaty specifying fresh emission cuts by 2015. This is supposed to come into effect by 2020. The important side development of the conference was "the shift in geopolitical certainties that could spell a substantial change in the way climate talks are conducted."[19] The agreement on legal constraints also subscribed by the former "Southern" countries and in particular the BRICS nations highlighted their taking a leading role in the issue, a fact that would have been unthinkable only a few years earlier. Possibly such shift came from the awareness that emerging countries are more vulnerable than the developed ones to the disastrous effect of climate change. As per the UNCTAD "the risk for a citizen to be exposed to a climate-related natural disaster is 79 times higher in a developing country than in an OECD one."[20] According to the same source the failure to mitigate the effects of climate change could cause losses ranging from 5 to 20 percent of the world's GDP, out of which 75 percent would be borne by developing countries. There is therefore a clear strategic interest for these countries to find a way to mitigate such effects. The fact that large investments in green technologies are foreseen during the coming years[21] and that the developing countries may be large recipients increase the said interest from their side. The

---

[17] Among these caveats the fact that developed countries should compensate developing ones for historical pollutions.

[18] This is an international agreement linked to the UN Framework Convention setting "binding targets for 37 industrialized countries and the European community for reducing greenhouse gas (GHG) emissions. These reductions amount to an average of five percent against 1990 levels over the five-year period 2008-2012," see http://unfccc.int/key_documents/kyoto_protocol/items/6445.php.

[19] See "The Great Regrouping," *Financial Times*, December 15, 2011, Dubai Edition.

[20] Energy Pact UNCTAD Conference November 2011, Geneva, Concept paper, http://www.energypact.org/energy_pact_conference/program.php?subject=concept_29_30_dec_2011.

[21] 750 billion USD per annum as per the same UNCTAD paper.

investment flows have already started and are coming from the developed nations but also being indigenously developed. In India the largest solar plant in the country (40 MW) was reported[22] to have started in April 2012, having been constructed in 129 days from concept to commissioning. This is expected to every year displace several million tons of carbon dioxide. At the opening of the plant the new and renewable energy minister is reported to have said[23] that India would soon become a global leader in solar energy since the government is making all efforts towards this goal. A more recent piece of news[24] reported that an Indian firm is to invest US$ 1 billion in wind farms in the country. Welspun Energy, an Indian independent power producer, is said to have signed agreements with the Karnataka Government to build two wind farms for a total of 850 MW in the next five years. Similar news on the green drive comes also from Brazil: recent reports[25] claimed that General Electric was building a wind power plant in the Northeastern state of Bahia, whereas another piece of news[26] talked about Alstom, a French firm, having been awarded a contract to build a 108 MW plant in the south of the country. Due to recent government legislative revisions in Brazil, the solar market is projected to realize a 350 percent growth rate in 2012, and continue to grow exponentially for the next several years.[27] Brazil has also seen increasing interest in wind power and has been adding during the recent past about 2,000 MW of new wind-power capacity every year as prices for wind power fall below the costs of other sources.[28] Russia is slightly behind the other BRIC nations, possibly due to the wealth of gas and oil reserves of the country that did not really create the urge to diversify. However such resources could face a decline in the future and it will be important to start looking at

---

[22] See *Business Standard Online*, April 9,2012, on http://www.business-standard.com/india/news/lt-commissions-indias-largest-solar-power-plant/162526/on.
[23] See same article quoted above on *Business Standard* online, April 9, 2012.
[24] Posted on June 13, 2012 on http://www.renewable-energy-technology.net/wind/energy-firm-invest-usd-1bn-indian-wind-farms.
[25] See http://www.renewable-energy-technology.net/wind/plans-build-usd-35m-wind-power-plant-brazil.
[26] See http://www.renewable-energy-technology.net/wind/france-bring-108-mw-wind-power-brazil.
[27] See "Chinese Firm to Develop Hybrid Solar Project in Brazil," posted on May 29, 2012, on http://www.renewable-energy-technology.net/solar/chinese-firm-develop-hybrid-solar-project-brazil.
[28] See http://www.renewable-energy-technology.net/wind/plans-build-usd-35m-wind-power-plant-brazil.

green energies. Thanks to its very vast territory the different regions offer unique renewable energy resources. The South-West region, Southern Siberia, and the Far East have significant solar energy potential, while the coastal areas in the north, low and middle Volga regions and the Urals offer wind energy potential. Hydro energy potential is mostly found in Central and Eastern Siberia and the Far East.[29] In the hydro field in fact there have been recent developments: a company called RusHydro, who has inherited 49 power stations, seems to be moving in the green direction and has created a New Energy Fund whose major objective is to develop a National Program for small hydro sector set ups as well as to implement projects. The positive fact is that Russian leaders have shown "the political will to support the development of renewable energy by adopting a target of 4.5 percent of all electricity generation and consumption from renewable sources by 2020. National Legislation on the electricity sector has been amended to move towards meeting this target. These steps have sent positive signals to potential investors and to the international community. On the other hand, specific support measures have been slow to develop."[30] Among the four original BRIC nations China seems to be the one who has shown the fastest progress. It was June 2006 when the State Council Information Office published a white paper entitled Environmental Protection in China. In the conclusions of the same the government committed a 20 percent decline in energy consumption per unit of GDP as well as other objectives of major pollutants discharge and reforestation. In order to achieve such objectives: "the Chinese government will make sure that the tasks to prevent and control water and air pollution are completed. It will strengthen the environmental protection of urban and rural areas and the protection of the eco-environment and ensure the safety of the nuclear and radioactive environments. It will undertake the key tasks of building national environmental protection projects and promote environmental protection work in an all-round way."[31] When the paper was issued not many believed that such commitments would have actually happened nor that the Chinese Government was really seriously intentioned to take such a drastic change in its energy policy. China has become some time back the world's largest polluter ahead of the USA and its emissions have doubled

---

[29] See http://www.engineerlive.com/Power-Engineer/Renewable_Energy/Russia_and_green_energy%3A_a_long_way_to_go/21123/.
[30] IFC, Renewable Energy Policy in Russia..., 2011, on http://www1.ifc.org/wps/wcm/connect/bf9fff0049718eba8bcaaf849537832d/PublicationRussiaRREP-GreenGiant-2011-11.pdf?MOD=AJPERES, page 4.
[31] See http://www.china.org.cn/english/2006/Jun/170355.htm.

during the last decade. Yet in reality various steps have been taken ever since and their results are already visible today. One of these has materialized in the province of Gansu in Northwest China, which had been home to the first oil field and several coal mines, thus having contributed to China's notoriety as the planet's biggest polluter and carbon dioxide emitter. Today this is becoming the theater of an important transformation thanks to massive investments in new energies happening in the area. The plains of Jiuquan are now the base for more than 50 energy companies[32] and the wind turbines installed in this area have the capacity to generate 6 GW of energy, with a plan of more than tripling the capacity by 2015, thus becoming the largest word wind farms.[33] This is part of the Chinese Government's long term plan to supply by 2020 15 percent of the country's energy from alternative and renewable sources, against the current 8 percent: if this actually happens China may become the world's first green superpower. In fact a recent report from The Economist Intelligence Unit[34] suggests that by the end of the decade the combined share of renewable energy and nuclear power will rise to over 16 percent, and the use of renewable energy would be roughly equivalent to the annual energy consumption in Canada. According to sources[35] China was in 2010 the world's biggest investor in clean energy with over 54 billion US dollars invested. In fact China, apart from hydro and wind power, has set a record in the solar panels industry too. Suntech Power, the world's largest producer of solar panels, has recently announced that "its industry-leading Pluto cell technology has set a world record 20.3 percent efficiency for a production cell using standard commercial-grade p-type silicon wafers."[36] Such an announcement follows another one from Swinburne University of Technology and Suntech on the "development of the world's most efficient broadband nanoplasmonic solar cells."[37] These kinds of developments have contributed to drastically reducing the cost of solar panels around the world and making solar power, which used to have high investments and installation costs,

---

[32] See guardian.co.uk, Monday, March 19, 2012, on http://www.guardian.co.uk/world/2012/mar/19/china windfarms renewable-energy.
[33] See the article in guardian.co.uk quoted above.
[34] See "EIU: A Greener Shade of Grey," special report on renewable energy in China, 2012.
[35] Leslie Hook and Ed Crooks, "China's Rush into Renewable: The Way the World Turns," *Financial Times*, November 28, 2011. Also available online at http://www.ft.com/intl/cms/s/0/0502a28a-15c9-11e1-a691-00144feabdc0.html#axzz2DQEgnRU5.
[36] See "China Sets World Record in Solar Cell Efficiency," posted on March 13, 2012, on http://www.renewable-energy-technology.net/solar/china-sets-world-record-solar-cell-efficiency.
[37] See "China Sets World Record," quoted above.

accessible to many households. Seven out of ten of the world's largest producers of solar photovoltaic modules are Chinese.[38] Chinese firms have understood the business opportunity of going green and are now exploiting the know-how they have developed in recent years to develop business also out of their native country. Sunbelt International, a company from Beijing, after having secured a multi-million dollar project in Tanzania, is now to build a hybrid solar technology in Brazil.[39] Two Chinese companies, Sinovel and Xinjiang Goldwind, rank among the largest wind turbine manufacturers (by megawatts of capacity sold) in the world.[40] Some of these companies are also investing in developed countries: Goldwind is now building a US$ 200 million 110 megawatt wind farm in Illinois, amongst the fears of local competitors who are hinting at the alleged poor quality of the Chinese products to try and limit the consequence of Goldwind's aggression. Interestingly the BRICS are not the only emerging countries where the business of going green seems to be developing at a fast pace. In the Middle East and Africa region investments in renewable energies grew by 104 percent during the year 2012, though starting from a small base.[41] In January 2012 the Dubai Government launched an AED 12 billion (US$ 2.5 billion) solar power park that, when completed in 2030, will produce 1000 megawatts of power. We have already mentioned in chapter 9 about Masdar city, a development in the vicinity of Abu Dhabi defined as a "cleantech cluster ...designed and operated to provide the highest quality of life with the lowest environmental footprint."[42] There are at least two reasons why the UAE as well as the other Gulf countries need to look at green energy for the future. The first is linked to the increase in the energy demand in the region: between 2000 and 2009 this grew by 7.5 percent in UAE and 13.4 percent in Qatar, and at an average rate of 5 percent across the GCC countries. By subsidizing the fuel the region adopted high energy intensive consumption patterns that have burdened the countries' budgets and made the area among the highest per capita energy consumers in the world. On top of this the region is particularly vulnerable to climate

---

[38] See "China's Rush into Renewables," *Financial Times*, quoted above.
[39] See "Chinese Firm to Develop Hybrid Solar Project in Brazil," posted on May 29, 2012, on http://www.renewable-energy-technology.net/solar/chinese-firm-develop-hybrid-solar-project-brazil.
[40] See "China's Rush into Renewables," *Financial Times*, quoted above.
[41] The source is the United Nations Environment Programme, as reported in "The Business of Going Green," *Gulf News*, January 18, 2012, Dubai Edition. The investments in 2009 were reported to be US$ 5 billion.
[42] Quote from the Project's website, http://www.masdarcity.ae/en/.

change due to the reduction in precipitation consequent to global warming in a territory already affected by water scarcity.[43] A fantastic opportunity to plunge into the green energy business is there for the African Continent too, since nearly two thirds of the additional energy capacity needed for 2030 still need to be built.[44] Geographically and geologically speaking the continent has high potential renewable energy sources, given the large coastal area where wind and wave energy are abundant, the sun shining for over 300 days a year in many of its countries and high intensity geothermal potential spread across its land.[45] As of today only a few States among which Morocco, South Africa and Rwanda actually exploit this natural wealth, also due to the fact that the cost of installing renewable energy projects here is still rather high.[46]

Climate change and its implications cannot be underestimated. The good news is that many of the doubts about how this phenomenon is affecting the world have eventually been dispelled, in spite of those skeptic minds who, maybe backed by strong lobbies, still try to question the evidence of facts. Worldwide investments in clean energy increased by 30 percent in 2011,[47] and this proves that the majority of nations are not only aware about the issue but have already started acting. Also in this case the role of the emerging countries is becoming more and more prominent and hopefully, with their growing geopolitical clout, they will lead the world leaders towards ensuring a sustainable growth for a cleaner and healthier planet.

---

[43] See "The Business of Going Green," on *Gulf News*, quoted above.
[44] "Renewable Energy Projects in Africa Can Generate Jobs," *Gulf News*, March 2, 2012, Dubai Edition.
[45] P. E. Malin, "Establishment of Geothermal Resource Center to Accelerate the Development of Eastern Africa," as reported in Wikipedia on http://en.wikipedia.org/wiki/Renewable_energy_in_Africa#cite_note-14.
[46] "Renewable Energy Projects," *Gulf News*, quoted above.
[47] As reported in "Renewable Energy Projects," *Gulf News*, quoted above.

EPILOGUE

The topic of emerging countries and their markets is fascinating. The continuous changes happening in those countries and their vibrant business climate make living and working there an extremely enriching experience. The incredible developments witnessed since the 1990s have focused the world attention on these countries, which have progressively gained larger shares of the world's trade, GDP and geopolitical clout.

More and more the world has become "flat"[1] and interconnected: the proof of this is in the immediate reaction of the Asian stock markets and currencies to facts happening in North America or Europe. The financial meltdown of 2008 and 2009 seemed to be almost over when the troubles in the Euro zone started surfacing and negatively impacted the world economies. In such circumstances also the BRIC countries' rates of growth seem to have slightly slowed down. Though in 2012 we are still seeing growths around 8 percent in China and almost 6 percent in India, Russia may hover around 4 percent for the year whereas Brazil may stay at a lower level similar to 2011 (2.7 percent), though should cross 4 percent in the subsequent years.[2] Three of the four BRIC countries should therefore keep on growing in excess of the world growth in 2012, with the fourth catching up during the coming years. The world is also getting "hot and crowded,"[3] with the huge expansion of the population and middle classes of the emerging countries, their increasing energy consumptions impacting, together with other factors, the world climate.

---

[1] Term borrowed by T.L. Friedman, *The World Is Flat: A Brief History of the Twenty First Century* (New York: Farrar, Straus and Giroux, 2005).
[2] See Reuters on June 11, 2012, http://www.reuters.com/article/2012/06/11/us-brazil-economy-survey-idUSBRE85A0JG20120611.
[3] T.L. Friedman, *Hot, Flat and Crowded: Why We Need a Green Revolution—and How It Can Renew America* (New York: Farrar, Straus and Giroux, 2008).

The Rio+20 event of June 2012 was supposed to take concrete steps to ensure a sustainable development, but unfortunately has not provided many tools for a pathway towards the Sustainable Development Goals[4] that were to succeed the Millennium Development Goals stated in 2000 by the United Nations.[5]

It is becoming clear that Africa will be the last business frontier due to the fast economic growth of the continent that will eventually end up becoming a major engine for the world economy, like Asia has been for the last two decades. On the other hand Europe is in the middle of one of its worst economic crises. While this book is being written the Spanish banks bail out and the results of the election in Greece seemed to have given some hope that both the countries will remain in the Euro, thus providing temporary relief to the markets and currency. However the situation is not very clear, since also larger economies like Italy seem to be at risk and Germany has so far refused to take a leading role in the Euro crisis. Even the outlook for Germany, despite its much stronger economy compared to other European ones, was downgraded by a rating agency in July 2012.[6] In the USA the situation is not much better. Contrasting signals come from the data on the economy and employment, at times improving just to worsen some time later. The huge USA debt remains a sword of Damocles hanging on the world's economy. The declining populations of the "developed continents" further suggest that their geopolitical importance will drastically decrease in the future to the advantage of the emerging ones leading to a new global equilibrium.

I shall now shift the focus from the macro global environment to the tiny microcosm of my life and work, the main topic of this book: the link between the two matters being the emerging countries. I have just completed the "silver jubilee" of my career. It seems just yesterday when I drove to a remote location of the Roman countryside to join Johnson & Johnson, but over 25 years have already passed in the blink of an eye. My work has been the center of gravity of my adult life and has helped me evolve into a different person. I used to be extremely ambitious, a workaholic and self centered during my first years of works. While the ambition may still be part of me, I think I am

---

[4] See Rio+20 comments, on RTCC, http://www.rtcc.org/policy/rio20-comment-summit-whimpers-to-an-inevitable-conclusion/.
[5] See http://www.un.org/millennium/declaration/ares552e.pdf.
[6] See "Moody's Downgrades German Outlook to 'Negative'," *France 24*, July 24, 2012, available on http://www.france24.com/en/20120724-moodys-downgrades-german-economic-outlook-negative-netherlands-luxembourg-ratings-agency.

today a more balanced person. Work is very important but family has become the priority. I keep on striving to improve myself but my children are the focus of my thoughts and their health and upbringing increasingly drive my personal and professional choices.

Looking back there is hardly anything I would change of my last 25 years. At times I think how my life would have changed had I decided to join Berkley University, in California, where I had gained admission for further studies at the beginning of the 1990s. After completing those studies I would have perhaps found a job in the USA; hence I would have not been exposed to life and work in emerging countries and I perhaps would have neither written this book nor my first one. Probably I would have not met my wife, I would have had a different family and a completely different life. At times one decision dramatically changes the course of one's existence. So it happened when I decided to apply for the posting in Asia and start a new life there.

What next for me? During my 30's I kept on saying that I would want to retire very early to compensate for the very hard work during my university years and the working years thus far. I used to quote the age of 45 as the threshold to stop working, at least full time work. The age shifted to 50 later on and now that I am not so far from that deadline I see that it will soon be further delayed. I was lucky to be in the Indian subcontinent while this was experiencing a radical change driven by its accelerated economic growth. Now that our group has moved the first serious steps into the African continent I would like to dedicate the next years of my working life to ride the wave of growth and transformation also of this region. If I manage to do so this task would easily take me to the retirement age, that, incidentally, is becoming higher and higher in Italy as a consequence of the large Government debt. Ideally during the coming years I would like to devote more of my time to social works. The extent to which I shall be able to do so depends also on the agreement I would be able to reach with my company on this matter. During the years in India, apart from my personal time and contribution to charity and social activities I had been able to convince the shareholders to invest in CSR in the Indian Subcontinent. Tomorrow we may follow similar steps in African countries too.

In parallel I would like to keep on sharing my experiences by researching, teaching and writing. When in India I used to be invited by management institutes to lecture on various topics. I realized that I enjoyed that and I thought that I should try to have more regular opportunities to interact with students and the academic world. Since 2007 I have been lecturing in some

Universities and Business Schools in Italy. Perhaps at a different stage of my life I may decide to fully embrace academics and leave the corporate world. In the meantime the storage space of my home office is getting crowded with cutting of interesting articles on various subjects I find in the countries where I travel. Every few months I take time off to file them properly and read the most interesting ones seeking inspiration for a new writing adventure.

ACKNOWLEDGMENTS

Writing a book is a fascinating journey: from the initial idea to the researches, the first planning, the actual writing, the revisions, and the final details, every step is linked to the next one. The parallel with a trip, where one plans a destination, does some research about it, books the tickets, reaches and discovers the various places, and possibly takes pictures to remember the same seems quite relevant to me. Even more in the case of this book where I write about the journey of my life. Therefore to be fair I should thank all those people who have had a certain role in my life. They would be too many though, and I would certainly end up forgetting some of them. Hence I limit my thanks to the people who have been directly involved in this book and have in some way helped me complete the work. I shall thus mention the SAGE publishing team and more specifically Sachin Sharma and Chandra Sekhar. Thanks to the former I started thinking about writing the book, an idea that was far from me till a phone call approximately one year ago hinted to me the opportunity. They both gave very valid inputs on the tone and the contents of the book and closely followed the development of the same in its different stages. My colleagues, and particularly those in India and in the UAE, helped in many aspects. Harsh Arora's help was once again fundamental in recalling anecdotes of earlier years; Hitesh Chakraworty helped a lot in coordinating the communication with the publisher; Ramesh Jayaraman was involved also this time in the difficult task of finding an appropriate title for the book, and in this matter Abhijit Awasthi (Keenu) from Ogilvy & Mather India was so kind to offer his always original and unique contribution. Blesson David and Farah Bosco in Dubai also helped in some practical issues. Ubaldo Traldi and Anna Re in Italy took out some time from their very busy schedules to read some chapters and provide valid suggestions. Among the friends Ayhesha Hoda in Pakistan was the person who had suggested having a bit more of myself in my books: I have thoroughly followed her advice this time. Akash Arora in Sydney was the first one to read the initial chapters and encourage me to go ahead and write the rest of the book, and so I did! The planes, where I spend a considerable amount of my time, offer a very good opportunity to write in a quiet and relaxing environment that helps concentration. In these planes a substantial part of this book has been conceived: the balance time had to be found at late nights or early in the morning, and often during the weekends. I must thank my wife for the unusual patience she displayed in coping with my lack of attention towards her during the peak writing periods, and apologize to my kids for the same reason. Last but not least I must thank the readers who have bought or are planning to buy this book: through your contribution the COIN (Children of India Now), a trust I created some years ago and where all proceeds from the book due to me will be deposited, will have more funds to help children in need.[1] It is a drop in the ocean indeed, but drop after drop, even the hardest stone is pierced.

---

[1] You can also contribute directly to the COIN trust. Contributions may be sent to our bank account number 0016324221 at Citibank NA Delhi. Our PAN number is AABTC0897Q.

ABOUT THE AUTHOR

Stefano Pelle obtained a Master's Degree with Honors in Economics from LUISS University of Rome and a Post Graduate Diploma in Marketing from the School of Management of the same university. He completed his second Master's Degree in Political Science from La Sapienza, University of Rome. During his career he attended executive education programs in renowned institutes such as HEC, ESSEC, INSEAD and London Business School.

He joined Price Waterhouse in 1985 but started his marketing career in 1987 with Johnson and Johnson. After spending six years in the FMCG sector, he moved to the services industry as Head of Marketing of Iberia Airlines. He subsequently joined the Italian Railways as the Marketing and Sales Director, and later took over the responsibility of the High Speed Train Division. In 1998, he joined the Perfetti Van Melle Group, the third largest sugar confectionery group in the world, to oversee the India operations of Perfetti Van Melle as the Managing Director.

Since September 2005, Stefano Pelle is the Vice President and Chief Operating Officer of the Perfetti Van Melle Group, with direct responsibility for the South Asia Business Unit. He operates out of Dubai. For three years he also handled Russia and the CIS countries in addition to South Asia. Since April 2012 he is Executive Vice President and COO for the PVM Group and handles South Africa, Middle East and Africa.

Stefano Pelle also holds the position of Chairman for the Indian operating company, Perfetti Van Melle India, as well as for PVM Bangladesh and Sri Lanka. For his work in South Asia, he received the highest award of Knight Commander (Commendatore) from the President of Italy in 2006.

Despite his busy schedule in the Perfetti Van Melle Group, Stefano dedicates his free time to academics. He was invited as a speaker at the meeting of the Academy of Management, in August 2011 in San Antonio, Texas, USA.

He published in 2007 the book *Understanding Emerging Markets: Building Business BRIC by Brick* as well as several essays. He has taught International Business and other topics in the European School of Economics, Rome, and is Honorary Professor in IMI (International Management Institute), New Delhi. Since 2007 he has been cooperating with LUISS University of Rome, Faculty of Economics, as Lecturer for International Marketing and International Business and with LUISS Business School for their executive education programs. He has also published several articles and essays in newspapers, management journals, and magazines.